LOSING IT

Yale

UNIVERSITY

PRESS

NEW HAVEN AND LONDON

LOSING IT

WILLIAM IAN MILLER

in which an aging professor

LAMENTS

his shrinking B R A I N,
which he flatters himself
formerly did him Noble Service

* * *

A Plaint, tragi-comical, historical, vengeful,
sometimes satirical and thankful
in six parts,
if his Memory does yet serve

Published with assistance from the foundation established in memory of
Calvin Chapin of the Class of 1788, Yale College.

Yale University Press books may be purchased in quantity for educational, business,
or promotional use. For information, please e-mail sales.press@yale.edu (U.S. office)
or sales@yaleup.co.uk (U.K. office).

Designed by Nancy Ovedovitz and set in Monotype Times New Roman type by
Duke & Company, Devon, Pennsylvania. Printed in the United States of America.

The Library of Congress has cataloged the hardcover edition as follows:
Miller, William Ian, 1946–
Losing it : in which an aging professor laments his shrinking brain, . . . /
William Ian Miller.
p. cm.
Includes bibliographical references and index.
ISBN 978-0-300-17101-3 (hbk. : alk. paper) 1. Old age. 2. Aging. 3. Old age
in literature. 4. Aging in literature. 5. Miller, William Ian, 1946– I. Title.
HQ1061.M534 2011
305.26092—dc22   2011014102

ISBN 978-0-300-18823-3 (pbk.)

A catalogue record for this book is available from the British Library.

10 9 8 7 6 5 4 3 2 1

For my teachers:
to own up to debts
I can never repay

And as with age his body uglier grows,

So his mind cankers.

—*The Tempest*

CONTENTS

Striking Out

The phrase *striking out* can suit an enterprise launched in grand hope no less than one that ends in humiliating failure. It may also invite an editor to strike out the first sentence and tell me to start over, or just to give it up. If the general themes of this book may strike some as glum and grim, others will find solacing compensation in the joie de vivre of its gallows humor, some of which is intended. But such joie, like all joy, will soon be followed by a letdown. The figurative trapdoor opens and you drop, and are left dangling.

In common usage, the "it" in *losing it* can stand for any number of things. But in this book, "it" refers mainly to mental faculties—memory, processing speed, sensory acuity, the capacity to focus. Sometimes "it" will mark general physical decay outside the brain, as when I complain about joints and organs, sags and flaccidities, aches and pains. This "it," whether mental or physical, is more general, and the process of losing it more drawn out, than when "it" stands for a cell phone or virginity, each of which can be lost in mere seconds of thoughtlessness.

You will discern, however, that now and then I lose it in the sense of *flipping out*. That kind of losing it describes a fit of rage, usually thought of as losing "control," when the expectation would be of a more modulated show of irritation, or of feigned indifference. That particular idiom is quite recent. The *Oxford English Dictionary* dates its earliest recorded use to 1976, from England, not America, which might count as a minor surprise.[1] But to lose it in that sense was already latent in the sixteenth and seventeenth centuries when one could lose, if not the pronoun "it," then nouns like one's patience or one's mind, something less concrete than the head you could lose to an executioner's ax already in fourteenth-century usage.[2]

The discussions that follow circle around the theme of growing old, too old to matter, of either rightly losing your confidence, or wrongly maintaining it, culpably refusing to face the fact you are losing it. Yes, you can grow old gracefully. But what does that mean? Does it require withdrawing quietly without making others feel guilty, accepting, if not quite invisibility, then a quiet confinement to the shadows, from which you politely tell the economists measuring national happiness or the psychologists who study the well-being of oldsters that you couldn't be happier? And these experts, coding your response, are stupid enough to believe you.

Does growing old gracefully mean that you don't fight old age with unseemly cosmetic surgeries? That you alter your personality to fit what properly respectable old age is supposed to be? Will you have to affect a certain look? But what if you are not blessed, like Robert Frost was, with thick white hair and the appropriately etched wrinkles? Just how are you to face decline and the final drawing down of blinds?

I hate confessionalism (except, it seems, my own, which I can manage on terms of my choosing). I am compelled, however, given the subject, to be self-referential at times, though I will mostly do so by attributing my anxieties to you, the reader; or, when not making "you" the bearer of the burden, it will be "we," share and share alike.

Though most of you are not professors of law, and even if you are, you will not be one who teaches law students Icelandic sagas in a course called Bloodfeuds, or one who offers seminars, depending on the year, on topics such as disgust, humiliation, charlatanism, and revenge, and then gets paid as if you were teaching corporate law or bankruptcy; and though only half of you will be male, and even fewer of you Jewish, and almost none of you have grown up in Green Bay, Wisconsin, or have read an Icelandic saga and had it transform your life, I operate under the reasonably sincere belief that my experiences are those of Everyman. "Everyman," by the way, with its medieval associations, is gender neutral.[3] We are still plagued in English by the politics of the third-person neuter pronoun, for which I mostly use *he, him, his,* and an occasional *one,* when it does not seem too prissy. I do not employ she/her as a neuter pronoun, settling instead for the good husbandry of neutering males, which is what old, even middle, age effectively does to males anyway.

The "you" and "we" of my exposition is a claim of my averageness and yours too. Please do not be insulted: in our culture of inflated self-esteem, to be average, and to recognize yourself as such, is to bear a mark of distinction. And unless you suffer from incurable positive thinking and its attendant imbecility, my experiences should be readily comprehensible to you, if not always exactly shared. (Caveat: I will not quite be able to repress all my irritation with and contempt for so-called positive psychology and the related field of positive emotions, with their fatuous takes on old age, wisdom, happiness, and well-being—not to mince words, these fields are either culpably moronic or a swindle, one in which its purveyors, it seems, believe their own con.)[4]

The first four chapters—part I—retail the ways of losing it in unsettling detail; they are largely about brain rot. The book's middle will be in good part historical before we turn to more reflective (timeless?) matters in the last parts. In history or in ancient tales, we find more interesting people than either you or me: the likes of David, Joab, Beowulf and his grandfather Hrethel, Lear, of course, Enrico Dandalo (who, blind and over ninety, led the Fourth Crusade), Saint Anskar, apostle to the blond beasts of the North, various ancient Egyptians and curled-bearded, dark-haired beasts of Assyria, some Talmudic sages and magic men, several cagey and ruthless denizens of the Icelandic sagas—a berserk Viking, a wily lawyer, two homicidal poets—together with other old cynics, ascetics, and geezers—old Jews, old Christians, old pagans, and dying in the end with Jezebel. It will be impossible not to respect their tough-mindedness, to recognize their laudable as well as their blamable differences from us, but mostly to experience their deep kinship with us. They are never so different as not to be recognizable and comprehensible, even or especially when the concern is whether you are too old to take revenge and may wish to retire from such stern duties.

I treat wisdom in part II and show it is not all sweetness and light, rather the contrary, if wisdom is to be wise. Wisdom suffers greatly at the hands of modern psychologists who claim to study it, but then so does old age, when they patronize it with positivity. What can the quality of the wisdom you achieve be when it comes to you, if it indeed does come to you, at the same time your mental abilities are on a bullet train heading south?

No different from us, people of yore complained, and the three chapters in part III will be devoted to complaining. How much are you allowed to complain, and in what style? Are there strategies of compelling others to take your complaints seriously, especially when you complain about losing it, or about plain old aches and pains? What about complaints to God, when he reneges on his promises? What too of sorrow, despair, emptiness, when complaint gives no relief, and you end by turning your face to the wall?

Beds figure prominently in this book, for not only might you be put into one or be unable to get out of one, but you might actually choose to take to one. Sickbeds and deathbeds are dense with meaning and play an important part in one retirement ritual I examine in some detail in chapters 10 and 11. Retirement from active life, and from life plain and simple, can be graded on style points which, if we do not live so long as to be demented, we have much control over. How is one to go down? With all guns blazing, raging against the dying of the light, or in bitterness consumed by fantasies of revenge? With whining and whimpering self-pity or in garish self-abnegation, as the renouncers of the *Upanishads*? Doped up in hospice or hospital? In apathy, whether abject blank dementia or cold stoic firmness?

And what about your property? Are you still with it enough to know what to do with it, if you have any? The soon-to-die worry about their property and what to do with it: should one waste it in riot? Burn it? Bury it in a mausoleum? Pay it over to doctors? Pass it on to heirs who are impatient for it and not willing to concede it to be wholly yours to begin with? Or take it with you, just to annoy them? And just how do you do that?

Like gravediggers, morticians, and archaeologists, a medieval historian, which in part I am, owes the dead for giving him a job and feeding his family. Part of this book, thus, if not quite a Book of the Dead, is a prologue to one. And thus I deal with those end-of-the-road reflections, those that lead you to recognize unpaid and unpayable debts, uncollected ones too. These kinds of musing lead to related matters in parts IV and V: Hamlet's defying augury, his heebie-jeebies—a signal not always false that something's up, maybe rather lethal, and getting ready to face the end is all. I wonder too about taking stock of one's life, and how that is to be done with an ever more spongiform memory. Some of the emotions that play their part as you become increasingly aware that awareness of any sort is ever harder to achieve get their turn. And would you do it over were you offered the chance? Are do-overs desirable, if by some trick they were possible?

Throughout a good portion of history and a wide range of cultures, old age was (as it still is) more likely to subject you to ridicule than to respect. If you were rich and powerful, the ridicule would be behind your back, unless you were nearly blind or deaf. Rollicking good fun was to be had by setting stumbling blocks before the blind or by shouting insults into the ears of the deaf. The biblical injunctions not to treat the halt, blind, and deaf to such abuse are not metaphors. These unfortunates were given no special privilege, unless it was a negative one. One chilling example: David, after having been mocked by the Jebusites, who claimed they could beat him with their blind and lame, the Jebusite way of saying "with both hands tied behind our backs," responds: "Whoever would smite the Jebusites, let him get up the water shaft to attack the lame and the blind, who are hated by David's soul" (2 Sam. 5.8).[5]

The Jebusite blind and lame are about to find themselves props in David's cruel joke, whose wit is to force literalism upon Jebusite trash-talk metaphors. And while at it, why not trick a blessing from your blind old father, rendering him a fool and filling him with anguish? Little kids mocked old bald men who, if the particular bald man happened to have God on his side, could avenge himself by calling down two she-bears to maul the brats. Forty-two mischievous town tykes of Jericho got eliminated that way, getting their comeuppance when the prophet Elisha decided their taunts regarding his baldness were not to be borne (2 Kings 2.23–24). What the crippled and blind, the old and bald, would not have given to have had Elisha's connections.

John of Trevisa, in a late fourteenth-century treatise discussing the ages of man, minces no words about *elde* (old age): "Everyone has contempt for the old person and is annoyed and bored by him" (All men dyspyse þe olde persone and ben hevy and wery of hym).[6] Consider yourself lucky, I guess; it is better to be old now than it ever was,[7] not because you will not be despised and found to be a bore, but because there are drugs to alleviate much of the pain of your greater life expectancy, psychologists who get richly funded to flatter you by "proving" your sense of well-being is at an all-time high, the Internet to fill the emptier time, and old-age pensions, still possibly solvent if you do not linger too much longer, to keep you housed and fed.

Life is a desperate struggle not to be laughed at, sneered at, or looked down upon. It is next to impossible to cheat others of the small pleasures they achieve at your expense. Even if you accept being ignored, in fact seek to be ignored, you still risk ridicule. Minding your own business when you are old, ugly, and deformed seems to provoke little boys and teen girls. They do not even have to be your own children, nor do they need to know you at all. And no, I am not even close to paranoid. I hardly feel persecuted or singled out, nor am I. I am only growing old, and with it comes that sense of self-estrangement I remember last from puberty.

Say you are, as I am, in your sixties. We take it for granted that dividing up humanity by decadal age cohorts starting at thirteen—into teens, twenties, thirties, and so on—is a perfectly natural way to carve up a population. But making a plural of the multiples of ten to indicate an age cohort is rather recent. True, we have girls referred to as in their teens as early as 1673, but for the other multiples nothing is recorded before the last third of the nineteenth century. Until then the plural of a multiple of ten was more likely to be used to refer to a decade in a century, and not before the eighteenth century at that. Marking age cohorts in this fashion is of an ilk with those older traditions that divided the "ages of man" variously into three, four, six, and seven stages.[8]

These older traditions of dividing up the course of life have been much studied in the past couple of decades. The schemas show wide variation. In John Burrow's words: "Anyone who goes to medieval discussions of the ages of man with the intention of ascertaining at what age youth was then thought to end, or old age to begin, will find no easy answer. The texts offer, indeed, a bewildering profusion of different answers."[9] Old age can begin anywhere from thirty-five to seventy-two in the various ages-of-man schemes.[10] In classical Rome, Livy calls Hannibal *senex* (old) when he is forty-four, while Cicero refers to himself as *adulescens* at that same age.[11] Cicero, though never short on self-serving estimations of himself, is sixty-three when he calls himself adulescens at forty-four, so there is some excuse. He may not have classified himself that way when he was forty-four.

Youthfulness is somewhat relative and the stage of life is partly in the eye of the beholder. My mother, who is a preternaturally fit eighty-nine (she still swims a half mile a day and plays eighteen holes whenever the weather does not prevent it), refers to her golfing partners as young. When I press her, she says they are sixty-five or seventy. Middle age has been pushed back. Thirty-five could qualify when I was a child and forty surely would. Some say I am middle aged at sixty-five, but that is because they are already forty-

five and have revised in a transparently self-interested way the ages
of man, in order to avoid having to think of themselves as middle
aged. Old age is pushed back even more forcefully by people already in it. More than half the people between the ages of sixty-five
and seventy-four surveyed in a National Council on Aging study
in 2002 thought of themselves as middle aged or young, as did a
third of those over seventy-five.[12] Only the AARP pushes the other
way, sending you membership solicitations when you reach fifty.[13]
Seventy is not young, for the Bible tells me so, and fifty does not
yet qualify as old except to people in their twenties and thirties.
Yet strangely, the teens in my father's high school yearbook look
to me like men and women. In the picture of my dad going off to
war, he looks like the man he indeed was; in more than one way
he was older at twenty-three than I am now.

Do not think that because of miserable life expectancies old
people were a rare sight in ancient, medieval, or early modern times.
The big culling took place in the first few years of life; in a population in which life expectancy at birth was twenty-five years, if you
made it to twenty, you could expect to get to fifty-four, and if you
made it to forty, you were likely to get to sixty-three.[14] One could
expect a not insignificant 6–8 percent of the population to be over
sixty.[15] Females stood a better chance at all ages than males, child-
bearing years notwithstanding. War, violence, and occupational
accidents ensured that men died at slightly higher rates.

Even under the brutal demographic regimes that made surviving
childhood a bet against unattractive odds, the notion of dying in
childhood, or later, in the so-called middle of one's life—the very
term *middle* indicating it was not properly an end—was thought
unnatural. It was considered natural to die only in one's old age.
In medieval times the law did not excuse people on account of age
from the onerous legal obligations of attending courts or from owing various services, military or otherwise, until they had reached
sixty, sometimes seventy. Then as now, sixty often served as an
excuse, and seldom as a qualification, as when it served as the
minimum age for membership in the *gerousia,* the Spartan sen-
ate.[16] Nowadays, we do not find it natural to die even in old age.

It has become quite rare to hear that someone has died because he was old, and not from a more specific cause: cancer, diabetes, liver, heart, pancreas, brain failure. Rather than blame the czar, we blame his evil ministers.

I began writing this book in my sixty-fifth year. Some will say I am still too young to undertake this enterprise, that I am jumping the gun. They, I suspect, are patronizing me. My fear is that if I delay much longer, I will be not be able to write it, or anything else; there is no stopping the downward slide. I am troubled about how and when to close up shop, about justifying my salary, which was hard enough to do when my wits were still there. Will I know when I am an embarrassment? Do my younger colleagues, sometimes very much younger, already know? Am I missing the hints that they are sending my way?

A metaphorical gibbet casts a shadow over the discussions that follow as undeniable decline and incipient decrepitude force one into thinking about hanging it up. And images of hanging intrude whether I decide to hang in or hang on longer than I should, wearing out whatever welcome I may have once merited, oblivious to no longer measuring up. Will I, or better, will you retire in full exercise of your will, or will you be gently, yet firmly, escorted, not to a gallows, but to an ice floe thinned by global warming, where death by drowning rather than by freezing is the likelier end. Hanging might be preferable to either of these if, like Sam Hall, you can snarl a defiant "Damn your eyes" from the gallows.

Will anyone show up for your retirement dinner? Will you? Will your memory still be good enough to recall everyone who did *not* show up, so that you can even the score? But how will you manage the revenge except by fantasy? Will you be able to come up with their names, should you manage to recall their faces? And why are you consumed with fears about that dinner some five years before it will take place in exactly the same way you would lie awake at night worrying about botching your bar mitzvah three years before you had to go onstage and man up in the Jewish way? But then once you stop worrying about ridiculous things like this, you know you will have lost touch not only with the world, but with yourself.

PART I

The Horror

CHAPTER 1.

The You behind Your Eyes
Is Out of Date

Digression, cast adrift on the buoyant Dead Sea of your own narrations, is a sign of old age, remarked by ancient moralists and proven by modern neurology and brain science to be a symptom of the natural decay of the aging brain. Says John of Trevisa, old age is characterized by a "faillynge of wyttes,"[1] and the failing occurred, as far as we can tell, roughly at the same chronological age back in the old days as it does now. More of our ancient and medieval ancestors died before their brains had a chance to rot, but if they lived into their sixties and beyond, their old brains fared no worse than our old ones do. And though a higher percentage of us will make it to old age, we have been unable to budge the upper limit of the human life span ever since the Israelites entered Canaan after their forty years in the desert and mythical life spans gave way to reality. Eli the priest could still make it to ninety-eight, but Psalm 90 provides us with the famous and eminently reasonable three score and ten, with another ten years of a misery bonus if you are in good shape: "The days of our years are threescore years and ten; and if by reason of strength they be fourscore years, yet is their strength labor and sorrow; for it is soon cut off, and we fly away." Predictably, in a triumph of genocidal irresponsibility, we are trying to extend our lives well beyond not just eighty but beyond ninety and a hundred. Thus the spate of articles in the mainstream press about how near-starvation diets keep mice, and by extension humans, living ever longer. The grim joke being that the best recipe for living a long life is barely to live a life. Recipes generating gustatory satisfaction kill you. Longer life turns out to be just as the misanthropes suspected: a prolongation of misery, though some argue staying drunk on red wine will achieve the same result with greater joy. I can barely restrain my own misanthropy: those who wish to live forever on this earth, without having the good grace to remove themselves elsewhere, either to heaven or to hell, are—dare I say it?—morally defective, miserable Swiftian Struldbrugs.

I got sidetracked a few pages ago in the Introduction by the history of naming age cohorts by the plurals of multiples of ten when I had meant to offer you this vignette instead: you are in your sixties, even fifties, and you are walking by a shop window, or in some area in which a security monitor shows a scan of the line you are in. You sneak a look. You see someone in the space where you should be but you do not recognize the interloper. Then, after an unseemly lag of a second or two you are forced to remake your own acquaintance; it seems you no longer know yourself at first sight. The you behind your eyes believes you look like you did twenty years ago, and it assumes that dated image is the real you, even if recent photos tell a horror story. But photos seldom confirmed your self-image, even when you were young, so you can dismiss the latest batch. In high school you accepted only one or two out of fifty on the contact sheet as satisfactory, though none of your friends or family, when asked, could distinguish the person in the photos you thought reasonably flattering from the many in which you looked like a total doofus. To them they were all indistinguishably you. They were not even putting you on, as you vainly believed, when they thought the best picture was one you felt the most loathsome.

Now, at age sixty-five, you supply yourself with the appearance St. Augustine says you will be accorded at Judgment Day, when you will rise with your thirty-year-old body and looks, which approximates Paul's making your resurrected body match Christ's: "Till we all come in the unity of the faith, and of the knowledge of the Son of God, unto a perfect man, unto the measure of the stature of the fulness of Christ" (Eph. 4.13).[2] The resurrection of the dead heels to our vanity.

The belief in the resurrection of the thirty-year-old body is sustained by our inability to think of our real selves as the wretched old people we are destined to die as, if we are lucky enough to live so long, just as we are unable to imagine ourselves as the babies we once were. We are alienated, in different ways to be sure, both from the present real image of ourselves as old and from distant images of ourselves before age four. Both are in some sense not us. The old us is made strange by the self-deception I am in the midst of discussing, while we are alienated from the infant us by our inability to imagine, let alone remember, what it was like to be that baby or toddler pictured in the family album.

What bodies are the staggering numbers of babies and toddlers who fell victim to the mortality tables to be provided with at the Last Judgment? Does the baby arise as a baby? Or with the body it would have had had it not been nipped in the bud? Opinions differed,[3] but the anonymous poet desperate with longing who, sometime in the second half of the fourteenth century, wrote the moving Middle English poem known as *Pearl* to mourn the death of his two-year-old daughter, sees her in a vision as a queen in heaven, a beautiful maiden, not as a toddler. Yet he is still able to recognize her as the precious pearl he has lost. She rather firmly reprimands her father that his grief is out of order, since she is now a bride of the Lamb. The poet wants to be consoled by the vision, but in the end it only augments his sorrow and grief. The consolation that his faith offers him fails to console him. Some believers, evidently, were unable to shrug off, or become inured to, the grim demographic realities of their world.[4]

If we construct a fantasy of childhood as a time of an unalienated unity of being, then that sense of unity, the actual feeling of it, cannot be recovered by memory but must be accepted on faith, or by supposing it for our own children when they are happily (we think) lost in fantasy and play. But as soon as memories begin, so do memories of fear, anxiety, and shame, of not fitting in, of a vivid image of being mocked at age four in nursery school by a girl a year older because I dribbled chocolate milk down my shirt.

I must say I do not know what older adults those psychologists have been testing, those who, these researchers insist, remember only pleasant feelings, no particulars, mind you, just pleasant feelings from times long past.[5] Have they regressed to that supposed unity of being we impute to children? Once our selves start to multiply in order to handle the various roles we are called on to play as moderately well-socialized actors, good-bye, unity of being and good-bye, lack of self-consciousness. I never felt I properly learned to play the role of a mature adult. I have tried to discuss interest rates as if knowledgeable about them; I tried to act upset over one of my kid's lousy grades. But I never felt one with the part. If I had a hard time adjusting to the roles demanded in the prime of life, then what am I to do with old age, where I am not even sure I know what I look like?[6] Maybe playing the old man properly requires thinking you are twenty years younger than you are and acting the fool who thinks such. If that is the case, then my very failure to recognize myself in the shop window proves me perfectly immersed in the role of the old man I thought I wasn't.

But with recognition comes deflation and shame, because you fear that others can see your pathetic vanity, that they caught you in the act of such egregiously self-flattering complacency, that they caught an old guy checking himself out in the shop window. Any minimally astute observer, such as one of your students, can see the pretense in the way you talk, or try to hold yourself, which you believe is ramrod straight, but the sag at the knees and the crick in your back betray you. Yet that shame is also its own sort of vanity. It assumes people, younger people, to be exact, are looking at you, or looking at you as anything other than a sixty-something, cancelled soul. As one female student told a female colleague of mine, which my colleague, reveling in Schadenfreude, hastened to relay to me: "Oh, Professor Miller, he's such a cute old man." That was rather more painful than the specter in the shop window, though I still vividly remember when I was twenty how someone forty might as well have been a member of a different species, or a shade in Charon's boat crossing over. The idea that such moribund souls could be objects of desire or have any themselves was beyond my imaginative powers. And still is. The student and my colleague were instruments of cosmic comic revenge, punishing me for having somewhat too good self-esteem, which like so much self-esteem had become quite unhinged from reality.

Comic for a while. Eventually the genre switches to horror. When you were a little kid, very little, four or five, the old were not cute, especially the very old. Grandparents were excepted, but it was an easy exception to make because they were only in their late forties. The very old, however, were images of death and blight and scared the bejesus out of you. One of my earliest memories is of meeting an old withered soul from our small synagogue in Green Bay in the grocery store and tearfully asking my mother when we escaped if that would happen to me too. The wrinkles, the blotched skin, the gnarled hands that reached to pat my head, the wart with a hair like a dog's whisker sticking out of it—little kids see the world as Gulliver saw it in Brobdingnag—the thick glasses that monstrously magnified the eyes, the goiter on the neck.

I am not quite there yet. Even the shop window did not disconfirm that. The genre I live in is still broad comedy. I get angry when my wife or kids tell me that they responded to my question and that I just did not hear the answer. Am I getting hard of hearing too? More likely they are disdaining to answer and falsely claiming that I did not hear. But that is what my truly hard-of-hearing mother thinks too. Lately, though, when speaking with students I do find myself leaning too close, violating their personal space, using up my one permissible "What?" then hastily jerking back while taking a stab at a sensible response, only to burden them with what turns out to be a non sequitur.[7]

Yet within hours of the encounter with my reflection, even as few as five minutes, I reconstitute the false me so recently exposed as a delusion. I guess I succumb to positive thinking. You would need the uncompromising eye of Rembrandt to keep seeing yourself as others see you. As long as that false you knows its place and does not make any embarrassing demands on others to confirm overtly its truth, you are welcome to your vanity. You might, for an instant, feel a fool for having your self-conception so divorced from reality, yet you can always find a support group ready to congratulate you for not giving in to ageism, to "socially constructed" categorizations unfavorable to your deluded upbeat view of yourself.[8] And worries on this score cease altogether once you bottom out in true dementia, as in the case of some Alzheimer's patients who neither recognize their written name nor know what they presently look like and are thus unable to find their way back to their rooms when meandering the nursing-home corridor unless there is a picture of themselves outside the room, for they do not recall the room number either.[9] Not just any picture will work, though. The person captured in a recent photo would be a stranger, unrecognizable, but put up a picture taken in their thirties, the prime of life, and they know the room is theirs. Eventually, it seems, you lose the capacity to be embarrassed by the self-serving image that the you behind your eyes thinks is you.

We look at ourselves in the mirror every morning without it producing much anxiety. Our face is much easier to deal with than confronting the disgusting transformations below the neck (actually, the neck has its problems too). The mirror was much more dangerous when you were fourteen and a humongous zit had erupted on your forehead hours before the Friday dance. So why the shock of the shop window? Because we are ready for the mirror in the morning (most of the time, anyway); it is a ritual we perform on autopilot. The task at hand occupies us: shaving or combing hair, should there be any. We make sure to see only the part addressed. The stakes are very low, though not so low that I have not taken to shaving in the shower sans mirror. If we must confront the whole countenance, we put on a game face. We have taught ourselves to see not our face but our mirror face, a creature with its own independent existence, like the picture in our high school yearbook, which is no less strangely unreal and out of date.

The horror of the morning mirror is not so much what you see but what you have managed to miss until it is too late. How could that single hair sprouting from your ear have reached a half inch in length before you noticed it? You hasten to shave it off, cutting the ear in the process, unable to stop the bleeding because of the anticoagulant effect of the 81 mg daily dose of aspirin you take so that you can—the joke of it—live longer.

Others serve as truer mirrors that force upon us these abrupt realizations of our own decline. Can it be that my high school friend looks so terribly old? Wasn't he a year behind me? The theme is treated in exquisite detail by Proust in the last volume of his magnum opus, and much earlier and more briefly by Seneca who, when seeing an old slave at the entrance to one of his estates he had not visited in years, asks the bailiff the identity of the "broken-down dotard." The slave answers: "Don't you know me, sir? I am Felicio; you used to bring me little images. My father was Philositus the steward, and I am your pet slave." Seneca has no defense against the truth that that pet slave represents.[10]

The shame of such self-flattering blindness. Shame seems to crop up in everything I write (shame is by and large a good thing; it helps keep us moral, honorable, and socialized): humiliation, fears of exposure, the anxieties that attend the simplest interactions—muffing a routine handshake—or the torment of replaying those interactions afterward. Honor is always at stake and always being lost or threatened in the commonest of interactions. And with honor and its discontents come revenge, or fantasies of it, at least when it is someone else who has made a fool out of you, rather than you making one of yourself all on your own. But what revenges can there be at my age? What honor? Honors, should there be any, should not be confused with honor. Honors come in the form of plaques and awards and retirement dinners; honor comes in the form of others envying you.

FISHING FOR COMPLIMENTS

At the end of one's career one is asked to give talks on topics one wrote about fifteen or twenty years earlier. To prepare, I reread my past writing on the theme, hoping to reawaken, or to ram back in, the knowledge I had back then. Rereading one's own work is a fraught experience. I lose either way: if I feel a surge of pride—"Wow, Miller, the muse was really singing when you wrote this"—no more than two seconds into indulging a fantasy of posthumous glory or even of belated present acclaim, my daydream crashes into the sea before the oxygen masks can drop down. Thus chastened, should I reexamine the work and conclude yet again that it is verifiably inspired and ever so unjustly ignored, then I despair that I could write anything approaching it today. I cannot remember that I ever knew the things I was talking about in that book. Wherever did I come up with that example to make my point? I would not even know where to look to find it now, even with the Google crutch, available now but not then.

More frequently, however, my reaction is this: no pride at all, just a chastening recognition of superficiality. I hope no one has read it, a hope that has pretty much been fulfilled, unlike most hopes. Presumably the dean hadn't; all he cared about was that it got published. This second reaction rings truer than the one celebrating my own genius. Negative self-judgments, because they must overcome our tendency to self-flatter, are likely to be more reliable than positive ones. Or as La Rochefoucauld put it: "Our enemies get closer to the truth in their judgment of us than we get ourselves."[11]

Like that shop window that forced upon me a moment of painful truth, so too surprise attacks of painful truth occur in one's professional life. One reads the work of some fellow medievalists—friends, in fact—and its excellence reveals to you with painful clarity your own shortcomings, your corner cutting, your lack of gravitas: gravitas bearing not the sense of dull pomposity but rather an enviable refusal on your friends' part to dishonor their subject matter by making themselves, their anxieties about their relationship to it, even minutely their theme. They are real scholars, needing no genre mixing to provide a defense against failure by claiming to be playing a game halfway between essayist and historian—a law prof to historians, a historian to law profs, a half-baked moral psychologist to both, a jack of a middling number of trades to flit among so that you can always claim, when challenged, that you are not really in *that* field.

You do not, however, completely trust such negative judgments, either, for you surely do not believe them with all thine heart, with all thy soul, and with all thy might, in the idiom of Deuteronomy. These painful self-castigations, like the painful knowledge of the shop window, decay quickly or are shunted aside again and again. Merely to state them, to publicize them, is to fish for a compliment, to seek reassurances, even to display confidence. But should the fished-for compliment not be granted, if the begged-for reassurance is not proffered? Then these essays will have run afoul of the imitative fallacy, which holds that you should not be boring when writing about boredom or stupid when writing about stupidity. If one has lost it, one should not write about losing it. You do not want the proof of your fears showing up in the pudding. But who am I to taste the pudding and pass on its quality? Old age has deprived my sense of taste of its nuance.

Yet this half-posed self-abnegation I have been indulging for the last few pages is more than a vulgar fishing expedition. It is also meant to work some magic. By claiming more decay than may have actually set in, or by owning up to what has set in, I hope to ward off more, and perhaps reclaim some ground already lost. The gods will reward my self-flagellation, the modest stripes of blood on my back, for not presuming on their beneficence. By counting chickens of negative value before they hatch, you expect to trick the gods into treating you better than it is certain they would had you counted unhatched chickens of positive value, in which case you can rest assured they would take a hostile interest in your presumption and kill the chicks or smash the eggs.

CHAPTER 2.

Can You Recall
What You Had for
Dinner, Cronus?

A competently socialized person knows that a welcome has a half-life; he senses when to leave, graciously saving the host from having to hint that it is time to do so. The adept actor anticipates a hint before it needs to be given. But we make mistakes sometimes and misread the situation. It is one thing to misread by ten minutes when we should have left a dinner party, and quite another to misread by ten years when we should have left the job, or by thirty years when we should have left off breathing. Since age takes its toll on our perceptual acumen, we may lose the capacity to discern even the heaviest-handed of hints, nor are we in any mood to take the hints we do perceive. Instead of taking our leave, we mobilize politically and demand third and fourth helpings, to be put up for the night too, thirty more years of nights, our bodies still insisting on staying long after our minds have lost the ability to know we have put our hosts in the poorhouse.

To hell with taking polite leave: there are more of us merry old souls than ever before, and we vote, which the young, whom we fleece, are less likely to do, and will be outnumbered even if they do show up at the polls, mightily armed as we are with obedient mortality tables. The withered hands of the old are now rather more powerful than they were in earlier times; it does not take much strength to feed a ballot into a voting machine, or to send in an absentee one if your arthritis is acting up.

As Western populations age, the costs of maintaining the old could justly activate in the young an image of the old as so many Cronuses and Saturns devouring their offspring.[1] (The myth or truth of the cannibalistic old is of long standing.) The riotous and stoned youths of the sixties, now in our sixties, who did much to pave the way for our no-gratification-left-behind culture, take to this mythic role with no shame, cramming our craw with everything in sight, not caring that it is chunks of our children and grand-children that are the tenderest meat on our well-presented plate.[2]

Me, Cronus? Occasionally I flatter myself that I am earning my keep, contributing more than I am consuming. And unlike those football players and boxers who do not know when to quit, profes-sors like me cannot be cut. Tenure and age-discrimination laws let us keep working, which somehow does not seem the right word. Besides, there are always a couple of lazy colleagues whose real contribution to the enterprise is to make less lazy ones feel like we deliver value for the price. Never mind that my keep would fund four entry-level scholars in history or anthropology who are now unemployed: I still have kids of my own to feed, though I might be feeding them with someone else's. Self-deception and wishful thinking, looking on the bright side in a self-interested way, keep us conveniently color-blind to our real value, seeing black when the ink is red. Or simply not caring if it is red when we see it.

What of my clearly decaying scholarly capacities? Of being unable to continue learning or, if able, then unable to retain what I have recently learned? I can't even reliably come up with words like *refrigerator* or *kitty litter* and must endure my wife's hand ges-ture of irritated contempt to "get on with it." Can I ever get lost in a book again without my mind wandering? I have always been

Figure 1: Saturn (Cronus) eating his son.
Francisco Goya, Prado Museum, Madrid.

suspicious of those parents who claim that their dull normal and badly behaved children are really geniuses suffering from attention deficit disorder and need to be dosed with Ritalin. But now it seems, in some kind of poetic justice, that I have come down with ADD, the only difference being that I really do have it. My doctor actually prescribed Ritalin for me, which, as it turned out, my health insurance refused to cover for anyone over eighteen. Not willing to pay the unsubsidized price, my avarice, itself an attribute of old age, has kept me Ritalin-free and my mind wandering.

Everything distracts me. Being interested in something has become unmoored from my ability to attend to it. Ambient noise, intrusive trivial thoughts, e-mail, stock prices, Green Bay Packer blogs variously and predictably plague me.[3] Ambient quiet is distracting too and sent me to the Internet to buy a white-noise machine. I interrupted the writing of this paragraph to play a game of solitaire, and then when I lost I allowed myself to play until I won, and then one more in case I won two in a row, and then I kept on until I won two in a row. Says the ancient rabbinical *Pirkei Avot: The Ethics of the Fathers,* written some eighteen hundred years ago: "If a man is walking by the way and is studying and then interrupts his study and exclaims: 'How beautiful is this tree? How beautiful is this plowed furrow?' Scripture considers that it is to be regarded as if he has forfeited his life (or as if he bears guilt for his soul)."[4] If the beauties of nature cannot justify distraction, what of solitaire? My offense is (*as if*) capital; if only I could remember which circle of hell awaits me. My will—an element of my name, no less—never strong to begin with, has become weaker. The "I am" that remains in Will-*iam* is thus a ghost of its former self. If William James is right, and I find that he usually is, then I am in trouble: "*The essential achievement of the will, in short, when it is most 'voluntary,' is to attend to a difficult object and hold it fast before the mind*"(italics in original).[5]

Has Nemesis gotten even with me for the contempt I did not quite disguise for the dead wood of twenty years ago by making me petrified wood in the eyes of my younger colleagues? You see them, don't you, giving signals that they want to break off the conversation you are holding them to almost out of spite, but desperately too, telling them, Oh, just one more thing, but talking faster as a concession to your perceiving in some primitive part of your brain that you are boring them silly, which they can perceive that you can perceive and so on in an infinite regress. You even find yourself following them down the hall as they head for the hills, still chattering at them, self-destructively unable to break off.

BLANKING

There is no small amount of self-flattery in the lament of losing it: it claims you once had it to lose. Have you inflated your own past abilities? Complaining about how much "it" you have lost is a claim to a reasonably worthy past, and in your attempt to claim such former heights, even if you acknowledge your descent, you are sneaking in a claim to being still plenty high in absolute terms.

But unless you are one of those insufferable souls with self-esteem of such quality that no disconfirming evidence, no matter how devastating, can dent it, or unless you are already well embarked on dementia, these delusions about our minds are harder to maintain than the falsehoods we maintain about our appearance. You get caught once too often having forgotten things that are shameful for someone in your field not to have at your beckon. You fear too that you may be pretending to have once known them, that in fact you have forgotten nothing. Claiming forgetfulness is a way, pathetic as it is, of saving face. Where once you could blame things on drink, you now blame them on inevitable decline, on having sampled a few sips of the River Lethe. (Drink, whether from rivers or bottles, figures in many myths of memory and forgetfulness.) In the questioning after a public lecture, you find yourself unable to deny that the questioner is thinking better about your subject than you are. You tell yourself: At least I am still capable of shame. I can still recognize when someone is a whole lot sharper than I am. How many clowns in my racket can be skewered by a questioner's comments and not even know they were shown up for frauds and fools? But that ungenerous thought, despite its truth, dares the gods to make me one of them, if they have not done so already without my knowledge.

Being bested, even on your own turf, happened when you were younger too; big deal, that is part of learning. The shame it triggered spurred you to learn more, to do better. But when it starts to happen more frequently than is seemly, the earth beneath you no longer seems so firm, and your confidence starts to wane. You find yourself stuttering, losing track of your train of thought, just plain blanking.

A runner or a swimmer can prove exactly how much his abilities have decayed; so too there are ways of measuring the decay of mental abilities, even if not quite stopwatch accurate. Things just do not happen as quickly in my brain as they once did. Always a slow reader, I could count on about thirty pages an hour for a novel I was not distracted from. Now it is twenty-five if I can stay focused, but the distractions are more frequent too, so that the real rate is closer to fifteen to twenty pages. I have to look up Old Norse and Old English words that twenty years ago I did not. I cannot add, subtract, divide, or multiply numbers without writing them down, something that used not to be the case. Just the other day I struggled figuring out the crew size of a Venetian transport in the Fourth Crusade when the book I was reading claimed that the two hundred Venetian ships requisitioned would need a crew of twenty-seven thousand to man them. This sounded high and I figured it must have mistakenly included the troops, but I needed a pen and paper to write out 27,000/200 and then cancel out the zeroes to figure out the average per ship. I cannot remember the scholarship I have dutifully read within the past two weeks, let alone two months ago. Though most of it was eminently forgettable, I also cannot recall the most gruesomely lurid of accounts in a medieval chronicle that I did not think I would need to take notes on because I could trust myself never to forget something that perversely entertaining.[6]

The slowing down seems to mimic in many respects the mechanics of conversing in a foreign language, one that you are not able to think in and so must translate in a race against time into

English what your interlocutor is saying to you in French so that you can respond. I now find myself conscious that I am translating English into itself before I understand what is being said. By the time I have parsed the first part of the speaker's sentence, I have already missed the next part. Maybe it is not my memory that is at fault, but rather that the processing speed of all my mental functions is slowing down. You feel every couple of minutes that you got plunked down in medias res, in the middle of things, yet again, wondering what had happened and is happening. It is as if I were driving through an infinitely long school crossing zone in which I am the only one obeying the speed limit.[7]

Worse still, I cannot remember what I have written, whether perhaps I have not published this very paragraph somewhere else. Self-plagiarism does explain the extraordinary productivity of a few well-known academics; why should I be any different? Didn't I already say that in my *Faking It* book?

I just stopped typing and started to get out of my chair because I had formed the intention to . . . I forgot what I was getting up to do. Was I going to check *Faking It?* Then why would I have started to get up since I have a searchable version on my hard drive? Was I going to look up a word in the Latin dictionary? If I were, the thought that I might have been thus embarked does not prompt a rediscovery of the intention. I am certain that I did form an intention. That much I know. There is some good evidence. I made small initiatory movements to carry it out—I stopped typing, I started from my chair, and I am consumed with a panicky sense of being stuck in a satanically inverted *Amazing Grace:* I once was found but now I'm lost; I could see but now I'm blind.

This total loss of an intention is more unsettling than the more frequent failures that kick in a little later in the unfolding of an intentional action you are already well in the midst of. When that happens, I know there was a word I meant to look up or a book I meant to pull from the shelf, but I have forgotten which word or which book. Those things usually come back to me eventually, or so I think. This sort of lapse seems to be happening more often, too, and I now consider them of minor moment if I recover the goal within a few seconds, successfully pulling Eurydice back from oblivion. At least in these kinds of forgetting I know the rough domain of my intention: some word or some book. But this time the blank is blanker, for I have no clue what I roughly intended at all, only that I intended something.

This kind of failure is not like those dully common failures of forward memory that seem more frequent among teenagers than among sexagenarians: forgetting to discharge a duty or to do a chore that must be fulfilled sometime in the near future. My youngest son used to forget to walk the neighbor's dog, though it was his job to do so daily, more often than I forget a doctor's appointment. But I did forget to be in my office for my office hours last week. It seems that as I head for the infancy of old age I have already reached the irresponsible teenage level on my return trip back to diapers.[8]

I suppose I can take some consolation from these unnerving failures to remember an intention within seconds of forming it that I am hyperaware of the blank, that it torments me. Were the erasure so complete as to keep me blithely unaware that I had even formed an intention in the first place, I would be embarked on Herr Alzheimer's ship of fools. Maybe, though, horrifically, I never had an intention but only the illusion of one, the illusion taking the form of the panicky sensation of blanking. I cannot accept that or I would be in chains on the lordly lofts of Bedlam. What in hell did I get up to do? I have not a clue, and it never came back to me either. But then I cannot be certain that it did not come back, only that if it did, I did not recognize it as the intention that I had lost.[9]

These kinds of failures share a family resemblance with another kind of failure: blanking on names or words. This seems to be a special curse for sexagenarian teachers who fail to find the names of even the most intelligent and attractive of their students at moments when it is apparent to them and everyone else that you blanked. As William James pointed out, ever so perfectly, that blank is not just a formless blank. It has a shape: "a sort of wraith of the name is [in the gap], beckoning us in a given direction, making us at moments tingle with the sense of our closeness, and then letting us sink back without the longed-for term."[10] Much the same with the wraith of a lost intention. A small vertigo sets in. With a name or a noun you cannot come up with, you might run through the alphabet hoping that with the first letter the rest will fill itself out. This may work for a lost word, but not for recovering that fleeting intention that just slipped through the widening cracks in my consciousness.

Nor is the story just one of forgetfulness triumphing over memory. The productive capacity to forget is decaying too. Forgetting comes in more than a few flavors, some of them quite beneficent, like the ability to inhibit memories irrelevant to the task at hand that intrude and disrupt it, or the ability to forget insults or disses, or hated songs. For those things my memory is acuter than it ever was. It helps explain my late-onset ADD.[11]

Q.E.D.

January 13, 2010: I am defending to a colleague the wisdom of the police rounding up the usual suspects.

Me: Claude Rains was being more than a mere cynic, which of course he was also being, when he said "round up the usual suspects" because the usual suspects were not innocent but the known criminals of whatever the city was, Tangiers, Marrakech, I forget which.
Colleague: Casablanca.
Me: I am going to go shoot myself.[12]

CHAPTER 3

Shrink Wrap

One not very rare and mildly mystifying trick of the mind is that it can block out or miss knowing something, a word or fact, so common and obvious that one would have to be a flatworm not to have internalized it. When the word or fact finally forces itself into your word-hoard or knowledge bank, you inevitably hear it used or referred to several times within the next week. The coincidence, you feel, is uncanny, the world strangely enchanted. The only enchantment, however, is the one that put some part of your brain to sleep for so many years. You were faced with that word or fact hundreds of times in your life and somehow remained oblivious to it.

Let me offer this example of a fact that finally impressed itself upon me when the stakes were such that I had no defenses against the information. A month before he died three years ago, my father, a good and dignified man, suffered a sudden major insult to his brain. Within the space of a couple of hours he had become seriously demented, having avoided that fate for eighty-six years. A CAT scan was ordered and the doctor showed the image to my mother and me and said: "There is nothing here that looks unusual, only the normal shrinkage that one would expect in the brain of a person his age."

Normal shrinkage? You mean the brain actually shrinks? It is not just that it wears out and silts up? It actually shrinks? Yup, said the doctor as she pointed to the frontal lobe region. Within a week of accessing that distressing knowledge, I saw any number of references to it: several articles in newspapers, a PBS program. But that was three years ago. Now it seems that every week the popular press has some piece on it, targeting aging baby boomers and accompanied by antiwrinkle cream advertisements when you call it up on the Web. I must have thought it was a metaphor, apparently seduced into that belief by the influence of the word *shrink,* meaning psychiatrist or therapist. Shrinking turns out to be only part of the sad story. Take the hard truth from professional brain researchers: "With age, the number of dopaminergic receptors declines; many brain structures show volumetric shrinkage; white matter becomes less dense; and brains of even very highly functioning individuals are frequently characterized by destructive neurofibrillary plaques and tangles."[1] Plaques and tangles to add to the volume loss, spongy white matter, even if I should be lucky enough to qualify as one of those "highly functioning individuals."

Best not to know such things. Since that chance revelation, I have become consumed with self-doubt. I no longer could satisfy myself that it was mere anxiety about losing it, and not really losing it, that was generating the symptoms, causing me to forget student names, Norse words, the authors and titles of books I had read two weeks before, and just last week blanking on President Obama's first name. No, I was suffering from nonmetaphorical brain rot. Add to that the power of suggestion, working as a demonic negative placebo to generate the need for care rather than as a magical cure, as would a proper placebo. I started to feel as if my brain was balsa wood floating in a helium sea. Maybe I took too much blood pressure medicine today and that is why I almost passed out when I stood up, or was it that I also had just found out that hypertension accelerates normal shrinkage and decline of the brain?[2]

The only solace I took from the reading I did on the shrinking brain was that brains are already heading downward by one's early thirties, even late twenties, some parts faster and more precipitously than others.[3] The prefrontal cortex, where a good chunk of *you* resides, is last to develop (thus helping explain why teenagers are teenagers) and first to start its slow drift and then increasingly rapid plunge downhill. Luckily, I had lived more than twice thirty years in blissful ignorance of that fact. I make sure to tell my younger colleagues about it lest they be caught unawares as I was. I am considerate in that way. How could I have been surprised, though? Why should the brain be any different from the muscles I used to run with?

COMPENSATIONS AND CONSOLATIONS: A POLEMIC

So what if your brain has shrunk and you are no longer quite as tall and your never very enviable amount of muscle lies closer to the floor? It is not as if being a teenager was so great either. Welcome the escape to the contemplative. Contemplation, in our culture, evokes ideas of communing with something. Thinking and communing always seemed to me to be at war with each other. Contemplation brings up images of sitting in a rowboat or over a hole drilled in the ice of Green Bay, impatient that the fish were not biting. (These experiences were not of my own choosing, but at the kind invitation of friends.) The true fisherman is patient, enjoying the process, the bugs in summer, the frostbite and alcohol in winter, sitting, sometimes standing, and waiting. What were these guys thinking about that could prompt such quietude and oneness with the world? I suspected it was the achievement of total inner emptiness, the complete escape from thinking—Buddhism on ice.

The attraction of waiting like this for a fish eludes me. For me, waiting is part of a nexus of ideas that includes being stood up, being dealt with cavalierly by a colleague I was to meet but is late, late enough to kill all possibility of forgiveness. Fish were no better than humans in that regard; both annoyed you, the difference being that I entertained no murderous fantasies about the fish. Waiting is the experience of the emergency room or doctor's office. When waiting is not making you frustrated or mad, it can bring its own fears and dreads, as in waiting for the other shoe to drop. Contemplation was too closely associated with phony meditation, with new-age vacuity, with plain old snake oil and hokum. Contemplation, I know, was also the hard discipline of certain religious devotions and spiritual exercises, but my view of it got poisoned by having come of age in the sixties, when gurus were no less insipid than the positive psychologists of today. No St. John of the Cross they. I do not mean to be unfair to this kind of contemplation, but I could never engage in it without feeling foolish. And since I knew so many verifiable fools to be taken with it, that was proof enough for me.

Now that my brain has lost no small amount of its mass, maybe contemplation will come on its own. Patience will at long last be achievable, forced upon me by having nothing much to look forward to, except looking backwards or looking around at the present state of affairs, and then presto: I lose it. We live in a culture of cowardice triumphant, a refusal to face mortality—or even minor bruising, as when I watch my colleagues' children learning to ride bikes in suits of armor. We can even keep screwing no matter how disgusting our bodies have become, until finally even Viagra must admit defeat in the face of dementia. This is not youth culture triumphant. Quite the contrary: it is the *reductio* of our obsession with health, which in the end turns out not to be so healthy for the polity as a whole, nor for the demented body and its family in its final years. *O tempora, o mores,* and all that. But what, I ask myself, would you have those old people pathetically remaking their sagging, rotting bodies do? Contemplate? Why assume that contemplation will do anything but confirm the justness of despair on one hand or, if you are lucky, set your mind at ease about using Botox, Viagra, or getting a face lift? Instead of feeling ridiculous, you might actually think you are quite the man or woman.

Why should I think that one's emotional life does not suffer decay in tandem with one's cognitive life, the two, emotions and cognition, being interdependent in the more consuming aspects of our consciousness? Respectable psychological research on aging has shown that old people have less ability to process and deal with complex emotional situations, since their ability to handle complexity of any sort shrinks with their brain.[4] But this being America, there is a large body of work that celebrates the shrunken brain. The ever-upbeat researchers who do these studies claim we are very much happier with it smaller.[5] Happy as a clam, or any other invertebrate, it seems.

These researchers, mostly adherents of positive psychology, are driven to impose on their doddering subjects their own irrational propensity to see an empty glass as three-quarters full.[6] What to most of us reasonable people seem to be obvious debilities are redefined in this work as rational adaptations. The literature most frequently cited in this happy-oldster school comes from Professor Laura Carstensen of Stanford, her students, and collaborators.[7] Professor Carstensen writes of things such as "the positivity effect in old age," her name for the upbeatness she finds in old people, and has a theory to match, which she calls "the theory of socioemotional selectivity." America, God bless her, has snake oil bearing the Stanford label.[8]

One of that theory's chief claims is that old people do not learn new things or pursue increasing their knowledge, not because they are losing it or have become dimwitted, but because they are being rational and wise. They instead "are motivated to pursue emotional satisfaction. They invest in sure things, deepen existing relationships and savor life. Under these conditions, people are less interested in banking information and instead invest resources in the regulation of emotion."[9] Except for the part about investing "in sure things," like their homes and mortgage-backed securities, her description of old people strikes me as more characteristic of adolescents and indeed of my students than of the geezers I know, though I must admit that I have invested the amount of my co-pay in Zoloft to help in the regulation of my emotions—the richness of which, their refinement and complexity, remember, have diminished along with my other brain functions.

Carstensen speaks of the "paradox of aging." By this she means that conceding the oldsters' undeniable cognitive and physical declines, old people show improvement in their sense of well-being. "How can it be," she writes, "that people suffer significant loss with age but experience life more positively?"[10] Paradox? There is no paradox here at all, even if we grant for the nonce that her surveys showing old-age upbeatness are reliable, ignoring that her subjects may well be on rather higher doses of Zoloft and Paxil than I am. These oldsters have lost the very means to make the critical judgments to evaluate accurately their situation. Remember that National Council on Aging survey mentioned in the introduction? Most of these old people do not even think they are old. Is that very delusion itself the *cause* of the positivity effect or the *effect* of the positivity effect, assuming there is such a thing to begin with? These deluded souls, apparently, make up a significant percentage of the people answering Professor Carstensen's questionnaires.

As a general rule, critical intelligence—mental acuity—wars with happiness. That claim can pretty much be proved by inspection. The ancient and medieval medical science of humors—no worse a theory for being old than the syndromes and personality types of DSM-IV (*Diagnostic and Statistical Manual of Mental Disorders*) are any better for being new—observed that melancholics tended to verbal wittiness and superior discernment.[11] Examine your own experience. Most occasions of happiness mean an escape from thinking too precisely on the event or from thinking at all. Bliss and distinction making are mostly at odds, as indeed the old proverb about ignorance and bliss would have it.[12]

The sense of well-being reported by Professor Carstensen's upbeat oldsters, if sense it is, owes much to their mental debility, to an increasing tendency to have false memories or to recall only the gist of things rather than the particulars because old people have a hard time dredging up any particulars, even false ones. There is, however, if not quite a paradox, a modest irony that Carstensen does not note: according to her "socioemotional selectivity theory," it is irrational for any oldsters to learn about it, it being by the theory's own premise a waste of their time.

I suspect Professor Carstensen has misinterpreted much of the positive feelings her subjects report. They are probably being merely polite, not wishing to complain or, more darkly, they are contented in the minimalist sense that word often bears—like Shylock's "I am content" after he has been stripped of everything—to have made it through it all still breathing, possessing no wish whatsoever to go through it again even should they have had a relatively good life. The contentment is of the sort that I felt as I lay vomiting on the track after having run a four-hundred-meter race: relieved it was over. Did she interview any old Jews?[13] She couldn't have, unless we have become more assimilated than I would ever have thought possible.

Let me make one softening qualification: I do not deny that some people do better than they otherwise would by thinking that they are better than they in fact are, if only because the truth would sink them into a depressed torpor rather than set them free. So, admittedly, some benefit can be had from preferring rosy error because it feels better than the depressing truth. As a society we might gain productivity as a consequence of this plague of self-serving self-esteem and positivity, but that does not make it less frustrating and tiresome on an individual level. Don't get me wrong; I am greatly in favor of people having small vanities, even in indulging them; they are absolutely necessary to human moral and social life.

But a line gets crossed when B+ students (formerly C students) think they deserve an A+, formerly an A, because they fully believe their work demands it. Show them an A+ paper from one of their classmates, better by far than the model answer you, the teacher, provided the class, and they still think theirs better. The cost of such self-esteem and so much positivity is less that it self-inflates beyond reason than that to do so it cultivates blindness to real excellence in others.

CHAPTER 4.

Old Views of Old Age

My views reproduce one very well-established view of old age: the negative one. Western cultures have been of two minds about old age since the classical and biblical periods, and the traditions have been well detailed in recent studies, so I will paint with a broad brush. Both views are still very much with us.[1]

In the positive view, which comes in several versions, pagan, Christian, gerontocratic, old age tends to be associated with wisdom, with prudence. Advantages, moral and intellectual, are to be had from finally being freed from the chief passion of youth—sex—and from the dominant passion of maturity—ambition. Old age was the time for the soul rather than the body, a time for contemplation. In the pagan Roman world, among the rich, old age could be a time of *honestum otium* (virtuous leisure), a retreat to one's villa to read, write, look to the farm (which meant watching your slave steward manage the slave laborers), and correspond with like-minded thoughtful old rich people. Old age allowed one to escape to belle lettres from the dangers and rough excitement of Roman public life, if, that is, you were reasonably healthy and still had your marbles. Cicero's friend Atticus, to whom Cicero addressed his tract on old age—*De senectute*—is the exemplar of this virtuous leisure: he succeeded in making his villa the ideal retirement home of today. Cicero's tract, however, assumes the dominance of the negative view.[2] Thus the tract's combative polemical tone, achieved by putting its arguments into the mouth of Cato the Elder, a man who was famous for taking uncompromising orneriness to unsurpassed levels, and who was not inclined to take prisoners in war or in argument. His opponent, like Carthage, was to be destroyed. His positive view of old age was hardly accompanied by upbeatness; it bristled with cantankerous combativeness instead.[3]

Plutarch thought positively about old age, but disapproved of the withdrawal from public life that went with honestum otium. He advocated instead that the old remain active in civic life, because, being old, they would be less inclined to pursue their own interests rather than those of the common weal.[4] One wonders at the normally acute Plutarch seriously claiming that old age prompts disinterest or selflessness. Tell that to the AARP, and to the old Cronuses who vote down any property tax to improve the schools as not being in their interest because their children are already out of school. Perhaps it is because the old, though not a rare sight even in the grim demographic regimes of the premodern world, constituted a smaller percentage of the population then than now, nor were they organized as a special-interest group. Their lack of organized clout can perhaps explain Plutarch's mistaking impotence for virtue.

Even Christianity could put old age to good use, if one were wise enough to be penitent, for its miseries could count as a partial atonement for the sins of youth. Old age served as a kind of premortem purgatory, a training ground for the tough work of expiation that lay ahead.[5]

The negative tradition, on the other hand, is often bound up with a general satirical misanthropy that visited special vitriol on

old age. Old age represented everything that is vile about embodied existence. The precursor of death, it looks like death except it
reproduces all the disadvantages of childhood with none of its excuses or hopes, or lovable bodies. It is about rot, meanness, avarice,
cowardice, peevishness, irascibility, moroseness, whining, bad eyes,
deafness, dripping noses, hacking coughs, baldness, loss of teeth,
reeking breath, loss of libido, sagging flesh, forgetfulness, repetitive
garrulity.[6] As pure description, this view rings no less true today
than it did more than two thousand years ago. Why shouldn't the
old be peevish, irascible, morose, irritable, given their aches and
pains, their loss of mental acuity, their not mattering anymore? I
find, for instance, that arthritic knees, hips, and left big toe, the
increasingly common morning experience of discovering I somehow injured myself while sleeping—that is if I had the fortune to
fall asleep in the first place—do wonders for the natural sweetness
of my disposition. A part of my body that had been safely ignor-
able, parked away in the unconscious, now invades consciousness
because it hurts. What must it have been like to be old, say, in saga
Iceland, with no ibuprofen, no naproxen, not even any whisky or
wine, and only small amounts of beer since they could barely grow
any grain, it being too far north and the growing season too short.
No wonder they were tetchy. The Romans at least had wine.

And avarice? Until the twentieth century, with only rare excep-
tions, the old had no pensions, no annuities. Squirreling away and a
tight fist were prudent planning for retirement: "Provide, provide."
Avarice had another virtue: it kept one's mind active. According to
Cicero, avarice keeps the old person's memory functioning acutely
in money matters, if in nothing else.[7]

Much was made of the fact back then that no one clings to
life more tenaciously than the old, and the old are mocked for it.
Why seek so unrelentingly to prolong life once it has largely been
sapped? Says Aristotle, giving his own spin on the positivity effect:
"[The old] are small-minded, because they have been humbled by
life: their desires are set upon nothing more exalted or unusual
than what will help them to keep alive . . . they love life: and all
the more when their last day has come."[8] Euripides has Admetus

make the same observation: "It seems that old men, who find fault with age and length of years, pray for death insincerely. For once death comes near, none of them wishes to die, and age is no longer burdensome to them."[9]

These ideas were and are commonplace and perhaps even truer today than ever. In every century quacks extorted money from well-heeled oldsters by providing them with potions and incantations to prolong their days. The difference now is that some science has actually delivered some goods for the billions that pour in from a rich and aging society willing to buy more life no matter what the cost or what kind of life is being purchased. Our days have been prolonged, prolonged in many cases to a time when we will no longer fear death, because with the insentience of dementia we will know neither that we are old nor that we are dying.

The meanness of this tradition in its most familiar form is captured by Hamlet as he insults Polonius, the sententious meddlesome old fool: "[It] says here that old men have gray beards, that their faces are wrinkled, their eyes purging thick amber and plumtree gum, and that they have a plentiful lack of wit, together with most weak hams" (2.2.196–200).[10] Body and mind, both shot, and of the consistency, if you will pardon me, of snot, but providing an occasion for Shakespeare to display his perfect ear. One gets stuck in the k's, g's, pl's, m's in "thick amber and plumtree gum," the very sounds of coughing and spitting goop and viscous mucus and phlegm.

In the early medical theory of humors, old age was the age of phlegm, and the phlegmatic character was sluggish and forgetful.[11] Phlegm combined the attributes of cold and wet in a matrix representing the properties of the four classical elements: hot, cold, dry, wet. Each pairing of the matrix was commonly matched with a season of the year and with one of the four ages of man, in its four-stage version. Old age was cold and wet and thus the winter of our discontent. An Old English rendering of the theory is so evocative that I will quote it in the original, and since every word has survived into Modern English, except perhaps the last one, whose onomatopoeia readily reveals its meaning as mucusy, it should not be too much of an imposition: "[Winter] *byð ceald and wæt; wæter ys ceald and wæt; swa* [as, so] *byð se* [the] *ealda man ceald and snoflig*" (Winter is cold and wet; water is cold and wet; just as the old man is cold and snuffly).[12]

No Santa Clausy image of the kindly old man in this tradition. There was no sanguinity in old age. Maimonides considered the aged so unmerciful that they were not eligible to serve on the Sanhedrin because of their cruelty.[13] The sanguine cheerful humor, depending on the scheme, was allotted to younger people. Even our sanguine Santa, one notes, must bribe his way into the hearts of the young. He is rich, inexhaustibly rich, and the rich old person will be flattered and fawned over, if not exactly respected. Santa used also to be armed with sticks to accompany the carrots, leaving a switch or a lump of coal in a stocking when it moved him to do so. He was not until very recently painted as jovial sweetness; he was rather a purveyor of justice, rewarding the good and punishing the bad. The idea of the kindly old man or woman had a hard time competing against the more dominant images that flourished in the negative tradition of old age. Do you not remember when you were little the terror Santa struck into your heart in the department store as he put you on his lap and asked you, ho, ho, ho, what you wanted for Christmas?

Add to that the more lethal dangers the old are thought to pose. The wise old woman, whose wisdom was held to be knowledge of the black arts, was feared enough to get herself burned at the stake in some centuries, tossed into "deviant graves" in others. Respectable medieval medical theory gave scientific backing to her dangerousness. Having passed menopause meant her poisonous menstrual blood was not purged but festered inside, promoting evil.[14]

And the old, if they were property owners, were not wished continued longevity by their heirs, their loved ones, who impatiently awaited their turn at the trough. To the young, the old were a burden. They did not have the good manners to know when to die; and if some young did not harbor such wishes, the old suspected they did, their suspicions being anything but paranoid. Among the nobility sons warred against their fathers, among the lower orders they stinted the frail old parent of his food and warmth when he, Learlike, had handed over the farm (or kingdom) to his children in exchange for care and maintenance. In their defense, the young were often in straitened circumstances too, and the old parent was at his most needy when his sons, who married older than his daughters, were struggling to feed their own children.[15]

Though a woman burned as a witch might disagree, it might be better to be seen as Saturn (Cronus), a terrifying eater of his own children, than as Santa, for the reason just noted: Santa must make gifts. To be considered benign is to be ignored. Look at what happened to Yahweh, that violent and irascible war god (and thus credible as THE LORD). How could one ever realistically visualize him as an old man and be faithful to the image he took care to project? An old man does not go looking for a bar fight—"And it came to pass by the way in the inn, that the Lord met [Moses], and sought to kill him" (Exod. 4.24). How in God's name did Yahweh get turned into a white-bearded old man, God the Father, inevitably morphing into God as Santa? If his followers in 700 B.C. dared envisage him, it was as a bull, a storm god, or as Ashurbanipal, king of Assyria, had himself depicted: with black beard, thick and curled, butchering his enemies, making mounds of their severed heads, or spearing defenseless, drugged lions for sport.

Revenge lurks in the strangest of places. Yahweh was a victim of it. I suppose there might be some poetic justice in that. Yahweh, in the Christian dispensation, bears some resemblance to Cronus; or mankind took him to be so and served up his son to him as a sacrificial lamb. The son, though, was not without his avengers, who got even on his behalf by transforming Yahweh from the warrior he was to an old white-bearded man, grandpa, thus castrating him as Cronus did his father, Uranus. Once aged in this fashion, he ceased to matter much. Imagine Yahweh's chagrin seeing that he had been displaced by a baby in a manger for part of the year, by an Infant of Prague, or by a soft and gentle young man for the rest of it, or, in some devotions, by a woman, Mary, who is seldom depicted other than as a young woman, whether in the Pietà or Stabat Mater, or by Jesus maternalized, as Caroline Bynum has shown.[16] The New Testament, the young covenant, transmogrified the grand Hebrew Bible into the *Old* Testament, and Yahweh grew old along with it.[17]

Christianity wanted its God young. In fact, it would not let him get old, having him die in the prime of life. One view, Thomas Aquinas's, is that Christ *chose* not to grow old. Suffering the degradation of being incarnated as fully human is one thing but, says Thomas, having God suffer the indignities and failing powers of old age is quite another: "Christ willed to suffer while yet young, for three reasons. First of all, to commend the more His love by giving up His life for us when He was in His most perfect state of life. Secondly, because it was not becoming for Him to show any decay of nature nor to be subject to disease. . . . Thirdly, that by dying and rising at an early age Christ might exhibit beforehand in His own person the future condition of those who rise again."[18] This is pretty grim, though it holds out for us the prospect of receiving that thirtyish resurrected body talked about earlier. But the core message is that had Jesus died an old man, there would be little notion of his suffering and death on the cross counting as a sacrifice.

OUTLIVING YOURSELF

To have been Keats, Mozart, Emily Brontë, Jimi Hendrix, or Alexander would you have been willing to die at their ages? And if you admit that glory was not worth that price, fantasizing your downward slide into old age in epic terms is not a fantasy that will provide much pleasure either: Priam was sitting on the top of the world at your age; so was Margaret Thatcher, before whom all trembled. There is nothing saga-worthy about a nursing home and dementia—or a retirement condo, for that matter—and though old broken Priam achieved the grandest memorability begging for the mangled corpse of his son before being butchered, few of us are likely to prefer such an end to one in a nursing home.

No disgrace inheres, obviously, in outliving those who mattered in the grand historical sense of mattering, for mattering in that way is the lot of only a select few. The horror is that you might outlive yourself, fading away in a demented haze. Several of the schemas of the ages of man distinguished between two stages of old age: *senectus* and *senium;* the latter is also sometimes indicated by *decrepitus,* which needs no translation. In those schemas in which senium or decrepitus appear, it indicates severe physical and mental breakdown, an image of being at death's door; it is Shakespeare's Jaques's "mere oblivion, sans teeth, sans eyes, sans taste, sans everything."[19]

Even cultures that do well by those in the first stage of old age, senectus, may engage in senilicide or other death-hastening actions when the old person is no longer with it—when he, in other words, has passed into senium.[20] The same distinction between two levels of old age has been considered useful up to today in a variety of cultures. In our common parlance we distinguish between the active old, the "with it," the young-old, and those unfortunates, the old-old, the out of it, the gone, demented, and senile. Categories like geezer, codger, coot, granny are still on the senectus side and make some amends for the ridicule and contempt that inform them by adding a pinch of moderately affectionate toleration.

Our biography effectively ends at the point senectus becomes senium, though in some sense we are not formally dead because the doctor or the Author has not signed the certificate. Stoics of a Roman stamp, Seneca, for instance, whose advice must be leavened with the knowledge that he tutored the young Nero, counseled taking death-hastening actions into your own hands, pulling the plug on yourself while you still had your wits about you, enough wits to discern that you were losing it. Suicide let you be reasonably sure that your life and your biography terminated at the same moment. I remain agnostic as to Seneca's advice, but it is hard not to find it disturbing as it makes its point:

To my mind old age is not to be refused any more than it is to be craved. There is a pleasure in being in one's own company as long as possible, when a man has made himself worth enjoying. The question, therefore, . . . is, whether one should shrink from extreme old age and should hasten the end artificially, instead of waiting for it to come. . . . If the body is useless for service, why should one not free the struggling soul? Perhaps one ought to do this a little before the debt is due, lest, when it falls due, he may be unable to perform the act. And since the danger of living in wretchedness is greater than the danger of dying soon, he is a fool who refuses to stake a little time and win a hazard of great gain. . . . I shall not abandon old age, if old age preserves me intact for myself, and intact as regards the better part of myself; but if old age begins to shatter my mind, and to pull its various faculties to pieces, if it leaves me, not life, but only the breath of life, I shall rush out of a house that is crumbling and tottering.[21]

Seneca did in fact commit suicide—and famously made a mess of it—not, however, to escape the degradation of extreme old age, but because Nero ordered him to commit it or suffer worse. It is good that none of my students have become emperors. Without imperial urging I would have neither the courage nor the cowardice to manage my end in that way.

PART II

Wisdom

CHAPTER 5

Older, Yes, but Wiser?

Oh, but there are compensations. You are wiser now, you have better judgment; besides, research on the aging brain offers evidence that we form alternate compensatory structures in different lobes or hemispheres to keep up appearances. At a price. The new areas, covering for the plaqued-up places that were meant to do the job, are now not available for what they were supposed to be doing, and the newly recruited areas are not what they used to be either. Even bleaker is that the increasing cross-hemisphere sharing of frontal lobe functions may be nothing to celebrate. This new bilaterality may not be compensatory at all, but rather part of the story of disintegration, figuring more as a cause of decline than as a response to it. An image of one half of the brain sucking the other half dry captures the idea.[1]

Is wisdom a sop, a payment in unverifiable coin to make up for the provable failings of focus and memory, for the manifest impairment of cognition and the ability to deal with complexity, for the "increasing incidence of white matter lesions"?[2] Is wisdom a fiction accorded by default to some construct of the old, because the young so manifestly do not have it, unless, as we shall see, they have a pro-geriatric attitude toward risk? Is wisdom three parts resentment of the young in one another's arms and their hopelessly long-shot hopes? Every virtue comes with a built-in rebuke to those who do not have it, and the wisdom granted the old is meant more as a rebuke to the young than as a sop to the old, for whom it is also a rebuke.

Your worst suspicions about the truth of the proverbial association of wisdom and old age, however, are confirmed by those academic psychologists arguing *for* the association. Similar to the way Professor Carstensen sees certain mental dysfunctions as adaptive and rational, their view holds wisdom actually to be produced or enabled by the slowing down of perceptual and cognitive functions of the aging brain. Brain rot, not fear of the Lord, turns out to be the beginning of wisdom. Not the least of the problems with this view is that it tends to flatten wisdom into a simple matter of look-before-you-leap, and then confers it on people who can no longer leap, nor see much when they look. This is Humpty Dumpty science: "'When I use a word,' Humpty Dumpty said in rather a scornful tone, 'it means just what I choose it to mean—neither more nor less.'" So if you in your wisdom believe that the slowing and shrinking brain enables wisdom, well, then, you are slow, real slow, on the uptake.[3]

Even in societies in which the wise old are given authority as healers, witnesses, dispute settlers, mediators, price setters, elders, age alone counted for little.[4] The culture depicted in the Hebrew Bible, for instance, is one in which the elders held positions of power, but not every old person could be an elder, and manifestly not the old women. Most old men were not elders, no more than in Rome they were senators. To qualify as an elder a man had to acquire standing before he was old, or in some cultures he had to inherit the title. Would the Lord need such threatening tones— "Thou shalt rise up before the hoary head, and honor the face of the old man, and fear thy God: I am the Lord" (Lev. 19.32)—if the cultural norm were to honor hoary old men for merely being hoary? Moreover, within chapters of sternly ordering one to honor the face of an old man, Leviticus more pragmatically prices the redemptive value of a man over sixty at 15 shekels, down from the 50 shekels that was his value between the ages of twenty and sixty years old, while an old woman declines in value from 30 to 10 shekels (Lev. 27.3, 7). These are markdowns one does not even see at a going-out-of-business sale. The price set on a hoary head pays it no respect.

SENEX AMANS; OR, NO FOOL LIKE AN OLD FOOL

The wisdom conferred by the positive view of old age is hardly a match for the forcefulness and greater vividness of negative images that deny wisdom. The wise old man is no less a stock figure than the old fool, who represents the pure distillation of the fool, as in "no fool like an old fool." In his most ridiculous of guises he is the *senex amans* (old lover), and a bore to boot. The senex amans is in our idiom the dirty old man who still fancies young ladies and thinks he stands a chance. He has been an object of ridicule for millennia.[5] Even powerful old men, kings, who as a perk of office get to treat the young women (and young men) of the realm as sexual slaves, though partly excused by virtue of their office, end up pathetic: Henry VIII, for example. To David's credit it was not his but his entourage's idea to order the services of the beautiful young Abishag as a cure for his chills and ills.[6]

The lascivious old woman, who knew a thing or two, got her thrills vicariously as the corrupt duenna who betrayed the chastity of her comely maiden ward.[7] Or in the saga world by finding teenage boys to initiate. She was wise enough not to look for satisfaction from our old male fool. She knew the senex amans was unlikely to be functioning down below and that even if he were he would not desire her anyway, having his sights set on younger flesh, his very own Abishag.

Lucky us: our Viagra culture encourages us old guys to be senex amans, utter fools. Instead of moralists railing against old geezers who do not know enough to keep their bodies clothed, or their fantasies in check, or who still cluelessly think that anyone would want to do it with them, we have ads—as many as for cars and beer (the Viagra of the young)—promising that we won't be let down by the little guy downstairs. Humiliation there will still be: this time from success, rather than the usual mortification of failure.

If Claudius at his orisons laments that his "words fly up" but his "thoughts remain below"(*Hamlet* 3.3.100), Chaucer's dirty old Reeve's thoughts remain up in his head, unable to fly down and trigger any surges below. His impotence makes him sour, mean, and itching for a fight. Leave it, however, to the young lecher John Wilmot, the Earl of Rochester (d. 1680), to have his imagined dirty old man, his "disabled debauchee," play the part of the wise old man by counseling high-minded, priggish, "cold-complexioned" youths to emulate his own youthful escapades. Like the conventional duenna, he gets his kicks vicariously, but unlike her—she really is in the know—the old debauchee might know a little less than he pretends to. He is something of a spinner of tall tales.

> Or should some cold-complexioned set forbid,
> With his dull morals, our night's brisk alarms,
> I'll fire his blood by telling what I did,
> When I was strong and able to bear arms.
>
> I'll tell of whores attacked, their lords at home,
> Bawds' quarters beaten up, and fortress won,
> Windows demolished, watches overcome,
> And handsome ills by my contrivance done.
>
> Nor shall our love-fits, Cloris, be forgot,
> When each the well-looked link-boy strove t'enjoy,
> And the best kiss was the deciding lot:
> Whether the boy fucked you, or I the boy.
>
> With tales like these I will such heat inspire,
> As to important mischief shall incline.
> I'll make them long some ancient church to fire,
> And fear no lewdness they're called to by wine.

Thus statesman-like, I'll saucily impose,
And safe from danger valiantly advise,
Sheltered in impotence, urge you to blows,
And being good for nothing else, be wise.[8]

How fine is that last line? Rochester's send-up has an astuteness that informs its bawdiness. He shows that the disabled debauchee, as wise counselor, is best advised to package his wisdom as an adventure story. You run a risk in so doing: by trying to establish your credentials with tales of your lurid experience, the better to purchase attention from your young audience, you risk beggaring belief. Given the way you look now, a wild past is simply not conceivable. Your interlocutor cannot help but imagine the wretchedly aged you, not the young you, as the fornicator, the brawler, the whatnot that you are lying through your teeth to present yourself as, and whether true or false the thought disgusts him.

PROVERBIAL BORES AND CURMUDGEONS

Even if you were a young wallflower, if you never had much experience to speak of, age gets you credit for experience. Merely because you have lived through more years, you are held to have lived through more. Does wisdom simply accrue as life's options close, without you so much as lifting a finger? Aging tends to modulate if not quite kill optimism and that surely counts as wising up, optimism being mostly for youth and fools and the old people positive psychologists dig up. So the old are, if wise, killjoys, dousing the exuberant flames of youth.

Should an old person by chance be truly wise that does not mean he will not burden you with other, more negative markers of old age: taking forever to get to the point or getting wholly lost on the way there. There need be no correlation between being wise and being interesting. Often they are quite at odds. Take Nestor, for example, the wise old man of the *Iliad.* Agamemnon would consider it a blessing to have ten such as he.[9] Nestor had just given excellent advice as to how to marshal the army for battle, and

Agamemnon was exuberantly appreciative. Nonetheless, on other occasions much of Nestor's wisdom is a mere recitation of old saws inserted into tedious tales of his glorious youth.[10]

The wise old do not just instruct youth; they also buttonhole them to tell them tales of how much better it was back then or, if not better, then nobler and harder, when people were not spoiled by material excess and indulgent parents. I really did walk through deep snow to school and there were no snow days unless more than a foot fell and certainly no days off for excessive wind chill. That index was not kept. Once it was kept, people as far south as Nashville could claim to have endured zero degrees Fahrenheit when it was thirty-three on a mildly windy day. Wind chill is yet another instance of grade inflation penetrating into every nook and cranny of our lives.

The old were also privileged to repeat proverbs and to insist that experience led to the validation of these often bitter clichés. Just the other day, trying to console a student abandoned by a spouse, I actually said: "You'll get over it, time heals all wounds." With a mite less political and military instinct Nestor turns into Polonius, the stock garrulous wise old man of comedy. Polonius, however, had the misfortune to have been cast in a tragedy, where he served as cannon fodder. Though any adolescent can cite a couple of Polonian proverbs and quickly learns to do so, having had them imposed on him many a time, the youth, even the adult, does not understand them. Just what does "This above all: to thine own self be true" mean? To me it meant I could lie like crazy as long as I knew I was lying and made some Jesuitical reservation, a crossing of mental fingers behind my back, as I breezed on mendaciously.

Moreover, for every proverb advising the wisdom of an action, there is another equally wise one counseling the opposite. This is oft noted and it is easy to rattle off examples. Haste makes waste, but he who hesitates is lost; absence makes the heart grow fonder, but out of sight out of mind. Or don't look a gift horse in the mouth, but beware of Greeks bearing gifts. One can find a proverb to justify any desired action or, after the fact, explain any failure or success. Far be it from me, though, to impugn the wisdom of proverbs. The fields of social psychology, sociology, and behavioral economics mobilize reams of paper, and legions of undergrads, to confirm proverbs, or tell us what we already knew, but without even a dash of wit. The true wisdom of folk wisdom, though, does not lie so much in the aptness of any particular proverb as in its great concession to practicality: wisdom demands attending to the particular and micropolitical. That is why sometimes you are wise not to look a gift horse in the mouth, and at other times it is wise to check to see if there are armed Achaeans inside it. It all depends.

The book of Proverbs largely accepts that wisdom comes in old age only to those who have been drilled in its lessons, who have been taught to be wise not only by experience but also by real teachers: "Train up a child in the way he should go, and when he is old he will not depart from it" (22.6). Ancient wisdom literature contemplates instruction, apprenticeship of a sort, especially as we move east to Hinduism and Buddhism. If you are to stand a chance of gaining wisdom by the time you are old, it seems that you needed to have learned from real teachers as well as from a few hard knocks, which often were delivered by the teacher. In these traditions wisdom did not accrue naturally. The teacher was important. Remember the veneration, even the love you had for many of your teachers from grade school on. They opened worlds for you.

Some consolation awaits an old teacher. The students love the young, good-looking teachers, of course, but it is one or two of the really old ones that are *be*loved. And those of us who fall in neither of those categories have ways of explaining it away. We refuse to pander to the students and stuff like that. But it seems you stand a better chance with them if you are not the age of their parents. If you are still young enough that they think you are one of them, or old enough to be their grandparent, you are better off. You can benefit from a certain image of grandpalike old age. Or from a cultivated curmudgeonliness, which camouflages reasonably well one's failing brain, and which enough of the students somehow find charming—or at least servilely pretend to, and you believe them anyway. Rarely do you need to say anything clever. Just a roll of the eyes, or a look askance, works rather nicely. This is less gender dependent than you might think. Some of my female age-mates can roll their eyes or smirk with considerable unsettling effect.

Curmudgeons get credit for wisdom for the high hit rate that comes with hostility to easy optimism; and being old, and thus not really counting, they, like children, have a privilege to say what would constitute an offense if said by a fully responsible adult. And like children, the curmudgeon is considered cute for it, but unlike the child, he is also considered wise for it. To the extent curmudgeonism suspends the rules of mandatory polite compliments, and indeed substitutes a rule of mandatory harrumphs when these compliments are given, the curmudgeon gets credit for seeing truth, or for telling it the way it is, and that counts as wisdom, even though this wisdom lies in everyone's knowledge that the polite compliments or obligatory upbeat statements are inane.

For some, curmudgeonliness is a conscious strategy, but for others it may be primed by the incessant bodily aches and pains and the depressing awareness that the Preacher was right: there is nothing new under the sun. But now you feel its truth in every sinew, every nerve. Even the new pains in a new location, though new to you, are not new under the sun. Near everyone blessed to have lived to a modest old age has endured them. But these thoughts are curmudgeonism gone sour. In fact, there is plenty of novelty for the elderly, thanks to our decaying memory. A book read before can now be read again with all the original joys of discovery. Would that that could also be said of hearing the same story a second and third time told by a colleague or friend.

REMINISCING AND REVALUING

Professor Carstensen says old age is a time for emotions—but mostly for positive emotions, whatever they may be—rather than for learning or thinking. One can guess that among the positivity crowd the list of positive emotions is treacly and pious: love, joy, happiness, sympathy, hope, pity. No room for the delights of

Schadenfreude, the triumphant feeling of getting even; no place for anger, which is an especially enlivening emotion (Aristotle listed anger in the plus column because it contemplated the pleasures of revenge).[11] I am positively generous in the emotions I would say have their own bright side, emotions I bet the positivity crowd would not let join their club. There cannot be a grimmer story than Carstensen's for killing whatever vestige remains of linking old age with something we think of as wisdom.[12] In a strange sense, she out-grims the likes of me with her defense of upbeat oldsters who no longer care to learn anything new, for whom, recall, learning is not rational given they won't have as long a time to realize a return on their investment in the knowledge acquired. They invest in good feelings, she says, where the returns are immediate. What, though, if you were one of those souls who got pleasure out of learning, for whom learning was an end in itself, each step gratifying for its own sake? Where are the joys of learning in her account? And what of the oldster whose main pleasure was in learning? What happens to his sense of well-being once his cognitive functions decay?

Let us look on the bright side: maybe there is some small truth to the positivity effect that is not just sour grapes or a sign of creeping dementia. Perhaps it is to be found in the pleasure the oldster gets in spinning his cautionary tales, of posturing as wise. For the cautionary tales you tell force you to romanticize the past; you thereby inject value into times you might not have especially valued as they were being lived. In striving to make the young hurt with having missed out on something nobler that you got to experience, you come to convince yourself that back then was indeed a better time as you spin tales only partly false.

Yet real pleasure of a bittersweet sort can be had in reminiscing with fellow lamenters of times past. It is a lament without the anguish, which is replaced more by wistfulness, a melancholic love song to the *neiges d'antan,* the snows of yesteryear, that wisp of melancholy that attends the setting of the sun on a clear cold winter day, that slant of pastel light that made you sad when a child. It is something like nostalgia and risks being cheaply sentimental, but there seems to lurk some wisdom in reflecting in such a way.

By engaging in valorizing the past, we pay it some homage and thereby, perhaps, pay off a debt or two.

Thomas Hardy, with a kind eye, captures the camaraderie that can infuse such reminiscence. His "An Ancient to Ancients" concludes with a list of ancients who delivered the goods in their old age, but the poem, read with an unkinder eye, has something of the feel of the thin books about Jewish athletes I was given by my grandmother when a boy:

> The bower we shrined to Tennyson,
> Gentlemen,
> Is roof-wrecked; damps there drip upon
> Sagged seats, the creeper-nails are rust,
> The spider is sole denizen;
> Even she who read those rhymes is dust,
> Gentlemen!
>
> We who met sunrise sanguine-souled,
> Gentlemen,
> Are wearing weary. We are old;
> These younger press; we feel our rout
> Is imminent to Aïdes' [Hades'] den,—
> That evening's shades are stretching out,
> Gentlemen!
>
> And yet, though ours be failing frames,
> Gentlemen,
> So were some others' history names,
> Who trode their track light-limbed and fast
> As these youth, and not alien
> From enterprise, to their long last,
> Gentlemen.
>
> Sophocles, Plato, Socrates,
> Gentlemen,
> Pythagoras, Thucydides,
> Herodotus, and Homer,—yea,
> Clement, Augustin, Origen,

Burnt brightlier towards their setting-day,
Gentlemen.[13]

Curmudgeonism's unkinder eye is forced to break the spell the
poet casts. Except for the brief mention of "failing frames," he
omits mentioning that so much of oldsters' conversation is recit-
ing litanies of their aches and pains, each trying to outmatch the
other. The real curse of the camaraderie of old age is that one's
health is usually the main topic. Hardy's poem is also no country
for old women; the ancient kills them off in the first stanza in
this excerpt.[14] Nor for the poor, either: his old men are gentlemen;
one sees the lament taking place at the club. The poem reverses
the game you played in your twenties and thirties of noting what
famous person was already dead by your age by finding a few who
were delivering after their sixtieth birthday. But what of stopping
the list at Origen (d. 254) and Augustin (d. 430)? No old worthies
since then? Kant delivered in old age, and Hardy the poet was doing quite well as an old poet, but the specter of old Wordsworth, I
suspect, who never understood that his formidable talent had left
him at a rather young age, might be haunting him. The idea that
old age is likely to undo poetic talent as it undoes any other talent
is an old one. Almost two thousand years earlier Longinus, in his
treatise *On the Sublime,* quite disagreeing with Hardy about Homer,
attributed the failure of the *Odyssey* to measure up to the *Iliad* to
its having been composed when Homer was old and his talents in
decline.[15]

PREMATURELY WISE, THE *PUER SENEX*

The book of Wisdom in the Septuagint and Catholic Bible con-
tains this oft-quoted passage:

For old age is not honored for length of time,
nor measured by number of years;
but understanding is gray hair for men,
and a blameless life is ripe old age. (4.8–9)[16]

The book of Proverbs also rejects a necessary correlation between wisdom and age. A wise son makes several appearances (13.1, 15.20, 23.24, etc.); a substantial portion of Proverbs takes the form of a wise father counseling, endlessly, his son to learn wisdom *before* he gets old. A whole lot of shaking goes on to hold the kid's attention: "My son, do not forget my words"; "My son, do not forget my teaching"; "Hear, O sons, a father's instruction." Evidently not all sons are uneducable or wake up to wisdom only when they have become older, sadder, and thus maybe a mite wiser.[17]

Wisdom, in a trivial sense, comes with age, just not with old age. No matter how unwise a thirty-something might be, he is likely to be wiser than he was at fourteen. The sad truth, however, is that wisdom is hard to locate anywhere. The old are mostly fools, or out of it, and the young are, well, young.[18] Not all the young are fools, though. The pathetic *senex amans,* old but not wise, contrasts notably with the *puer* (or *puella*) *senex,* the old youngster, who is wise but not old. In one strand of Christian hagiographical literature, the wise child is preciously and precociously devout, eschewing the vanity of play and games and, once puberty sets in, resisting the pleasures of the flesh. Such as these are marked for sainthood from the get-go.[19]

The idea that anyone could find cause for admiration of these spiritually precocious children makes demands on my sympathetic imagination that it cannot meet. The puer senex offers a real test for a medievalist's commitment to the period, even one like myself who can sympathize with many of the stranger religious devotions. I could never quell my sympathy for the Jews who could not endure the seven-year-old "litel clergeon" of Chaucer's *Prioresse's Tale* who belted out hymns to the Virgin everyday as he walked through the Jewish quarter to and from school.[20] Though they slit his throat and tossed him in a privy—anything to get him to stop—the little lad miraculously kept hymning. An insufferable puer senex nicknamed Father Time comes close to ruining Hardy's otherwise powerful novel *Jude the Obscure.* And various colleagues' precocious tots can be equally ruinous to an otherwise convivial occasion. The puer senex and his ilk are a part of the reason I fled to the lava fields of Iceland. Precocity in the young Egil Skallagrimsson was not only demonstrated at age three, when he composed his first poem, but also at age six, when he embedded an ax in the skull of an older boy who had pushed him down in a ballgame and mocked him.[21]

Yet there is evidence that the hagiographers and the pious boys and girls they celebrated met with more than their share of rolled eyes from their contemporaries. Medieval people too were suspicious of the saintly puer senex. Thus a proverb of considerable currency: "young saint, old devil." "What seems to one observer a youngster's preternatural and God-given wisdom," says John Burrow of the puer senex, "may strike another as odious precocity."[22] Ostentatious piety grated, not only when it was precocious. Early fifteenth-century pilgrims found the middle-aged Margery Kempe's company unbearable because of her constant weeping and preaching: "[The company] was greatly displeased because she wept so much and spoke constantly of the love and goodness of our Lord at the table and everywhere else."[23] Jesus himself frowned on the showy piety of those he called hypocrites.

One readily detects a whiff of Nietzschean *ressentiment* in these pious tales of holy toddlers. The hagiographers might themselves be getting even with their own childhood tormenters. It is not as if these most spiritually precocious youngsters would not wish to avenge themselves on the other children who beat them up. Little Jesus too. Thus the Infancy Gospel of Thomas (c. second century) relates of the child Jesus: "And after certain days, as Jesus passed through the midst of the city, a certain child cast a stone at him and smote his shoulder. And Jesus said unto him: 'Thou shalt not finish thy course.' And straightway he also fell down and died. And they that were there were amazed, saying: 'From whence is this child, that every word which he speaketh becometh a perfect work?' But they also departed and accused Joseph, saying: 'Thou wilt not be able to dwell with us in this city: but if thou wilt, teach thy child to bless and not to curse: for verily he slayeth our children: and everything that he saith becometh a perfect work.'"[24]

A puer senex, a real one, was rare, for his mere existence ran against the natural order. He was a sign of a world turned upside down.[25] One would think that to keep his risks more manageable, the precociously wise youngster would figure out ways to make his wisdom less painful to his age-mates, or to the parents of other children. The fifteenth-century mystery play *Christ Disputes with the Scholars in the Temple* depicts Mary in a panic wondering where her little boy has gone when he wandered off to Jerusalem to confute the sages. She fears for his safety: "Every childe with hym is wroth and wood [mad]" because of his great "wyttys and werkys good."[26] Resenting goody two-shoes appears to be a human universal.

But given his goals, the pious puer senex is no less practical than he is holy. In exchange for never risking giving God offense and jeopardizing the infinite payoff after death, he will risk the hostility of his age-mates and their taunting and occasional pummeling, unless he should be blessed with the power to perform miraculous revenges like Jesus in the Infancy Gospel. Not for our wise youngster to test God's promised forgiveness of sins, his paying the same wage to the person who shows up to the vineyard five minutes before quitting time as to the one who has been slaving since the morning whistle. And he is wise not to test final forgiveness. Can you be certain that if you begin a life of sin you will be able to call it quits in the nick of time? Best never to sin, except originally, even as an infant. The holy St. Nicholas "would not take the breast nor the pap but once on the Wednesday and once on the Friday."[27] One sees a contemporary version of this type in the preschooler, grade-schooler, high-schooler who is already building a résumé.

CHAPTER 6.

The Dark Side of Wisdom

Wisdom suggests gravitas, aged weightiness. The dom of its second syllable is a form of the word *doom,* meaning judgment, as in Doomsday, with the vowel shortened by virtue of its unstressed position. Subtract the weight of the suffixed *doom* and we are left with the adjective *wise.* The "dom" adds something of a jurisdictional sense, a sense of domain and terrain, as it does with kingdom, Christendom, freedom, even boredom. This chapter counts too as something of a modest polemic against the silliness of psychological treatments of wisdom and its association with old age. We saw in the previous chapter how that racket boils wisdom down mostly to the idea of look before you leap. We will see that the ancients were a whole lot wiser than our wise guys, who generate articles and studies and are armed with questionnaires and statistical regressions and who are "positively" on a mission. (Not all of them, of course; there is much useful psychological work and excellent brain research that I have drawn on.)

To be wise encompasses some very different skills, stances, and behaviors. Even within the wisdom books of the Bible, the wisdom of the book of Job is hardly that of Proverbs, nor that of Ecclesiastes. In other traditions, a person could be called wise for being good at any number of tasks: mediating disputes, piloting ships through tricky passages, predicting the weather, casting spells and cursing, healing, discovering thieves, insulating assets from creditors, reading and writing, figuring how many of a herd needed to be slaughtered in the fall to get the remnant through the winter, and more.

FEINTS, DECEPTIONS, AND WARINESS

In the poem commemorating the battle of Maldon (A.D. 991) the leader of the Essex militia opposing the Vikings is called *frod*. Frod means wise, prudent, and by extension it came to mean old in years. Byrhtnoth, the leader of the English force, is advanced in years, in his sixties, but he is called frod in the poem not for his age but for having the skill, the know-how, to guide his spear through the neck of the Danish "slaughter wolf" who had an instant before severely wounded him. Just because Byrhtnoth was frod in handling a spear, however, did not mean Byrhtnoth was wise in the way we would think to use the term. The poem goes out of its way to blame Byrhtnoth's imprudence for seeking a battle on unfavorable terms he could easily have avoided.[1] Wise as a strategist and tactician he was not. Byrhtnoth's frodness, his wisdom, has more to do with his muscle movements in close combat. Interesting too is that the Old English verb that describes Byrhtnoth's guiding the spear through the exposed Viking neck is *wisian,* formed from the adjective "wise" and meaning to guide, to direct. Good guidance, indeed. So we see that the sense of wise, of wisdom, is inevitably linked to guidance, counsel, know-how, instruction, teaching, and to skill in steering spears as well as steering youth or your own life.

The kind of wisdom that we think of as proverbial wisdom, as exemplified by being reducible to sayings—whether in the ancient Egyptian wisdom literature, in parts of the biblical book of

Proverbs or the book of Wisdom, or in the Norse god Odin's *Há-vamál* (The Sayings of the High One)—tends to agree on matters of practical wisdom. It is about getting on in the world without getting snookered or whacked. The book of Proverbs counsels five times not going surety for another's debt; the wise person does not cosign a note (6.1, 11.15, 17.18, 22.26, 27.13). Many of the maxims, aphorisms, or satirical definitions in the manner respectively of La Rochefoucauld, Nietzsche, or Ambrose Bierce pay homage to the form and substance of the proverb, parodic at times, but consciously part of a tradition that makes wisdom vaguely misanthropic because wisdom means being chary of trusting too readily anyone or anything.

Proverbial wisdom is prudent rather than heroic; discretion tends to trump valor. You do not count chickens before they hatch, you do not go looking for fights or get stuck in a web of deceits. (A carefully planned single deceit is fine, but webs are hard to manage.) The wise are constantly wary of the ubiquitous wicked, with their lies and snares, who always seem vastly to outnumber the righteous, among whom you are unsure whether to include yourself, for it sometimes takes fire to fight fire. Ecclesiastes is even more cynical: "All things have I seen in the days of my vanity: there is a just man that perisheth in his righteousness, and there is a wicked man that prolongeth his life in his wickedness. Be not righteous over much; neither make thyself over wise: why shouldest thou destroy thyself?" (7.15–16). Be good and wise in modest doses or you are either dead meat or have just wasted your time.

You are to assume a certain wary humility before the complexity of the world; thus "the fear of the Lord is the beginning of wisdom." So too the Boy Scout motto: "Be prepared." The motto speaks both to reducing the odds of getting lost in the woods and of increasing them for finding your way out when you do. The Boy Scouts, romantically and somewhat innocently, locate danger in nature—bears have a taste for your leftovers, snakes and centipedes hide in sleeping bags. Proverbial wisdom knows better: the dangers are people, not animals. This fallen world is a maze of false seeming and vice, deceptions and betrayals. With only minimal metaphori-

cal extension, life's journey was seen as getting lost in a dark and
dangerous wood, the *silva oscura* in which Dante got lost in his
middle age, the dead middle of his life, exactly half of the biblical
allotment of three score and ten. To know, as Dante did, that one
was lost in a silva oscura is itself a kind of wisdom, the wisdom
born of overwhelming anxiety about the point of your life, if it
has one, and about where the path you are on is taking you, if you
can manage to discern any path in the obscurity. By the time you
are sixty-five and you find you are lost in the woods, you will have
lost much of Dante's midlife acuity needed to get yourself out,
though, God knows, you will have the time, some roughly twenty
years by the present life tables, to stumble further into the brush.

Wisdom and cunning share considerable overlap across cultures
and time.[2] Proverbial wisdom always held it wise to play it close to
the vest, real close. So if you do not have anything nice to say, say
nothing. It might be best to say nothing even if you have something
nice to say, for once you start talking you are vulnerable. Wisdom
cunningly counsels the fool to fake being wise, which can be done
only if he keeps his mouth shut. "Even a fool, when he holdeth
his peace, is counted wise: and he that shutteth his lips is esteemed
a man of understanding" (Prov. 17.28).[3] The trickster god Odin
concurs: "When a stupid man comes into company he'd better be
silent; no one will notice that he knows nothing unless he talks."[4]
The lawyer's standard wise advice to his client to remain silent is
less the pernicious fallout of *Miranda v. Arizona* than a creature
of ancient wisdom.

But this advice, though wise, needs to be modulated with wisdom of other sorts. When words are expected, keeping silent is
itself a speech act. Too much silence might not be much wiser than
too much talk. Silence raises suspicions that you might be hiding
something, or are up to something, or are losing it, if an aging
academic. The advice to remain silent, it would seem, has to be
suspended for those who teach or who must make peace between
warring factions. Obviously there is a place for wise speech, but
how do you trust yourself to know that what you offer up is wise?
And what is a teacher to do with this: "He that hath knowledge

spareth his words" (Prov. 17.27)? The students who paid for an hour of your wisdom on property law four days a week would demand a refund if you spared too much knowledge. The trick, as the proverb intimates, is to dole it out slowly, lest your well run dry in the middle of the term. The grim assumption underpinning that proverb, confirmed by more than a few academic journals and books, as well as by the pestilence of pundits and talking heads, is that most of what passes for knowledge and wisdom isn't.

If saying nothing rather than something stands a better chance of keeping oneself out of trouble, then doing nothing might also qualify. Given the frequency with which the best laid schemes of mice and men gang aft a-gley, sitting tight may be no less prudent than buttoning lips tightly. No wonder we old are so wise; we cannot get out of the chair to screw something up. But if silence can qualify as a speech act, then some inaction can reasonably qualify as its own kind of action, as long as it is advertent and not merely a function of laziness. Fabius Cunctator was not doing nothing by avoiding battle with Hannibal, though his contemporaries thought him inactive and cowardly. When it became clear that his tactics turned out to be exactly what the doctor ordered for a desperate Rome, he was honored for what he did. Fabius, it should be noted, was well into his sixties when he was dictator and consul.[5]

This kind of doing nothing, saying nothing, by definition means going slow, but only when it is to your advantage to go slowly. It also means letting hindsight play to your advantage. Let the fools rush in, and then wisely break your silence when their actions turn out to have been ill-advised, reserving unto yourself the wisdom of hindsight. Hindsight gets rough treatment, not all of it deserved. It is not without its virtues; its exercise is one aspect of training up a capacity for wisdom. War colleges in modern nation-states take second-guessing very seriously. Tactics employed in battles fought twenty-three hundred years ago are criticized, commanders' reputations revised up- and downward. Historians and tacticians will still argue over exactly what the Roman consuls should have done at Cannae (216 B.C.) to save the situation or cut their losses.

Whoever would think that anything but the most general kind

of glib hindsight is 20/20? You screwed up; that much you can see, though it is hardly uncommon for people to refuse to admit they did, even as they are lowering their families into the grave. The hindsight that tries to replay the past in an attempt to determine what should have been done to have avoided screwing up in the first place needs cultivating to see clearly. Even then it rarely makes it to 20/20, as witness the endless and inconclusive arguments of Monday-morning quarterbacks. Forward sight does much better as long as the forward does not extend past the present. As historian Alexander Murray notes: "Historians can foretell the future after it has happened."[6] That might be too generous, for it ultimately depends on the quality of the historian's hindsight. He will know that the Great War took place, but did it end in 1918 or in 1945? Was it yet another German Thirty Years' War? And will there ever be a satisfactory answer for why it took place?

Wisdom has a paranoid streak. It assumes, in Proverbs and in other wisdom literature, as I noted above, that the world is thick with wicked deceivers, conmen, and enemies, a dangerous place indeed. Says Odin: "The careful guest comes to a meal and sits in wary silence; with his eyes and ears wide open, every wise man keeps watch."[7] The Egyptian Ptahhotep's late Old Kingdom advice— "Conceal your heart, control your mouth"[8]—makes its way to the book of Proverbs nearly two millennia later: "A prudent man concealeth knowledge" (Prov. 12.23). Such "knowledge" that the "prudent man concealeth" cannot be the kind your teacher desperately wants you to display in a seminar. Knowledge here means plans, intentions and, above all, what you have discerned about the intentions and plans of others.

The Hebrew word for "prudent" in that proverb—*'arum*—is the same word used to describe the chief attribute of the serpent in Eden. Hmmm. Why is it that no English rendering of *'arum* makes the snake prudent? He is subtil, subtle, crafty, clever, depending on the Bible translation, but not prudent, which suggests that unless you prefer making that devilish snake the most prudent of beasts, the proper translation of the proverb should be "A *crafty* or *subtle* man concealeth knowledge." So maybe the proverbial wise old person is just a snake in the grass, though more likely he is, in our day, a sucker, falling for the old pigeon drop or responding to a Nigerian e-mail solicitation, thinking he is about to get rich quick, saved only by his lack of proficiency with computers.

Prudence has always been something of a gray virtue, whether being a polite term for cunning or a euphemism for cowardice. But prudence has to make its peace with cowardice, for wisdom is needed in war and feud. The truly wise man should also have the virtue of not scaring easy. Wisdom thus becomes the science of knowing when and how to hit or hit back. Like Odysseus, the wise man makes a good military strategist. The wisdom of Odysseus, or even that of frod Byrhtnoth guiding his spear through a Viking neck, was something rather more than the wisdom that Humpty Dumpty psychologists argue is a function of brain slowdown. The book of Proverbs knows that one of the selling points of wisdom is that it produces winners on the battlefield and in war: "Every purpose is established by counsel: and with good advice make war" (20.18); and similarly, "For by wise guidance you can wage your war, and in abundance of counselors there is victory" (24.6, RSV). It reminds one of Agamemnon wishing he had ten Nestors.

Wisdom, at least in its Norse style, can sometimes take the side of the heroic. When it does, it enlists the loathsomeness of old age to make the argument and to give it cold rationality. Thus death in battle is better than the miseries of old age:

> The foolish man thinks he'll live forever
> > If he stays away from war,
> But old age shows him no mercy
> > Though the spears spare him.[9]

The book of Proverbs is rather less cynical than Odin, and thus grander. Proverbs is made up of several genres, not all of which are proverbial. Some of the discussions are ethical and moral rather than practical and prudent. One passage in fact counsels against wisdom's dominant grain of wariness and cunning, arguing instead for heroic action, because morality and justice demand it:

If you showed yourself slack in time of trouble,
Wanting in power,
If you refrained from rescuing those taken off to death,
Those condemned to slaughter—
If you say, "We knew nothing of it,"
Surely He who fathoms hearts will discern [the truth],
He who watches over your life will know it,
And He will pay each man as he deserves. (24.10–12, JPS)

DESPAIR

Wisdom literature is pessimistic stuff; it often ends in despair, despair being itself evidence of wisdom. In matters of grief, for lost loved ones or for lost youth, wisdom provides a perverse consolation. Don't get too upset because nothing matters, or at least nothing you ever thought mattered matters. How could it, for there is no justice: the wicked flourish. Moreover, wisdom itself is vanity, for the wise and the fool have the same end: "And how dieth the wise man? as the fool" (Eccles. 2.16). There is only endless repetition, none of which is remembered anyway, nor need it be, for it will happen again: "The thing that hath been, it is that which shall be; and that which is done is that which shall be done" (Eccles. 1.9). No hint of rewards in heaven or in the world to come in this tradition. No such place exists in this strain of wisdom until later Judaism and Christianity supplied it so as to make this weary wisdom less inimical to the idea of a just God.

By the end of Ecclesiastes, Solomon the Preacher's intellectual despair turns into coarse cynicism: "Eat, drink, and be merry" (8.14–15), though he has already shown that merriment cannot survive the least bit of reflection. It too is meaningless, but if you can drink enough and gain a kind of bestial oblivion, you might be able to keep thought and truth at bay, with a burp. This perhaps can be considered a pessimist's version of the chirpy positivity effect of the happy-oldster school.

This triumph of meaninglessness, to be sure, is not the only strain in wisdom literature, but it is a very well-attested one, and the one that drew the greatest poets and writers to its cause, whether in Ecclesiastes, *Lear,* Job, or the haunting exile elegies of the Anglo-Saxon poets. Some of this world-weariness is a pose. Writers in this tradition are knowingly engaged in a contest of who can express the miseries and vanity of human existence in the most elegant way so as to get honor and fame for their excellence at expressing despair with style. But the power of the genre, its obligatory cold eye, its bleakness, survive the posing and the contradictions implicit in the poet's desire for the inheritance of wind that is fame.

Ecclesiastes and especially Job and *Lear* are too grim for me, except in small doses. Very few people can think that way all day, every day, and not put a bullet through their heads. Such indulgences in the literature and the sentiments of the senselessness of life and death can be likened to vacations, negative ones, but vacations nonetheless. You take them once or twice a year, with mini-indulgences analogous to weekends or nights out. And if you find yourself taking longer ones you better head for the friendly doctor to prescribe some antidepressants. For all this glum talk of mine, I must confess to taking delight in simple vain pleasures (beer and a football game). Delight is not quite the right word though, for the Packers make me suffer, win or lose, and at my age so does the beer.

KING DAVID'S FINAL WORDS

The most chilling account of wisdom as Machiavellian calculation—and wisdom is the word used—is to be found in David's last words on his deathbed to his son Solomon. And David is very old indeed when he displays his brand of hard wisdom. David first gives Solomon the pious advice to walk in the ways of the Lord, to keep his commandments and judgments, and then the dying king gets down to business:

> Moreover thou knowest also what Joab the son of Zeruiah did to me, and what he did to the two captains of the hosts of Israel, unto Abner the son of Ner, and unto Amasa the son of Jether, whom he slew, and shed the blood of war in peace,

and put the blood of war upon his girdle that was about his loins, and in his shoes that were on his feet. Do *therefore according to thy wisdom, and let not his hoar head go down to the grave in peace.* But shew kindness unto the sons of Barzillai the Gileadite, and let them be of those that eat at thy table: for so they came to me when I fled because of Absalom thy brother.[10] And, behold, thou hast with thee Shimei the son of Gera, a Benjamite of Bahurim, which cursed me with a grievous curse in the day when I went to Mahanaim: but he came down to meet me at Jordan, and I sware to him by the Lord, saying, "I will not put thee to death with the sword."[11] Now therefore hold him not guiltless: *for thou art a wise man, and knowest what thou oughtest to do unto him; but his hoar head bring thou down to the grave with blood.* So David slept with his fathers, and was buried in the city of David. (1 Kings 2.5–10; emphasis added)

David has some scores to settle, but being old and sick unto death, and for particular reasons he indicates (and others he does not), he cannot pay quit to these accounts in his own person. Here is wisdom on display, cold, calculating, not missing a beat even as he breathes his last. David's explicit invoking of Solomon's wisdom is a kind of in-the-know talk,[12] insinuating and collusive: "Do therefore according to thy wisdom," "for thou art a wise man." One can discern a tough teasing of Solomon by suggesting that his already proverbial reputation for wisdom needs to test itself on the rougher ground of dealing death. No need to mobilize wisdom to repay the kindness owed to Barzillai's house. Repaying Barzillai's sons is a routine matter, the standard kind of preferments kings show faithful followers who can be trusted to know their place, who constitute no threat whatsoever. Nothing risky, so no wisdom needed, and none mentioned.

To kill Joab, however, David's own sister's son, who, moreover, is popular with a large segment of the army, who took care of necessary business when David would periodically go soft, as in the case of Absalom, and who did David's dirty work, as when David

lost his head over Bathsheba, was going to take political skill and
a fairly accommodating moral sense. Joab was efficient, competent, intelligent, and except on the two occasions David invokes,
loyal. David could not have been David without Joab. Joab minded
the shop. Joab was himself wise, but not so wise that he didn't
speak truth to power; he was a great warrior, a killer. And thus one
would need to handle killing him right, even though he was now
no youngster himself, but hoar of head. Hence the requirement of
wisdom, with a wink and a nudge. Solomon, as David knows, has
his own practical reasons for taking out Joab, since Joab supports
Solomon's half brother Adonijah's claim to succeed David. Here
David and Solomon's interests coincide.

Solomon, however, could care less about Shimei. David is asking for Shimei's death purely as a favor. David cannot bear that
someone who mocked and cursed him when he was down on his
luck should live out his life in peace. The trick, though, for which
wisdom is needed, is that Solomon must find a way to kill Shimei
without it violating the oath David swore to Yahweh that Shimei
would be spared. Solomon does so by setting up Shimei to violate
the terms of his sanctuary, so he can execute him on what can be
classified as an independent offense.[13]

Unlike the case of Shimei, where David is open about the grounds
for killing him, one suspects that David is not giving the real reasons he wants Joab killed. True, Joab's killing of Abner was a political disaster, and David was greatly beholden to Abner for delivering
Israel to him (2 Sam. 3.9–21). David had to engage in elaborate
humiliation rituals to save the situation (2 Sam. 3.28–37), and one
suspects it made his task holding the tribes of Israel more difficult
than it would have been for years, but he survived, and that was
some twenty years ago. As for Amasa, whom Joab killed toward
the end of David's reign, David could hardly be too concerned.
David had appointed Amasa in Joab's place as head of the army,
this same Amasa having been the rebellious Absalom's army leader.
David could hardly have been surprised that Joab would make
short work of this interloper, whom Joab would feel was occupying what was rightfully his (Joab's) office. David must surely have

meant to provoke Joab. If it cost Amasa his life, that was not to be unexpected or unwelcome. It looks like David set Amasa up.[14]

David in his last years would show signs of losing it. Absalom in fact relied on people's perceptions of exactly that to make his putsch possible; and David indeed was anything but sharp in his handling of the matter, but when it comes to settling scores, David is all there, sharp as ever.

Surely David's most compelling motive for killing Joab is that Joab killed Absalom against his explicit orders to "deal gently with the young man" (2 Sam. 18.5), and then for having implicitly to concede the rightness of Joab's harsh rebuke when David was incapacitated with grief: "Thou [David] hast shamed this day the faces of all thy servants, which this day have saved thy life, . . . for this day I perceive, that if Absalom had lived, and all we had died this day, then it had pleased thee well" (19.5–7).[15] Leakages of David's real motives appear in his words to Solomon. He cannot keep Absalom out of the text. But avenging Absalom, when Joab saved David's skin by killing him in a time of civil war, would not work as well legally and politically as the official reason for killing Joab as the ones David articulates, nor would avenging Absalom do much to motivate Solomon, who cannot be displeased that Absalom is out of the succession picture. Hence the reasons offered: that Joab killed Abner and Amasa treacherously, that is, in violation of a peace.

The wise Solomon does not miss a beat and the episode is so rich, I cannot stop without concluding the story. This is not a digression. Its point is to confirm the shallowness of the psychological literature on wisdom and old age that makes it warm and fuzzy, moral and pious, white-haired and Santalike, when the historical story about wisdom is grayer, more nuanced and intelligent. Watch Joab. He is not about to go quietly. He arranges to make killing him a cultic embarrassment, and thus hopefully self-avenging. As soon as the news reaches him that Solomon's purge of his brother's Adonijah's backers is under way, Joab flees to the tent of the Lord and grabs the horns of the altar. Solomon had already sent the formidable Benaiah[16] to kill Adonijah, and now directs him to get

Joab. Joab refuses Benaiah's order to come out and dares Benaiah to come in and kill him at the altar. Reluctant to violate the sanctuary, Benaiah returns to Solomon for instructions: "And the king said unto him, 'Do as he hath said, and fall upon him, and bury him; that thou mayest take away the innocent blood, which Joab shed, from me, and from the house of my father. And the Lord shall return his blood upon his own head, who fell upon two men more righteous and better than he, and slew them with the sword, my father David not knowing thereof, to wit, Abner . . . and Amasa. . . .' So Benaiah the son of Jehoiada went up, and fell upon him, and slew him" (1 Kings 2.30–34).

Solomon, at David's suggestion, legitimates the killing by making Joab's death, as an official matter, an act of purification for any bloodguilt the royal line incurred as a result of Joab's killings of Abner and Amasa. But there is good reason to doubt that either David or Solomon cares all that much about angering the Lord on those grounds. Solomon is not in the least bit hesitant to violate the sanctuary of the Tabernacle by spilling human blood there.[17] Fears of being accursed on those grounds do not seem to scare him at all. Indeed, it is Joab's last hostile manifestation of cold wit to expose the official account of his assassination as so much pretext by forcing his enemies to violate the holiness of the Tabernacle to accomplish their purely political goals. Even Benaiah, a steely hit man, fears spilling human blood in the Tabernacle. Not Solomon. The wise Solomon can also take satisfaction in his own wit, a match for Joab's. Just as Joab violated the rules of formal peace and truce to kill Abner, so does Solomon to kill Joab: a violation of sanctuary for a violation of sanctuary. Both David and Joab go out in style.

Wisdom in this account is the wisdom of Odysseus. It is about know-how, about how to steal a march on your enemy, how to catch him unawares, how to hoist him with his own petard, and how to kill wisely. This sort of wisdom strictly runs against the grain of forgiveness, unless forgiveness also happens to be wise in just this cold way. Wisdom literature is not sentimental about forgiveness. Forgiveness is a move in a hard game, a biding of one's time: "A fool gives full vent to his anger, but a wise man quietly holds it back" (Prov. 29.11, RSV). It is from Proverbs that St. Paul gets his warrant for turning deeds of kindness and forgiveness into revenge: "If thine enemy be hungry, give him bread to eat; and if he be thirsty, give him water to drink: *For thou shalt heap coals of fire upon his head*" (Prov. 25.21; cf. Rom. 12.20).

Those who claim wisdom is a consequence of the slowing down of the brain's functioning, so that going slowly and thus being prudent come more easily to the old, are perhaps simply pandering to aging baby boomers or, worse, have themselves fallen victim to the irrational wishful thinking of the positivity effect and their own declining cognitive abilities.[18]

PART III

Complaining

CHAPTER 7.

Homo Querelus
(Man the Complainer)

In the early fifteenth century St. Bernardino of Siena voices what was already an old adage on old age: "You strove to reach it, you desired to achieve it, you were afraid you'd not reach it, and now, arriving, you complain. Everyone wishes to reach old age, but nobody wishes to be old."[1]

We demand complaint as the first sign of life. No cry from the baby is not good news; we even rank newborns by how vociferously they complain in those very first moments outside the cramped comfort of the womb. Two of the criteria in the Apgar score depend on the quickness and volume of complaint. Complaining is one's essence in adolescence, when it is sometimes laced with edgy humor, those teen years producing some of the cleverest as well as the stupidest observations of our lives. It continues as the basis of a considerable measure of our conversation, occasionally interesting, often dreary: interesting when it functions in the small-minded comedic mode manifesting "the instinctive spite of local gossip"[2] as we pierce and expose the pretenses and vanities of others, and dreary when it is humorlessly self-referential. Old age hardly has a lock on complaining about one's lot, but as St. Bernardino notes, the complaining of the old is distinguished from that of those younger by the reflexivity of the complaining. The old complain about old age or its attributes, about their position in the life cycle. Not even adolescents, poor unfortunate souls that they objectively are, complain about adolescence as adolescence.

Something rings so true about Bernardino's observation that it must come close to stating a human universal. In the humanities, one is considered naive to invoke "human nature" or certain behavioral or moral universals. Social behavior is supposedly all mere "performance," unless, that is, you are adopting a baby or going to a sperm bank, in which case the same humanities prof becomes quite hastily and sincerely a rather vulgar genetic determinist. I will invoke a stripped-down, chastened human nature anyway. I admit cultural variation and variation within cultures by age, sex, and class as well as obvious variations across individuals. I make all the obligatory qualifications. Yet the core truth of Bernardino's complaint refuses to budge.

I cannot resist a detour of two paragraphs on some very small human universals that touch an old man's heart, and tickle that of, if not a sullen teenager, then surely a depressed grad student. Anyone who mucks around in old texts will have moments in which he forges a bond of kinship with the dead. These moments are sometimes suffused with an epiphanic sensation, which happens most touchingly when the behaviors are incidental, trivial, or comical. Constantine the African, an eleventh-century author (or translator) of a tract on cures for lovesickness, advises warm baths to cure the lovelorn of their sorrow because, he says, warm baths make people sing.[3] Substitute shower for bath, and one of the more attractively comical expressions of human well-being is captured to a tee. Singing in the shower. Why am I touched by that knowledge?

Scratching the inside of an ear with a little finger is a behavior you do not bother to think about, unless someone with whom you are eating is doing it and finishes by checking the end of his finger. But when you find an early twelfth-century Latin translation of a ninth-century law of King Alfred in which Alfred's Old English "lytla finger" is rendered *auriculis,* "ear finger," someone with an itching inner ear emerges from the gloom of the Dark Ages into the light to bond with you in comical kinship.[4]

A comic kinship of a slightly different sort, tinged with Schadenfreude but no less capable of eliciting fellow feeling across not just centuries but millennia, emerges from the records of the small miseries and the interminable battles of dealing with loved ones. As soon as there are letters between family members, we have what looks like our own families at their most annoying—and most recognizable. And here we are back to our present theme: complaint. It is hard not to feel a sublime connectedness with one or both of the parties in what follows. In Akkadian more than four thousand years old we find: "Thus says Babi to Shartum: I have been distressed about you. Why are you quarreling with Ibbi-ilum in the house? Live in peace with each other. Send me some sesame oil."[5]

In ancient Egypt marital quarrels continued beyond the grave. This from a husband to his dead wife in the nineteenth dynasty (c. 1250 B.C.): "What have I done against you wrongfully for you to get into this evil disposition in which you are? What have I done against you? As for what you have done, it is your laying hands on me even though I committed no wrong against you. From the time that I was living with you as a husband until today, what have I done against you that I should have to conceal it? What have I done against you?"[6] His wife continues to hound him from the grave. His aches and pains, his misfortunes are her doing, and she, he insists, is not justified in treating him like this. He gets himself so worked up that later in the letter he threatens to sue her in the court of the dead.

In the following letter from Ugarit (c. 1300 B.C., a port city in what is now Syria), one can sympathize both with the hurt feelings of the sister and the brother who hurt them: "Now the heart of your sister is sick because they have treated me ill and I was never consulted. In the month of Hiyyaru—when nobody consulted me—a fattened bull was slaughtered and nobody gave me any. As you live and as do I, I swear that nobody gave me any and my heart is very sick. . . . Now you know how sick the heart of your sister will be if there is any more enmity. . . . As for the money that you granted me, send it to me so I may cause you to sleep where your 'soul' is going. Why do you delay sending your messenger to me? Don't you know that my heart is sick?"[7] Not invited to the party, and perhaps no wonder. Her style of complaint is so painfully familiar to any Jew that I was tempted to absolve the eastern European shtetls of responsibility and instead blame it all on a long-enduring northwestern Semitic style of complaint three millennia old, until an Irish friend, and then an Italian one, indicated that it sounded exactly like their relatives too. Complaining, like singing in the shower, unites us in one big unhappy family. There is something almost sublime in such mundane and predictable complaints that are four thousand years old.

Complaint is everywhere; it colors the world and much of our inner lives. Human society, family life, international relations: all are unimaginable without it. Solitude too is inconceivable without it. Much of the inner monologue, or inner dialogue, we carry on with ourselves is cast in the form of complaint. We thus complain to ourselves about God's disfavor, about not being properly appreciated, about aches and pains, insomnia, the person writing a check in the express checkout lane, the decibel level of the cell phone user twenty feet from the seat you found where you had hoped you would be able to read as you waited for your flight, which is already two hours late, about the ice cream truck that pollutes your residential neighborhood with an endless loop of "Turkey in the Straw," which caused you to lose your one serviceable thought that day.

You even complain to yourself about yourself, playing both complainant and defendant. What a disgrace you are for being so easily annoyed, for being so unpleasantly unstoical on the one hand, and so cowardly on the other, that you do not go throttle the check writer or punch the loud cell phone talker. To *homo necans*

(man the killer) and *homo sacer* (man the accursed), we can supply
a third *homo* that can be understood to have generated the first two:
homo querelus, man the complainer. He is none other than man as
defined by the ill-favored eye of Dostoyevsky's Underground Man:
"a creature that has two legs and no sense of gratitude."

Complaining is often formally ritualized. Lawsuits are ritualized
complaints and openly acknowledged as such. The moving party
is the plaintiff or complainant. Courts exist to provide a forum
to hear complaints. Prayers, when they are petitional, often take
the form of complaints or laments; and when they are prayers of
thanksgiving for a good harvest, or for witnessing the defeat of
one's foes, they are grateful acknowledgments that God or the gods
responded favorably to an earlier complaint made in a petitional
prayer.

In the later Middle Ages complaining gave rise to a subgenre
of poetry, the complaint—mostly lovers' complaints regarding the
miserable course of true love, but also courtiers' complaints about
the corruption of the king's court, the advancement of flatterers
at the expense of the complainant, and general complaints about
the evils of the time. One can understand most social satire to be
a complaint genre, especially when it goes after the standard array
of human vices and follies. Even the idea of the good old days, of a
golden age, of the Garden of Eden, is born of present complaints
about the human condition generally, or about more specific gripes
against particular novelties and failings of the present. I now find
the age before organized sports leagues for six-years-olds golden
for that reason alone.

Complaining obviously has its proper place. No teacher could
teach, no preacher preach, no moralist praise virtue or blame vice,
no parent set standards for his children, if unable to complain
about inadequate performance. These people have a privilege to
complain. Their complaining thus gets more favorably categorized.
Instead of begging and soliciting, grieving and whining, teachers
and parents are mostly heard to instruct, to exhort, to cajole, or to
look justly disappointed, though there are limits to the privilege:
cajolery and coaxing, okay, but these decline inevitably into empty

threats, finally bottoming out in whining, which is the price to be paid for no longer having the privilege to box the ears of a child or student every now and then. The old, though, have no privilege worth the name because our complaining has no legitimating function such as the teacher or parent can claim. But when the old stop complaining and descend into vacant grins and positivity effect, they no longer are losing it: they have lost it.

OF WHINES, OYS, MOANS, AND GROANS

There are different styles of complaint within a culture as well as across cultures.[8] Not all, for instance, are made in the same tone of voice. Complaining can accommodate several timbres and tones, though some tones are wholly monopolized by complaint: whining, for instance, for which nothing good can be said. A justified complaint that is whined loses much of its justness. The aversiveness of the whine may be hardwired into us. Children use the tone before they have the words. We must beat it out of our children, to whom it comes as a lightning-quick reflex when an expressed desire is met with refusal. But given that the child soon learns that he was born in a time in which nothing merits a spanking, he also soon learns to whine the initial expression of a desire in order to forefend what has already been reduced to the remotest possibility of refusal. The parent will cede to the merest soupçon of a whine, grant anything not to have to endure it. So why, thinks the child, wait? When my wife gently ordered my then three-year-old daughter Eva to "stop fussing," she fired back: "I'm not fussing; I'm whining." The little girl did not want her whining euphemized out of its force.

A child's whining also carries something of a threat, the threat of continuing, the threat of it becoming a character trait, a trait that will trump all others to create that rather detestable being: the whiner. Unlike whining youngsters, however, complaining oldsters are mostly ignored when they complain, and completely ignored when they do not, which then prompts the more stoical or happier of them to complain, which is risky, for if we can barely deny thoughts of the ice floe for a whining child, then woe to the whining oldster.

Adults whine (students surely do); we may have, with mortification, heard our own voices take on the tone. We can whine in prose
too, many an e-mail I have received qualifying nicely, no idiotic
emoticons necessary. The remarkable Amarna Letters, 1350 B.C.,
preserve a stream of missives to Pharaoh and his officials from the
vassal mayor Rib-hadda of Gubla (Byblos), a city on the central
coast of present-day Lebanon. His incessant pleading for military
assistance, coupled with the obligatory groveling of a vassal petitioning his superior in that world, seems worthily characterized as
whining. The tone comes through the conventionalized epistolary
style. Rib-hadda is among the very few whiners in history one ends
up feeling sorry for. He is not trying to get candy, a toy, or a grade
changed; he wants help against his enemies. His requests, however,
are heard as whines by the people he is petitioning. They take the
repeated urgency and frequency of his letters as so much crying
wolf. Rib-hadda himself provides the proof that he is heard as a
whiner by his addressees. Here he quotes a letter that Pharaoh (or
one of his scribes) sent him: "You [Pharaoh] keep talking like this:
'You [Rib-hadda] are the one that writes to me more than all the
other mayors.' Why should they be the ones to write to you? They
have their cities, but my cities Aziru has taken."

In his penultimate surviving letter we have a barely surviving
Rib-hadda in exile in Beirut, having been driven from Gubla, lamenting: "I am personally unable to enter the land of Egypt. I am
old and there is a serious illness in my body."[9]

In Rib-hadda's world there were always wolves at the door; one
had to distinguish among them. Now, with no city left to lose, Rib-
hadda complains, predictably, about old age and his health, though
he finally is too demoralized to whine. His tone is one of resigned
lamentation. It is hard, though, not to find Rib-hadda comical; he
did not have the necessary mettle to play politics in his rough world.
Never mind that you and I would have broken down in tears and
changed jobs; Rib-hadda stuck it out, complaining the whole time.

With the whine at one unpardonable end of styles of complaint
(there is no such thing as a cute whine, unless it comes from the dog
shut out from the dinner party or is openly self-satirical, but even

then . . .), we can move to groans and moans which, except when completely unbidden, play a large part in the world of complaint. They mark one's suffering in a way that cannot help but be a performance, and they are often mistrusted, especially by one's spouse, as *mere* performance even when the pain is real. It figures as a request for solicitude, for commiseration, and partly as an unarticulated prayer for relief. Underground Man, not a very generous observer, refuses to concede even the possibility that the moaning induced by a toothache can be uttered in good faith. To him, it is all show.[10]

Then there is the Jewish "oy," especially the oy of old Jews. Unlike the whine, an oy admits of irony and shtick. Unlike the moan and groan, it asks its own pardon; an oy is as much a sign of resigned acceptance as a claim for relief. What else could a Jew expect anyway? In some settings, one can even discern in the oy an affirmation that surpasses resignation, an embracing of one's Jewishness. One might even grant it some small charm, as long as you do not exceed your modest number of allowable oys. The charm fades quickly and it soon starts to be heard as a whine.

Yiddish *oy,* it would seem, can claim descent from Germanic woe, *weh, vei,* which goes back to an Indo-European root that also gives us Latin *vae;* but oy seems more likely to come from Hebrew oy, אױ.[11] The expression *oy veh* is thus half Semitic, half Germanic, with the oy from אױ and the veh, obviously, a form of Germanic weh/woe. Oy vey, then, is a neat double complaint, coupling Hebrew and Germanic in a double blast of woeful interjection, Semite and Teuton united in a brotherhood of complaint and mutual dissatisfaction, but hardly issuable from German mouths. It captures Jewish, not German, ambivalence and confusion.

The oy proper is not available to the goy, nor is it really properly available to an assimilated Jew without it smacking of affectation (or a kind of hostile exclusivity), especially when coming from someone who is more than two generations removed from the shtetl, whose middle name is Ian, and who grew up in Green Bay. My oys, I must confess, lack authenticity, but the restriction on the authorized use of oy hardly produces a complaint vacuum, either for assimilated Jews or for Christians. Other interjections of complaint abound, and one can always settle for generic moaning and groaning.

Dress up the moans and groans, grace them with more parts of speech than interjections, and we can be said to lament, or, somewhat archaically, "to make moan." Laments, though dotted with interjections, sighs, wails, and groans, demand a more elevated and articulate style; otherwise they sink back into mere pissing and moaning, the adult equivalent of a toddler's fussing.

We could further divide the domain of complaint and distinguish among grumbling, murmuring, kvetching, griping, bitching, and remonstrating, in addition to the whining, oying, pissing-and-moaning, and lamenting already noted. This list does not come close to exhausting the words and phrases English speakers use to get a fix on this genus of behaviors, and the terms are not close to being synonyms. Each one implicates variations on multiple scales of justifiability, seriousness, tone, offensiveness, formality, repetitiveness, and duration.

Many of the terms not only mark a certain style of complaint, they are themselves a complaint against the style. There is a dismissive fed-upness with the complainer who pisses and moans; the person of either sex who bitches must bear the weight of vulgar antifeminism of ancient vintage. Some of the terms are privileged for use by certain people and denied to others. Soldiers, for instance, are known to be expert in grumbling and griping. The Israelites in the desert were masters of grumbling and murmuring. But whereas soldiers from time immemorial are deemed to have a privilege to grumble and gripe, the Israelites had no such privilege. Even formal remonstrances, as when Miriam and Aaron confront Moses about his having married a Cushite woman, were deemed unacceptable (Num. 12.1), though that hardly put a dent in the chronic complaining.

One can also discern hints of kvetching in the Torah, and lo, it is a complaint about old age: "And Pharaoh said unto Jacob, 'How old art thou?' And Jacob said unto Pharaoh, 'The days of the years of my pilgrimage are an hundred and thirty years: few and evil have the days of the years of my life been, and have not attained unto the days of the years of the life of my fathers in the days of their pilgrimage'" (Gen. 47.8–9). Jacob does make it to 147, apparently having had a premonition that he would fall short of Abraham and Isaac, who attained 175 and 180. He has not one good thing to say about his life—"evil have the days of the years of my life been"—but he wants more of it, apparently so as not to lose a longevity contest with his father and grandfather. Not for him a conventional lament of lost youth and health. Had Pharaoh asked, "How are you?" Jacob, we can trust, would not have answered with the ritually obligatory "Fine."

Mumbling and grumbling is the lot of the subaltern, the slave, the rank and file, the grunts, the cannon fodder. Not all big players in the honor game adopt the tight-lipped Clint Eastwood style. The complaining of those higher in the hierarchy—the princes, kings, heroes, and gods—is often coupled with anger, petulance, and frustration, in the venting of which their status largely saves them from being heard to whine or kvetch even when that is in fact what they are doing: thus Achilles, Hera, Hamlet, and Yahweh. The highborn lament their fate and sometimes become subjects for tragedy; they complain of the times they were cursed to set aright, of the incompetence of underlings and allies, of the betrayal of family and friends, or of offenses committed against their honor. Achilles, Roland, and Egil are chronic complainers, but they get a pass where the lowly Thersites does not. Lear and Job complain too and at great length, which even the justice of their cause would not excuse were they not, we feel, pleading for us too, exquisitely articulating wrongs we have felt but lacked such perfect words to hurl at a wagering God in Job's case or against the malignantly empty heavens in Lear's. Job stands in a long line of complainers who preceded him in the wisdom literature of the ancient Near East. A Babylonian laments his lot, c. 1400 B.C.:

> My god has forsaken me and disappeared,
> My goddess has failed me and keeps at a distance.
> The benevolent angel who walked beside me has departed,
> My protecting spirit has taken to flight, and is seeking

someone else.

My strength is gone.[12]

Jesus too complains in much the same spirit. He would hardly have been human if he did not—"O faithless and perverse generation, how long am I to be with you? How long am I to bear with you?" (Matt. 17.17). His complaints are mostly cast in the form of rebukes, impatient when directed to humans, poignant when directed to his Father, where he borrows from the ritualized complaints against God that characterize so many of the psalms and the Babylonian lament just quoted: "My God, my God, why hast thou forsaken me?" (Matt. 27.46).[13] Part of the power of this complaint is that rather than attempt his own words, he borrows perfect ones already composed from Psalm 22, but without the tendentiousness we see when Jesus is in his self-conscious fulfill-the-prophecy mode. His complaint is psychologically and dramatically right in its resonances.

Lear's "our basest beggars / Are in the poorest thing superfluous" (2.4.264–66) holds open the possibility that the basest beggar who complains of his lot could still meaningfully be reprimanded with a "What do you have to complain about? It could be worse." The beggar would be compelled to agree. That was proved by the death camps and Gulag, where there was always a way to make "it could be worse" not lose its meaning.

Turn Lear's image around and for the basest beggar substitute the filthiest rich and most well-endowed investment banker, the man who has everything. Complaining, even whining, is still part of the picture. The servant is lazy, the help steals, and people keep agitating to raise your taxes; you are not sure you are loved for who you really are deep down inside. As you lie on the analyst's couch, you complain about the burdens that come with wealth. If others only understood how much work it takes to manage your money, how unfulfilled you feel, they would understand that you are hurting too. This, as you recognize, is an old complaint, one commonly invoked about the vanity of human wishes, in part put to use as a pep talk to keep monks and other ascetics to their vows by constantly reminding them that their giving up every pleasure in life was really not giving up any pleasures at all.

Suppose, though, your good fortune does buy you happiness; you have no complaints. Yet you must complain. Your continued happiness hinges on your fulfilling the complaint requirement. Happiness uncomplained about provokes the gods, and surely the evil eye of your neighbors. Thus the Yiddish "no evil eye" (*kein eyin harah*), upon hearing *good news.* Good news is dangerous stuff; it is a tax on your remaining supply of good luck. Best to protect against the harmful consequences of good luck and ward off the demons by knocking on some nearby wood. Beware, too, the envy of your neighbors. It is one of mankind's most predictable traits to find as much cause for complaint in another's good fortune as in one's own misfortune, the former being experienced as a special case of the latter. In a world in which one's standing is gauged relative to others and the competition is fierce, your good fortune costs your neighbors. They will, unless you go out of your way to make their envy less painful to them, plot to make your happiness painful to you. As the Bemba proverb says: "To find one beehive in the woods is good luck, to find two is very good luck, to find three is witchcraft."[14] If your luck is too good to be true, it might cost you your life.

SHMUEL THE TAILOR

Complaining and wisdom keep good company. Who would think otherwise? To the extent wisdom must criticize, must often be satirical, it must register complaints. Shmuel the tailor, who qualifies as the hero of Barbara Myerhoff's study of a Jewish old-age center in Venice, California, in the mid-1970s, is *the* wise man. Victor Turner, one of the giants of anthropology of the prior generation, describes Shmuel in his foreword to Myerhoff's book as "one of those rare spirits that a culture occasionally produces, ample and strong enough to contain all the complexities and paradoxes of the human condition and his own tradition." Shmuel is reflective; as he says, tailoring is good for the life of the mind: "In my life I have never been bored. If you cannot tell a story to yourself when you are sewing, you are lost anyway."[15] He has suffered as a boy in a Polish shtetl and as a struggling impoverished immigrant in a strange land. He does not complain about his hard past. His reconstruction of his boyhood is remarkable for how little hate and blame figure in it. In his boyhood poverty, "Aprille with his shoures soote" brought pogroms along with the spring flowers (Easter was not a good time to be a Jew in Christian lands). He remembers a "sweetness amidst the fear and repression. That is how the Jews lived and the Jewish language was born."[16]

He holds no grudges, and it annoys his wife that he does not. His acceptance seems to be accompanied with a kind of Yiddish shrug; and it would almost sound too sappily new agey in its accepting-ness if it weren't that he had suffered, and reflected, and relived it all many times over. Despite the tinge of fatalism, there is no sense of resignation. Real pain, real loss, hard and wise endurance save his wistfulness from sliding into cheap sentimentality. An older Polish boy stabbed him in the neck when he was eleven years old as he took a short cut through the woods to get home before dark. "He was a bully and a small Jewish boy was like a fly to him. . . . But it must be remembered there were Jewish bullies also."[17] When one is old, apparently one misses childhood simply because it was childhood, so that even an attempt on your life and being bullied is looked back upon with a sense of loss.

But Shmuel has a sharp edge. He has much of the satirist in him and he has little sympathy for the vanity of his fellow oldsters who frequent the senior center. About them he is judgmental, not charitable in the least: "What do they know from truth? They collect a few pennies, some old clothes, and they are saving Israel. They learn some poems, make a book report, and go to a couple of classes, and they are now educated people. They will tell you how much their children love them, how their cupboards are overflowing, and they take a bus miles away to a store so no one will see them using food stamps. 'Well,' you will answer, 'so they are proud, they don't want to complain. They don't want to be pitied.' But no, that's not it. Let them have a bunion on their foot and they send up cries to heaven. 'Lord, why am I stricken? Did I deserve this from You?'"[18]

Shmuel cannot abide the complaining of his fellow old Jews. And so he complains about them. The wise must frequently find themselves in such binds, necessarily guilty of some of the vices they wish to correct. Jesus gets caught up in an analogous bind by rebuking rebukers who can't see the oak beam in their own eyes but are able to discern with great particularity the dust particle in yours.[19]

It is easier to be stoical about the past that has been endured, as Shmuel is, than about the intrusive annoyances of the present, as Shmuel is not. Present annoyance even works miracles upon other present annoyances. Proverbial wisdom rightly recognizes that the appearance of a new annoyance can displace a present one, a new pain mask a prior pain. Thus the Norse proverb: "A good way to deal with misfortune is to suffer a greater one."[20] New discomfort can bring some relief from the previous misery as some small compensation for its arrival. Part of the therapeutic aspect of complaining about X is not that it helps you deal with X so much as it is a way of getting the equally annoying Y out of your mind. But not for good. In the vile surrealism of the death camps, Primo Levi found that there was not much solace to be had in the fact that the more immediate misery blocked perception of the remoter one. Relief of a sort was soon followed by a letdown when the prior misery resumed its role on center stage: "Human nature is such that grief and pain—even simultaneously suffered—do not add up as a whole in our consciousness, but hide, the lesser behind the greater, according to a definite law of perspective. . . . And if the most immediate cause of stress comes to an end, you are grievously amazed to see that another one lies behind."[21] You were punished by a disappointment that outweighed the little respite you had; you had committed the sin of a perverse form of looking on the bright side and were now paying the price.

The other oldsters do not like Shmuel, partly because of his anti-Zionism and partly, one suspects, because they feel the weight of his disdain. Though he wishes to cast these others as fools, Shmuel needs all his wits to deal with them. The people he is mocking are worthy opponents in one respect, if not in most others. These old men and women—verified by the tapes of the anthropologist who is recording their frequent bickering and constant interrupting of each other—have maintained and continue to hone a Yiddish cultural genius for insult, curse, and putdown, as part of and in addition to a talent for complaint. Wise man that he is, Shmuel mostly stays away from such "fools," for they get to him more than he gets to them. Shmuel is more thoughtful, wiser, more learned, but when it comes to giving as good as you get, they are his match.

The character of Shmuel is a complex creation. He is playing to the anthropologist as the wise man, the informant; she in turn creates him as a character in her book, a labor of mutual admiration and respect. Myerhoff finds in Shmuel a way to remold her suburban, secularized Judaism in a way that still pays homage to the wisdom of the old ways; he offers something more than the watered-down nothingness so much of it has become. Though Shmuel is not observant, he is not religiously ill informed. He knows his Torah, his Bible; he always has the perfect quote from the prophets to make his point (he sees himself as a kind of Jeremiah); he knows the rabbinic commentaries and lore. No longer a believer, he respects the wisdom of the faith he has lost and continues to worship its writings.

You will say, argues Shmuel preemptively with Myerhoff, that these oldsters' pretense of not being in need or not having been abandoned by their children is a sign of their dignity, that their keeping up appearances is the equivalent of suffering in silence. Shmuel will have it none of it. These efforts are, to Shmuel's thinking, merely what comes easiest to them. There is no self-overcoming, just pathetic vanity. It costs them less pain to be able to brag about their children who have abandoned them and to feign financial security than to complain about poverty and neglectful children. The proof, he says, is their inability to keep quiet about physical discomfort.

Shmuel is making an argumentative move that probably doesn't hold up. He assumes a single unified virtue of noncomplaint. He wants the virtue it takes to deal nobly with physical pain to be the same as the one needed to face psychic pain. Yet it is not rare to find that people who are good at handling some kinds of misery are weak in the face of others. He reveals, though, just how ungenerous we are likely to be about the virtuous capability of people who moan and groan about aches and pains.

As Adam Smith notes, the capacity for sympathy works better in some domains than in others. It is easier to sympathize with another's small joys than it is with their great joys.[22] If a friend wins a scratch-off for $100 you are pleased for him; should he win Mega Millions it would be unbearable. When, conversely, it comes to pain, your sympathy does not extend to the small pains of others, even when they are your own toddlers (some mothers excepted), and especially not if they are your spouse. We do sympathize, on the other hand, with the *great* pain and suffering of others, but not for long. Pity has a way of ending in indifference or disgust if too much is asked of it. Sympathy, Smith observes, works best when the sufferer puts on a brave face. If he does not crack under self-evidently demanding circumstances, we stand in awe, imagining our own inability to behave in the same manner. Such people end up worshipped as saints, heroes, or martyrs.

Though we know by experience that another's complaining about aches and pains will stop sympathy dead in its tracks, that it will indeed produce antipathy, we, or I, will still kvetch about feeling crummy from lack of sleep or about the arthritis in my hips and knees, notwithstanding my wife's withering contempt, and no doubt my colleagues' too. When I manage to keep my peace I wish to be recognized for my virtue, for my suffering in silence, but how can I be praised if I am too successful at suppressing my unsympathizeable discomforts? I have—perhaps you have too—cultivated a wince when I get in and out of chairs, just so people can appreciate how stoical I am.

CHAPTER 8.

Old Saints, Old Killers, and More Complaints

Christian moralists of the Middle Ages did not have much good to say about old age. If there was any virtue to be found in the decline that came with aging, it was, as we noted, that it put one in the mind to turn to spiritual matters, to prepare for a good Christian death. It was a time for penance. Instead of complaining about aches and pains, about declining powers physical and mental, you could take advantage of your misery to contemplate the evanescence of pleasure and the mutability and instability of embodied life.

Old age's miseries could thus be recruited to the cause of salvation. The decline of libido, erectile dysfunction, loss of energy, stomach disorders made it hard for several of the deadly sins to operate. Failing eyesight meant the senex amans failed to ogle as many desirables as were ogleable; failing hearing meant less cause for peevishness and anger. Rather than others annoying you with their humming, whistling, and mindless chatter, it was you who annoyed them by forcing them to repeat what they had just said. When it came to foods, your sense of taste was no longer as nuanced, and your stomach wasn't up to what you could taste anyway. In medieval times, gluttony was a problem only for the rich; the poor were on their low-fat, low-calorie diet by default. In our day the poor must pay for their gluttony too. Let us not even think about the collapse of the sense of touch, which now fails to warn you of large chunks of food you have managed to park on your chin, though your pain receptors seem to be working quite well, thank you.

The grounds of bodily complaint were not dismissed as so much hypochondria. You were hurting; no one denied it. The suffering old body did more than wake you up to the nearness of the end, it was itself a penance, the wages of your youthful sins. The poor old body. It pays the price but got none of the benefits of the sinful pleasure. Very few of the molecules that made up the young you are there now; your soul, such as it is, provides the continuity that makes the present you the successor to the you that had the fun long ago. And the soul, unlike the already unsalvageable body and brain, can be saved.

But what is the virtue in being chaste and abstemious when you no longer have the means to lust and glut? Rather more virtue was required to motivate a young man or woman, still lusty and good-looking, who was called to religion, than an old geezer trying to time his confession to finish it exactly as he breathed his last. Virtue meant giving something up when you had it to give.

There is a catch here too. Alexander Murray hypothesizes that the reason a disproportionate number of young noblemen in the twelfth and thirteenth centuries were drawn to the religious life and its celibacy was that their high social rank deprived them of the thrill of the chase. For them, sex was for the having, as were food and drink: they were perks of position.[1] Many of these young nobles, at the height of their youthful vigor, were soul sick, suffering the *tedium vitae* of having it all. Celibacy offered a new way; religion made demands that gave life more meaning than was to be had from the beer-commercial-like vacuousness of worldly pleasure that was at one's pleasure.

Yet, perversely, once the vow of chastity was taken, the thrill would be restored to what earlier had been tiresome luxury. Now sensual pleasure would not be for the having; it would thus regain a sinful allure it did not have before. The very giving it up, which cost you nothing because you did not value it when you gave it up, gave it value. The paradox is that having given it up, you now had it to give up.

ST. ANSKAR, APOSTLE OF THE NORTH, THE FAILED MARTYR

Even the most saintly of old men could not keep from complaining. Taking stock of one's condition could lead to more complaining. The case of St. Anskar (d. 865), the apostle of the North, provides a subtle and rich example. Early in his religious career, Anskar passionately hoped for the crown of martyrdom. Nor were these fond hopes. It was Danes and Swedes he intended to evangelize at the height of the first wave of Viking activity. But somehow he managed to be spared by the Vikings, who plundered the ship that carried him on his first mission to Sweden. They simply put him ashore, preferring instead to take forty books Anskar and his party had with them. Wise businessmen these illiterate pirates were; they had come to learn that books could be ransomed for a higher price than a few middling clerics would fetch; and books did not have to be fed or defended against while you held them hostage or ferried them to the slave market.[2]

Some years later Anskar barely escaped a Viking sack of his bishopric at Hamburg.[3] This time his books suffered a worse fate. They, including an exquisitely penned Bible that the emperor Louis the Pious had given him, succumbed to the fire that destroyed the church and monastery. From that time forth Anskar had no calls as close as these, and that did not please him. On a second mission to Sweden, which could easily have turned hostile, everything went his way.[4] Anskar was an able man, a skilled negotiator and administrator, and rather too likeable to get himself killed by those he evangelized.

Anskar felt himself a failure for growing old and having not gained a martyr's crown. Rimbert, the author of the *Life of Anskar,* knew him well, knew his hopes and fears. He was Anskar's disciple, friend, and successor to the see of Hamburg-Bremen. He records that when Anskar was sixty-three, "he began to suffer from a serious illness, namely dysentery. When after many days, that is four months, or even more, he was still in pain and felt that he was nigh unto death, he continued to give God thanks and said that his pain was less than his sins deserved." Anskar, we see, did not keep silent about his pain. He complained about it rather frequently: "He would *often repeat* the words of Job: 'shall we receive good at the hand of God, and shall we not receive evil?'" (Job 2.10; emphasis added).[5]

But Anskar mostly complains about not having died a martyr. He would "make known his grief" on this score to Rimbert "often." Rimbert tries to console the suffering saint. He gamely suggests to Anskar that he is dying a martyr if martyrdom is interpreted to mean suffering a miserable painful death: "In his eager desire to bring comfort [Rimbert reminded] him of all that he had suffered in God's service and how much bodily pain he had endured: he urged, moreover, that, even if he had suffered none of these things, his last grievous illness, which had continued day after day, would by God's grace more than have earned for him the title of martyr."[6] Anskar is not consoled by Rimbert's argument.

Anskar's complaint about not having died a martyr is a double complaint. It can be taken at face value as sincerely meant. At some level of his consciousness, he wanted a martyr's crown. But lamenting his failure to get killed by pagan Swedes or Slavs is also very much a complaint about his present physical discomfort: "Oh, God, why couldn't I have been killed in an honorable way, dying a holy martyr, over in an hour at most, instead of this drawn-out illness with its piercing pain and degrading lack of bowel control? Let me die, already, I can't take it anymore." Without wishing to impugn the sincerity of his faith and his commitment to laboring ably and tirelessly for his church, a desire to *have been* a martyr is not the same as a desire to *be* a martyr; a desire to have died young cannot meaningfully be acted upon, unless you can travel backward in time.

Anskar believes that when he was a young man, God, in a vision, had promised him martyrdom. Anskar is sufficiently consumed by bodily misery that he begins to doubt God, finding him not a God of his word, perhaps not even the Word. This puts God, rather quickly, and Rimbert two chapters later, to some remedial action on Anskar's behalf. First God intervenes, if not *ex machina,* then *ex visione.* During a Mass, Anskar "heard a voice which chided him earnestly because he had *doubted* God's promise." The voice tells him not to doubt and that "God of His grace will grant both favors, that is, He will forgive the sins concerning which you are anxious, and will accomplish all that He promised." What sins could Anskar be anxious about if not his doubts of God? What sins must he have committed to suffer a shameful death by dysentery? I suspect the sin is precisely Anskar's forcing God first to admit, and then to reaffirm, a promise He might never have made.

Though Rimbert on his own could not convince the sick Anskar that dying a painful natural death qualified as martyrdom, Rimbert undertook to reargue his position more fully once Anskar was dead, so that he could wrap up the *Life* by giving Anskar his place in heaven among those with whom Anskar wished to be included. The conventional saint's life usually ends with or has appended to it miracle stories attributed to the saint's relics. In this *Life of Anskar* the miracle is not one that Anskar or his body parts perform but one Rimbert works by argumentation. Expanding on an idea offered more than four centuries earlier by St. Jerome,[7] Rimbert argues there are "two kinds of martyrdom," the conventional martyrdom of being killed in the service of the faith by its enemies and the martyrdom "which occurs when the Church is at peace, and which is hidden from sight. . . . [Anskar] desired both kinds of martyrdom, but one only did he attain." One can suffer in peacetime for the cause of the church without getting killed; and that should count. Anskar was surely "a martyr because, amid the temptations of the devil, the enticements of the flesh, the persecutions of the heathen and the opposition of Christians, he continued to the end of his life unperturbed, immovable, and unconquerable as a confessor of Christ. He was a martyr, for, whilst the word martyr signifies witness, he was a witness of God's word and of the Christian name. Wherefore let no one be surprised that he did not attain to that martyrdom which he so greatly desired and which, he thought, had been promised to him."[8]

Rimbert is agnostic as to whether God actually made a promise to Anskar. But Rimbert is arguing with God nonetheless. A just God would give this good man a place in the part of heaven he so desired, would grant him his martyr's aureole. Who would it harm to accord him that honor? We could blame Rimbert for playing on words, for hairsplitting; we could accuse him of grade inflation. Or, more charitably, we could admire Rimbert's generosity of spirit on behalf of his teacher, superior, and friend. Rimbert's gift to Anskar is to constrain God to grant him his wish.

As much as he reveres Anskar, Rimbert does not paint a picture of a noble and stoical death for him. He does not disguise that Anskar complains continually about physical pain and about spiritual failures he fears might make him out to be a coward. Why cowardice? Because Anskar could so easily have arranged to have gotten himself killed by pagan Northmen in service to the faith. Here's one sure way. This incident happened 150 years later, but the option would also have been available to Anskar. The account comes from Adam of Bremen (late eleventh century). An Englishman named Wolfred, "inspired by divine love," went to Sweden to preach the word of God to the pagans (c. 1030). In the presence of a multitude of Thor's devotees he cursed an idol of Thor and smashed it with a battle-ax. The pagans, understandably, took offense. "And forthwith he was pierced with a thousand wounds for such daring, and his soul passed into heaven earning a martyr's laurels. His body was mangled by the barbarians and, after further being subjected to much mockery, was plunged into a swamp."[9] Wolfred could hardly have been surprised that Thor's worshipers would not be pleased when he took an ax to Thor; Wolfred surely desired and assured the end that befell him.

Rimbert's portrait is psychologically astute. He gives us clues that Anskar, as holy a man as he was, did not exactly delight in mortification of the flesh. His complaining of pain in his final months is foreshadowed subtly by Rimbert's account of Anskar's self-imposed ascetic regimen seven chapters and some years earlier. To find some relief from "ecclesiastical duties and the disturbances caused by the heathen," Anskar had a cell built to which he would resort to be alone. There he would weigh out his bread and measure his water, "as long as he possessed any part of his youthful strength." But Anskar, by his own admission, became proud of his humble regimen. "For the enemy of the human race endeavored to corrupt his mind by this evil and he appeared great in his own eyes, because of his abstinence."[10]

Anskar responded not by increasing the rigor of his abstinence, not by punishing his body, but by relaxing the regimen that made him proud of his own holiness. Rimbert makes some excuses. Neither the biographer nor his hero, though admiring the virtues of giving it a good try, are especially given to morbidly garish self-denying devotion. Not for Anskar the Irish style, or that of the desert saints sitting high up on their poles: "After he grew old, he could not abstain from food in this way, but his drink continued to be water, though, for the sake of avoiding vainglory more than for the sake of taking anything pleasant, he was accustomed to mix wine with the small amount of water he was about to drink. And because in his old age he could not practice his accustomed abstinence, he endeavored to make up for this deficiency by alms-giving, prayers and other good deeds."[11]

To our minds, how much better that Anskar took his wine and ate more robustly, making up for his failings in mortifying his flesh by substituting alms and good deeds. But is not this Anskar the very same and quite consistent man who in his old age takes little pleasure, spiritual or otherwise, in his suffering, and when younger got a little too impressed with himself when he managed some abstinential rigor?[12] Nor does he suffer in silence. He was not very stoical, but why blame him for that? In their own way, stoics do not so much overcome complaint as change its style and shift its locus. True, they keep quiet; they do not whine or kvetch. They keep a stony face, but the stiff upper lip is played out before an audience. The quieter the stoic, the more awe he elicits in the audience, which then gives voice to what the stoic is keeping mum about. Recall Adam Smith, who recognized that such cold reserve is the best strategy for eliciting the sympathy of others, for getting them, that is, to feel your pain. They will complain for you but in a style and quantity that they will find bearable. I can hear them witnessing his noble suffering: "Do you see how that grand man suffers? How could anyone endure what he is going through? It hurts just to think about it. God forbid that something like this should happen to me."

Is there a conservation of complaint in the world? Lessen it here and a compensating amount pokes up there, when things are good no less than when they are bad? If Underground Man is right about man being "a creature that has two legs and no sense of gratitude," then we should not be surprised to find as much complaining when things are going well as when they are going badly. When we have it good, we get soft, and our baseline expectations are set at a height that, in an inverse relation, lowers the complaint threshold. We sixty-somethings might very well complain more now, with all our magical drugs, than we would have complained had we had the misfortune to have reached our sixties in the ninth century.

BERSI THE DUELER: THE LAMENT OF AN OLD KILLER

One does not expect sweetness of soul in a man who boasts of having killed thirty-five men in verse so complex that only the number jumps out without having to spend hours parsing it. He appears in two Icelandic sagas. In *Laxdæla saga* Bersi plays a very small role, confined to the brief scene below, after which, as the sagas are wont to say, he is "out of the saga." One of the saga's main characters, Olaf the Peacock, Bersi's first cousin, gives his young son Halldor to the old Bersi to foster. Halldor was in his first year at the time. The saga continues thus:

> That summer Bersi took sick and was bedridden the rest of the summer. One day, so it is told, when the people were

outside haymaking at Tongue [Bersi's farm], the two of them, Bersi and Halldor, were home alone. Halldor was in a cradle, but the cradle fell and the boy tumbled to the floor. Bersi could not move. Then he said:

> Here we both lie
> Unable to move,
> Halldor and I;
> We have no strength;
> My problem's age
> Yours is youth,
> You'll get better,
> But not me.

People returned shortly and picked Halldor up off the floor, and Bersi got better.[13]

The delightful simplicity of Bersi's verse means more in the Norse world, where its simplicity defies expectation. Norse poetry in the skaldic style is famed for its obscurity. Bersi's poem is meant to call attention to itself by its ready comprehensibility and clarity. It comes straight from Bersi's phlegmatic heart. No need to ask Odin for inspiration, no giving up an eye for a drink at Mimir's well, just an old gunslinger's heartfelt equivalent of a Jewish oy.

This short extract is typical of the saga style: low-keyed wit, unpretentious sophistication. If Bersi is going to compose under-stated verse, then he is going to be guilty of overstatement by doing so. Bersi's lament is self-indulgent, and he gets a mild slap on the wrist for it: "People returned shortly and picked Halldor up off the floor, *and Bersi got better.*" He was not sick unto death in the least; he was exaggerating, just moaning and groaning about old age.

The saga pays special homage to the poem by finding the lamest excuse to include it, for Bersi and Halldor's fosterage do not figure at all in the saga's plot or character development. The motive seems to be that the poem is simply too good not to work in somehow. One can marvel at the remarkable delicacy, given the cultivated nonsentimentality of saga style, with which the saga deals with the embarrassment of showing sweetness and indulging an old man his exaggerated pessimism. *Laxdæla saga* leaves it at that. In the other saga that has a version of this same poem—*Kormak's Saga*—Bersi plays a substantial role. In it, he not only gets better from his illness but lives long enough to add a thirty-sixth notch to his belt. He kills the brother of his unloved wife, who was grazing his cattle on Bersi's land. In the vignette in *Laxdæla saga,* Bersi's rising from bed is only meant to mock gently his woebegone complaining, or we would expect a small mention of his further noteworthy lethal deed.

Bersi's pagan soul is revealed to be in remarkably good array. There is generosity in his lament. He cares to comfort the baby. He speaks wisdom to little Halldor, conventional wisdom, but exactly the wisdom associated with responsible old age. Bersi is smart enough to know that in his tightlipped, tough-guy world a lament must be packaged just right to avoid being ridiculed as unmanly. The complaint manages to buy its space by first seeking to console the baby. That very consolation funds his complaint, a complaint he tells Halldor that a baby has no right to make. The only one with real grounds for complaint is himself, a sick old man, who is competing with the baby as to who has it worse. The strategy is commonplace; a friend complains to you about his health, his lost love, his whatnot, and you console him by telling him a story about how you suffered the same, only worse.

Yet something else is going on too. The lament might just work the cure. It manipulates the gods by appealing to their delight in ridiculing human pretension. If Bersi wants to claim tragedy for himself because he is old and sick in bed, then the gods will make him look a little foolish by curing him. Had Bersi wanted to move the gods in the other direction, he would have employed a different saga convention, which takes the form of an old man getting sick and announcing that "I have never been the sickly type, so this illness means the end." These predictions come true and we revisit them in chapter 12. Nor is there a jot of complaint in them, just the facts: a cold recognition that one's time is up.

The small joke about Bersi's moaning and groaning, a joke also at the expense of the culture's pessimistic style, depends on a truth about the chronic complaints of life's daily annoyances. The particular annoyance you are complaining about generally goes away or ceases to matter, unless you are complaining about old age. The moaner and groaner is consumed by the present and suffers a loss of imagination that the future could hold anything other than this particular unpleasant present moment extended forward interminably, and this is true whether the complainer is a yowling infant or his parent, trying to get him to quiet down because it is 3 A.M., or any old, old person. Each believes that the present misery *is* the future.

I am not about to complain about pessimism. Whether sincere or an affectation, it has more capacity for irony than optimism, and thus a better sense of humor. Contrast gallows humor or cynical wit with a squirting flower in the buttonhole or with jokes "that will really make you laugh." Nonwhining pessimists on average are easier to endure than optimists; grumbling phlegm wears better than chirpiness, though I must concede that an optimist with any social awareness learns to avoid chirpiness, if female, or motivational speech upbeatness, if male. Do not confuse generosity of spirit with optimism. One old Icelander, a certain Glum Thorkelsson, got himself immortalized for the prayer he would say to the cross sometime shortly after 1000: "Good luck to the old, good luck to the young."[14] The sweet simplicity, the generosity, the universalism of this prayer, perfectly pagan and nondenominational, makes no complaint and excludes no one, absolutely no one, from its good wishes. It also rather depends for its force on unoptimistic assumptions about the world. It shares something of the sensibility of Bersi's complaint, its sweet simplicity. No wonder both these texts were thought worth remembering.

Yet it is possible, almost, to match the seductive charm of Bersi's poem and Glum's prayer with the meaner spirit that generates the Yiddish prayers/curses of the sort voiced in a former colleague's yiddische grandmother's remark: "As for the third vorld, I vish them luck." Or the delightful curse "May you have my luck," which with exquisite economy turns a kvetch into a malediction, self-mockery into hostility, comic enough to save the author the revenge of the curse's target, maybe. But pessimism's wit can grow tiresome too, if too frequent and predictable. That is when the pessimist needs to follow the advice of the wisdom literature and keep his mouth shut.

CHAPTER 9.

Complaining against the Most High

This chapter deals with more formalized complaints made in an attempt to get back what you are owed, to claim your due, lest you lose it, the "it" being something withheld from you that is owed you. Specifically, the problem is how to compel a person to repay a debt or to deliver on a promise he has made. It is more like filing a formal legal complaint or going to what used to be the complaint window in the department store.

What if you are not even remotely the equal of the person you have a complaint against? What if he is a big man, your king, your lord, or the Lord himself? What means—legal, psychological, social—can you, a lowly soul, muster to gain your ends? What can you do to get a big guy, like God, to remember his covenant, whether it be to defend you against invasion from Assyria or Babylon or to protect you from your neighbors down the street in Kiev, York, Mainz, Lodz, Seville, Buenos Aires? The complainant need not be old, just weak, but since the old were inevitably that, I envisage my archetypal complainant as old and broken: Priam before Achilles, or Lear before his daughters.

GROVELING WITH A PUNCH

There is a close connection between penitential rituals of self-abnegation, like fasting, donning sackcloth, defacing oneself with dirt and ashes, rending one's garments or flesh, and a not so veiled attempt to force the hand of the person one grovels before. One seeks to shame him into fulfilling his promises or doing his duty by ostentatiously degrading oneself in his presence.

Groveling of this sort, bowing and scraping, even when merely a routine accompaniment to greeting one of superior station, was, along with harems and "Asiatic despotism," how most Western children, by age twelve, imagined the East. No need to read the Amarna Letters: *1001 Nights* for children, with an assist from the Bible, did the trick. And if the child checked a real petition to Pharaoh or to a Mesopotamian king, he would find that they began with "flopping formulae."[1] In the Amarna Letters we find: "[I] am the dirt at your feet and the ground you tread on, the chair you sit on and the footstool at your feet. I fall at the feet of the king, my lord, the Sun of the dawn, seven times and seven times."[2] Unfashionable as it has been to say since the appearance of Edward Said's *Orientalism* (1978), the twelve-year old got it right.

All cultures must have rituals of self-abnegation or, for instance, there would be no apology. And I venture to claim that human society is unimaginable without apology. Still, some cultures go in for more lurid versions of abnegation than others and extend the domains where it is deemed appropriate and mandatory well beyond apology. Certain religious systems generate ostentatious forms of asceticism; others do not. Certain hierarchical societies make garish groveling fairly routine; in others it would prompt disgust and be mobilized only rarely. The contrast between, say, segments of Hindu culture and the roughly egalitarian saga Icelanders could not be greater, nor for that matter the difference in proper displays of deference due Sennacherib of Assyria compared

to those due Henry II Plantagenet of England, or what any Herr
Professor Doktor at a German university expects from his students
and what I get from mine.

But it was not all risk-free for the person who got to use you
as his footstool. The dirt beneath the feet sometimes had a trick
or two up its sleeve. The groveler could waft a whiff of threat
about the hall. In the midst of Psalm 6, a complaint to the Lord
to heal the psalmist of the illness that threatens his life, and to
save him from his foes too, the psalmist shifts gears for one verse
and explains to the Lord why it might be a good idea for Him to
heed his plea: "For in death there is no remembrance of Thee: in
Sheol who can give Thee praise?" (6.5, RSV).[3] The latent threat
is blasphemous in its implications. Nor is the threat much veiled:
Lord, if you don't heal me, if you do not rescue me, if you let me
die, you, oh Lord, will die with me, for in death there is no remembering thee. Moreover (as indicated in other psalms),[4] my enemies
are my enemies because of my devotion to you. It is on account
of you that I am afflicted. So let me remind you: you need me as
much as I need you.[5]

One would think Psalm 6 would be hidden in a closet somewhere, but in the Jewish liturgy it features prominently in a portion
of the daily morning and afternoon service called Tachanun, meaning supplication, a formal assuming of the submissive, a groveling
before God.[6] In fact, Tachanun has an alternate name, Nefillat
'payim, which in Hebrew means "falling on one's face," literally
on one's nose or nostrils, groveling in the ancient Near Eastern
style.[7] Three years ago, when I began the eleven-month period
of saying the traditional mourning prayer, Kaddish, daily for my
father, I was startled to find Psalm 6 just a couple of pages before
the Kaddish. (I was something of an innocent about the liturgy of
the daily service until my father's death brought me to it.) There I
was threatening God, in the persona of the psalmist, which threat
I was to follow shortly thereafter with magnifying and sanctifying
his name, which is what the Kaddish does: "Magnified and sancti-
fied be God's great name."[8]

The pure praise prayer, the Kaddish, shares much genetic material with rituals of obeisance that are meant to constrain the selfsame Mighty One you are groveling before. Prayers of praise attempt to paint God into a corner, and are often meant to do just that. Praise constrains its object when delivered down the hierarchy. Any teacher or parent knows that. Praise, to be sure, can be heartfelt at the moment delivered, but that does not mean it cannot also be part of a general strategy to get a child to do what you want by tilling the ground for future rituals of shaming him when he is less inclined to do praiseworthy actions. Praise can also work quite well up the hierarchy, hence the consistent and lamentable success of sucking up and flattery, always hard, if not impossible, to distinguish from praise.[9]

Kaddish and Psalm 6 work together in a world of shaming—in a kind of good cop, bad cop routine—to make the deity more compliant. Moreover, it hardly needs saying that context can shift a prayer of praise into one of admonition, into a "friendly reminder." Saying Kaddish, sanctifying God's name, as one is marched into a gas chamber means what, exactly? One might discern latent blasphemy in the term "Kiddush ha-shem" (sanctifying the Name) as the Jewish term for martyrdom. Is there not implicit in that sanctification a blame, a shaming? Can it not be read as showing up God for not showing up? From a Jewish Chronicle recording the pogroms in the Rhineland at the outset of the First Crusade (1096), we find this remonstrance: "They were killed and slaughtered for the unity of the revered and awesome Name. . . . Were there ever a thousand one hundred sacrifices on one day, all of them like the sacrifice of Isaac the son of Abraham? For one the world shook, when he was offered up on Mount Moriah. . . . What has been done this time? 'Why did the heavens not darken?' . . . when one thousand one hundred holy souls were killed and slaughtered on one day, . . . infants and sucklings who never transgressed . . . 'At such things will you restrain yourself, O Lord?'"[10]

Can lords be shamed by the complaining of mere peons? Yahweh is not shameless. His ready anger reveals a keen sensitivity to affronts or what he takes as shameful treatments of his person. He has his honor to defend, and not just against mere mortals but against other gods he is competing with. More than a few psalms follow Moses's lead by invoking the incentives of this competitive world the gods play in to get God to do one's bidding. Says Moses: "Let not Your anger, O Lord, blaze forth against Your people, whom You delivered from the land of Egypt. . . . Let not the Egyptians say, 'It was with evil intent that He delivered them, only to kill them off in the mountains and annihilate them from the face of the earth.' . . . Remember Your servants Abraham, Isaac and Israel, how You swore to them by Your Self and said to them: 'I will make your offspring as numerous as the stars of heaven'" (Exod. 32.11–13, JPS).[11]

Moses argues two points in his appeal: one depends on God's sense of competitiveness with other gods whose adherents threaten to gloat at his expense ("let not the Egyptians say"), the other to his sense of duty to fulfill his covenant with the patriarchs and his people. Each point presumes God has a sense of shame, and each is directed to different aspects of it, one to his competitors—other gods—and one to his clients, his people, his covenantees.

If God has his honor to defend, then shaming rituals should work on him. Thus time and again he is called upon by those addressing him in supplication to *remember* his covenant. The notion of remembering in the Hebrew Bible, especially when coupled with covenant (or Sabbath) as its object, need not refer to the mental state of calling up an image from the past. "Remember" is rather a pointed obligational term, a legal term.[12] "To remember" means to fulfill a duty one is obligated to perform. And not just in the Bible: "Remember me," says the ghost in his charge to Hamlet, his son, to avenge him, the duty to take revenge being the primal obligation defining the close kinship of parent and child, of siblings, and even of spouses, and of friends who by becoming blood brothers thereby undertake to avenge the other as if they were brothers. In our usual sense of remembering, Hamlet is completely consumed by remembering the burden the ghost lays on him, but that is not what the ghost means when he says remember, and thus the ghost returns to chide Hamlet's forgetfulness.[13] The ghost uses remember to mean to be mindful of a duty *by discharging it.* The same is true with many uses of the word remember in the Hebrew Bible. Even today, I can be said not to have remembered a debt I owe if I do not pay it back, regardless of how much I actually may be thinking about the debt and how I can avoid paying it.

HUMILIATING THE TORAH

In Palestine sometime after the autumn holiday of Sukkot, the festival of booths or tabernacles, God promises rain, and if he reneges, he will be called to account. In the Talmud tractate devoted to fasts, *Ta'anit,* one finds a ritual designed to prompt tardy rains in a time of drought. A series of three fasts is decreed, then another set of three slightly more rigorous fasts should no rains have come. If still no rain, seven days of fasting is ordered, but here the ritual is ratcheted up with a novel addition:[14] "They carry the ark out to the open area of town, and they place burnt ashes on the ark, and on the head of the Nasi [the leader and chief elder], and on the head of the president of the court, and each and everyone else places ashes on his head."[15]

The elder is to preach words of admonishment, referencing the successful repentance of the people of Nineveh in Assyria after Jonah prophesied doom to them. The congregation is then to be led in prayer not by the usual prayer leader but by a man called on especially for the occasion, who "is well versed in prayers and who has children and whose house is empty, so that his heart will be perfect in prayer." This is a drought and the stakes are high; they want someone who will mean it when he prays, not the usual racing through the prayers at the speed of light.[16] His desperate poverty, his starving kids, means, the rabbis suspect, that he will be no less sincere in prayer than the psalmist is when surrounded by his enemies.

One sage, Rabbi Zera, admits his distress witnessing the ritual: "At first when I would see the Rabbis placing burned ashes on the ark, my entire body would tremble."[17] In that trembling is an indication that, at some level of his consciousness, he recognizes that the Torah is being shamed, humiliated, threatened, and indeed punished. The Torah is being forced to grovel.

Yet the whole ritual is structured to maintain a certain amount of deniability as to what is actually going on. It is not we who are calling God to account, but he who is calling us to repent, hence the reference to Nineveh and that city's successful repentance. He is withholding rain because, yet again, we have offended him. But just maybe he needs a reminder that unlike some Near Eastern vassal treaties in which the obligations run all one way, his covenant imposes reciprocal obligations, obligations he specifically assumed and delineated: "how You swore to them by Your Self," as Moses reminds him.

This is a humiliation ritual: the ark, the Torah, exposed in public, covered with ashes. The Talmud makes clear that ashes must do the humiliating, not dirt, because ashes are in its view more demeaning and because the ashes symbolize "the ashes of Isaac." In answer to why we put ashes on the ark and on our heads, one rabbi says, "So that He may remember the ashes of Isaac on our behalf."[18] The ashes are thus the symbolic remains of a human offering, the ultimate placatory sacrifice.

But Isaac was saved, was he not? He was not burned on the altar. The Bible leaves no doubt on the matter. But many of the rabbis refused to buy the plain meaning of the biblical text. They, it seems, were not quite willing to let the God off the hook so easily. A last-second staying of the hand and a substitution of a ram for a son was not sufficient compensation for so toying with Abraham and Isaac.[19] By this strange association of ideas, the rabbis reveal that they see a connection between the sacrifice of Isaac and the humiliation of the ark and it is a connection in which shaming and humiliation provide the connecting tissue. When we debase the Torah with ashes and force it to grovel, it is not just any ashes but the ashes of Isaac,[20] whose ashes are a shame unto the Lord. Am I blaspheming by suggesting that this ceremony pointedly means to shame God? That there is a strong hint that the Torah is being put through what Isaac was put through? If I am, there are more than a few analogous rituals to justify the claim.

TAKING YOURSELF HOSTAGE

The faithful of other dispensations punish their saints and gods when these do not deliver, do not answer prayers, do not send rains or protect their followers against their enemies. Not to put too fine a point on it, they may even kill their god, crucify him, tear him to pieces, abandon him, or shame and humiliate him. The religious and the legal meet here. These rituals are legal, because we are talking about the fulfillment and enforcement of obligations covenanted to. They are religious when the debtor is God or a saint, or when the gods must be understood to provide part of the sanctioning force when a lowly creditor tries to collect on his debt from a more powerful person.

Let us first take two legal rituals whose near identity in style and purpose was noted in the nineteenth century by the legal historian Sir Henry Maine. In India, the ritual is called "sitting dharna." A desperate creditor places himself before his higher-status debtor in abject squalor and starves himself, sometimes to death. Should he die, the debtor would be considered his murderer. The British found the custom barbaric, about at the same level with suttee, and tried to ban it. If one sees in Gandhi's form of resistance an avatar of sitting dharna, then the ritual survived quite robustly.[21]

In the ancient laws of Ireland—the dating of which remains problematic, but for our purposes seventh-eighth century will serve—when a poor man sought to collect against his powerful debtor, lacking the power to take the debtor's cattle and hold them until the debt was paid, he instead went to the door of his debtor and fasted. Indeed, the Old Irish term is properly translated as "fasting *at*" or "fasting *against*" his debtor. The legal compilation known as *Senchus Mor* says that, against persons of distinction, fasting is the proper procedure rather than entering on the land and taking his cattle as security. "He who does not give a pledge to fasting is an evader of all; he who disregards all things shall not be paid by God or man."[22] Remain unmoved by the fasting creditor and there is a suggestion God will aid the poor man, though perhaps there is more force in the stricture that makes the "evader of all's" own loans to others now appear to be uncollectible.

As with sitting dharna in India, the Irish tradition of "fasting against" has been alleged to account for their style of politics. Thus the infamous hunger strikes in 1981 at Maze prison, when ten prisoners starved themselves to death in protest for being classified as "ordinary decent criminals," rather than as prisoners of war.[23]

Add this Norse variant employing similar shaming techniques, in which debt collection narrowly conceived is not the issue but constraining a more powerful person to grant your demand is. A man named Hrapp is being chased by people intent on killing him, and who have a strong claim of right to do so. He had impregnated his host's daughter, killed his steward, mortally wounded his son, and robbed and burned down a temple. Hrapp throws himself face down before a man named Thrain, begging him to help him escape. Says Hrapp to the reluctant Thrain: "I'm not going to move from this spot. They shall kill me here before your eyes, and all men will speak of you with contempt." Thrain, much against his interest, grants the request.[24]

Back in Ireland, St. Patrick found himself, via an angelic intermediary, in a negotiation with God over some matter. The angel informs Patrick that God is not going to give Patrick everything he is asking for because the request is excessive: "Is that His pleasure then?" asks Patrick. "Yes," says the angel. "Then this is my pleasure," says Patrick. "I will not go from here until I am dead or until the requests are granted." God, like Thrain, relents.[25]

These rituals all operate by inflicting or threatening self-harm as way of forcing another to feel compelled to save you from yourself. Think of children throwing tantrums, losing it in the way a toddler loses it, holding their breath, refusing to eat their food (fasting against you, in other words) or, in more extreme cases, smashing their heads against the floor. In a more restrained version at a later age, even now in your looming dotage, think of the fantasies you entertain of dying or suiciding, just to imagine how sorry your spouse, friends, or children will feel for not treating you right. Old Shloyme, eighty-six years old, in Isaac Babel's story, hangs himself before the door of his son's house for all the town to see to protest his son abandoning the home, his faith, and him in his old age: "Shloyme would tell God of all the wrong that was done to him here. . . . Shloyme began to sway before the door of the house in which he had left a warm stove and the grease-stained Torah of his fathers."[26] Sitting dharna in the shtetl.

In short, in these rituals one is taking oneself hostage. If such threats against yourself are not quite sufficient to prompt the desired action, you can also hold something you know is sacred to the person you are fasting against: his son, his Torah, his mother, a saint's relics.[27]

The issue of hostage taking, strangely, arises in the same section of the Talmud in which the humiliation of the ark takes place. The rabbis move to discuss the manner in which Nineveh repented. "What did the [Ninevites] do? They tied the animals separately and the young animals separately. They said before Him: 'Master of the Universe, if You do not have mercy on us, we will not have mercy on these.'"[28] This is pure brinksmanship. Show us mercy, God, or we let the young calves and lambs we have separated from their mothers die for want of milk. This story of the Ninevites is not to be found in Jonah, and is wholly invented by the rabbis. But it fits in with the rabbis' earlier discussion about the ashes of Isaac. In both cases innocent kids are threatened with death, as we are too by the tardy rains.

Humiliation rituals abound in the Hebrew Bible; Mordecai sits dharna before the king's gate in the book of Esther (4.1–2).[29] We have plenty of sackcloth and ashes, ropes around necks, sittings in the mire, shavings of heads, putting dirt on one's head, rendings of garments, but what about accosting your upper-status debtor? Is there an analogy to the Irish and Hindu rituals purely in the context of debt collection?

There seems to be. Deuteronomy 24 deals with various aspects of creditor-debtor relations, primarily with pledges. Verse 15 requires paying a laborer his wages promptly on the day earned: "You shall give him his hire on the day he earns it, before the sun goes down (for he is poor, and sets his heart upon it); *lest he cry against you to the Lord,* and it be sin in you" (RSV; emphasis added). Suppose the worker's crying against you to the Lord is not a metaphor, but in fact a formal cursing. If the wages are not paid, the laborer cries unto Yahweh and shames his employer. The rather clear indication of the Hebrew, in light of the general methods that the lowly have of extracting debts from their superiors we have been discussing, reveals that Deuteronomy too has its dharna-like procedure to recover a debt owed.[30]

MAKING OTHERS SQUIRM

Sitting dharna, fasting against, or lying down threatening to die before the eyes of a reluctant protector are humiliation/shaming rituals. The complainant humiliates himself in order to shame the person he is pleading to. The ritual is also meant to be embarrassing and painful for those witnessing it. While its ostensible purpose is to shame its target, the target may well be impervious to feeling much shame on account of such a lowly soul. The ritual is thus meant to be hard for the audience witnessing it to endure, and it will be performed publicly so that it is sure to be witnessed. The pressure the ritual brings to bear is that it makes everyone uncomfortable. Should the debtor himself not feel the pain of his groveling creditor, he may find it harder to ignore the discomfort of the audience witnessing the spectacle the beseecher is making of himself.[31]

An example from nineteenth-century Balkan feuding practice demonstrates nicely the contagion of embarrassment generated by a humiliation ritual. I quote from an account given by an informant to the intrepid Edith Durham in the first decades of the last century:

And the [peacemakers] decreed . . . that I should hang the gun which fired the fatal shot around my neck and go on all fours for forty or fifty paces to the brother of the deceased Nikola. I hung the gun to my neck and began to crawl toward him, crying: "Take it O Kum,[32] in the name of God and St.

John." I had not gone ten paces when all the people jumped up and took off their caps and cried out as I did. And by God, though I had killed his brother, my humiliation horrified him, and his face flamed when so many people held their caps in their hands. He ran up and took the gun from my neck. He took me by [the hair] and raised me to my feet, and as he kissed me the tears ran down his face. . . . And when we had kissed I too wept.[33]

Ten paces are all the audience can bear. The observers force the successful conclusion of the ritual. One might detect a small hint in the narrator's "I had not gone ten paces . . ." that he knows he got off easy; indeed, he got away with murder. But what can the brother of the dead man do? He too feels the unendurable awkwardness of the situation, and he is the only one with the power to spare everyone more of it.

Repair to the monasteries of northern France in the tenth and eleventh centuries for a ritual known as the humiliation of saints, definitively studied by Lester Little, from whom I borrow these examples.[34] Suppose the saint whose relics a monastery houses—the monastery is his house—has of late not been answering the monks' prayers meant to stop a local lord from interfering with property the monks claim belongs to them. After argument and prayer has gained them nothing, the monks ritually and literally humiliate their saint in a solemn ceremony. They take their saint, his bones, his body, out of his reliquary on the altar and put him in the dirt or on the ground, the *humus,* whence the word humiliate. This is on all points identical to the ceremony in the Talmud. The monks will prostrate themselves along with the saint who, like them, is understood himself to be prostrated in the dirt, joining with the monks in the ceremony in which he is made to participate, though in fact the ceremony is in significant part performed *against* him. But they make sure the word gets out to the offending lord in order to worry him that it will be against him that the saint will avenge his humiliation.

Sometimes the crucifixes would be laid down on the floor, the doors of the church barred with thorns, and services would be discontinued. God and the saint were not going to get their due until they made sure the monks got theirs; no sacraments, nothing, until the saint or God wakes from his sleep and attends to duty. Recall Psalm 6: "In Sheol who can give Thee praise?" The saint is getting a not-so-gentle reminder.

No different from the rabbis, so too the monks vaguely misrecognized that they were punishing their saints, that they and no one else had placed him in the dirt. The rabbis claim that the ark was really joining them, helping them out: "And why do we place burnt ashes on the ark? Rabbi Yehudah ben Pazi said, 'as if to say, "I will be with him in trouble."' Resh Lakish said, 'in all their affliction He was afflicted.'" The modern explicator, Rabbi Steinsaltz, explains that placing ashes on the ark "is a way of saying that God is with His people in their time of affliction; for just as the people cover themselves with ashes so too does God."[35]

Rabbi Steinsaltz, like the rabbis in the Talmud, stands the ritual on its head and attributes to God his own act of humiliation, absolving the congregants, you and me, of fasting *against* him by forcing him to fast *with* us, though it is not as if the ark covered itself in ashes. The rabbis are blind (or feign blindness) to the muscling they did to get God to join them. The monks said much the same during their humiliation rituals. Some humiliators of saints, less sophisticated, did not repress the truth. Peasants would take whips to the saint's relics to wake him up. "'Why are you sleeping? Why do you allow us to perish,' they shout. 'If you are a true martyr of God, help us now in this moment of great need.'"[36] By the fourteenth century the church came down hard against this ritual, declaring it a "detestable abuse" done by persons of "unspeakable impiety" who would place sacred objects on the floor amidst brambles and thorns.[37]

The person being groveled to knew these rituals of self-abasement were often meant to do more than merely register obedient submission. He might even try to steal the ritual, shifting his role from supplicatee to supplicator. In Ireland and in India, it was possible for the person fasted at to join in the fast, in a competitive fast off.[38] In various rituals of submission and pardon seeking, we sometimes can find the person beseeched rushing to get a flop of his own in before the would-be flopper can flop, to beat him to the shaming ritual and turn it against the person intending to perform it. Gregory of Tours, in his *History of the Franks* (sixth century), describes the trial of Bishop Praetextatus before a convocation of bishops and King Chilperic. Praetextatus suddenly throws himself on the ground and confesses to plotting against the king; the king, not to be outdone, himself flops before the bishops. "The king knelt at the feet of the bishops and exclaimed: 'Most pious bishops, you hear the guilty man confess his execrable crime.' We wept as we raised the King from the ground."[39]

Or we see the powerful take over the ritual entirely as when they "humbly beg" a favor or a donation from their inferiors. "Humbly begging" can be seen as a way of graciously setting the inferior at ease when the superior could simply extort what he wanted without engaging in a humiliation ritual to get it.[40] Or, more ominously, ritually denying one's obvious superiority works as a threat. Beware lords who play the beggar, for their requests are a form of taxation.[41]

INEPT PERFORMERS VS. PROFESSIONALS

Any ritual can be commandeered by skillful players and turned against those who were supposed to benefit from its performance. Or a ritual can be made a mockery of by overplaying it or underplaying it. A ritual of humiliation can also be performed with all sincerity and yet be performed ineptly because the person does not know when enough is enough, when it is time to pick the Torah up from the dirt, restore the saint to his reliquary, or stop clamoring and get off the dung heap and wash up. You had to make sure you performed these kinds of rituals in a way that sold well. You thus had to perform them at the right time, the right place, with the right amount of passion, and for a bearable length of time, not too short, not too long. Botch the self-abnegation and you become a laughingstock, a byword. Appian relates this of Cicero:

Clodius impeached Cicero for breach of the constitution because he had put Lentulus and Cethegus and their followers
to death without trial. Although Cicero had displayed a most
noble spirit of resolution in the affair itself, when it came to
being prosecuted he collapsed; he put on miserable clothing
and threw himself down covered in filth and squalor in front
of those he met in the streets without even being ashamed
of bothering people who knew nothing of the matter, so that
thanks to his inappropriate behavior he became of figure
of fun instead of an object of pity. . . . When Clodius even
insulted him by interrupting his pleas in the street, Cicero
abandoned all hope and . . . embraced exile voluntarily.[42]

If one could botch humiliation rituals and rituals of self-
abnegation by overdoing them, one could also get a reputation
for being really good at them; one could become a professional
performer of them and compete for honors in the self-abnegation
sweepstakes. Maine reports that certain Brahmins offered themselves for hire by creditors to sit dharna for them. It would take
a brazen debtor to risk the supernatural sanctions, in addition to
the this-worldly ones, that would follow upon letting a Brahmin
starve to death on his doorstep.[43] One would think that the ritual
would lose some of its moral force if it were performed by a hired
gun, Brahmin or not. We should not, however, underestimate the
power even "mere" ritual can bring to bear when its goal is to
shame or curse. The high-status debtor no more wants a professional dharna sitter showing up than he wants his low-status creditor on his doorstep.

A somewhat different problem is raised by the Irish saints, by
the early pole-sitting ascetics, or by the pus-drinking saints of the
later Middle Ages.[44] They often openly engaged in asceticism contests. They fought to win and were proud of their ability to out-
self-abnegate their competitors. Unlike St. Anskar, they were not
about to give up the competition because of scruples about being
proud of their ability to self-mortify better than others. Would such
glorying in one's skills at "fasting against" undo its magical powers?

The Talmud tells of a certain Honi HaMe'aggel (Honi the Circle Drawer) who was asked to pray for rain to relieve the community from drought. In an incident that could have been lifted from an Irish saint's life or from Hindu debt-collection rituals, he drew a circle around himself and announced to God that he would not step outside the circle until it rained. First God sends a mere couple of drops. Honi is not satisfied and stays in the circle complaining that this was not what he had asked for; then God sends a damaging torrent and Honi says this was not what he asked for either. The third time God caves and sends a proper gentle rain, because Honi, like St. Patrick, was not going to leave the circle until he got what he wanted. The threat not to leave the circle is a threat to die, to fast to death. Jonah did much the same in anger outside Nineveh. For hapless Jonah, though, the ritual did not work.

Honi's behavior drew a remonstrance from the president of the Sanhedrin, who said: "If you were not Honi, I would decree a ban upon you [for addressing God disrespectfully]. But what shall I do to you, for you act like a spoiled child before God and He does your will for you, like a son who acts like a spoiled child with his father, and he does his will for him."[45] The president of the Sanhedrin recognizes Honi's circle-drawing ritual to be on all points comparable to a child's temper tantrum, a holding oneself hostage, just as we saw earlier.[46]

The next time your child throws a tantrum, the next time you indulge the thought of how sorry you hope people feel when you are dead, remember that falling to the floor, bowing and scraping, getting lower than the other guy, is often exactly the best way to upend him or get him to fulfill his obligations to you. The risk, of course, is that you might die in the process. Sometimes that might be precisely your intent. The Buddhist monks who brought down the Diem regime in South Vietnam by setting themselves on fire, to say nothing of Jesus adding to the humiliation of his Incarnation that of his Crucifixion, are cases in point.

But what if the high-standing debtor who is not paying his debt is Death himself? You have outlived yourself, and still, as when no rains come, he likewise will not come. Everyone else in your community, as in the Torah fasting ritual, prays to God to order Death to pay up on your behalf. But Death has no shame, and finally you starve yourself to death, as is not infrequently the form the most natural of deaths take. Unless, that is, some evildoers interrupt your sitting dharna and force a feeding tube down your throat.

PART IV

Retirement, Revenge, and Taking It with You

CHAPTER 10.

Giving Up Smoting for Good

A t the end of the one of the better revenge movies, *The Princess Bride,* Inigo Montoya, who has after years and years finally succeeded in killing the killer of his father, muses: "You know, it's very strange; I have been in the revenge business so long, now that it's over, I don't know what to do with the rest of my life."[1]

I have been in the revenge business too, a virtual revenge business, for revenge has been the chiefest of my scholarly interests. How could it not be, when I make a living reading the Icelandic sagas, the smartest of writings on the politics and strategies of revenge? That is to make a strong claim, given that revenge is probably the single most consistent theme in both the world's best literature and a good portion of its cultural, legal, and moral history.

Revenge does not discriminate among genres, either. It is equally at home in farce or in epic, and rather more so in comedy than in tragedy. Run-of-the-mill comedies feature nerds getting even, the loser getting the girl to the misery of the cool guy, and the pompous, who are often parents, brought low as they stand in the way of airbrushed true love, the audience's delight elicited rather more by the discomfiture of the losers than the happiness ever after gained by the winners. Two of the cruelest revenges in literature occur in comedies: the fleecing and Christianizing of Shylock in the name of mercy in *The Merchant of Venice* and the painfully drawn-out tormenting of Malvolio in *Twelfth Night*. Shylock's offense was being a Jew, Malvolio's was partly being a Puritan, but mostly that Feste the clown could never forgive him for not thinking him funny (1.5.83–89).

But such is revenge that it transcends genre. When Inigo at last confronts the killer of his father, a Jewish shtick comedy rises to tear-eliciting sublimity that one would expect from tragedy or epic. Quite simply, revenge provides a reasonably satisfying, even happy, ending to more stories than we care to admit.[2]

In one respect we are no different from the vengeful souls whose tales follow. Not very differently from revenge cultures, we still feel we are owed when a loved one dies, or else that someone has it coming. Welcome the market, which answered the need rather nicely, doing the pious work of assuaging rage that might otherwise have been directed at God, or burned the old lady next door whom the shaman fingered as a witch. Life insurance provides compensation in lieu of revenge. Somewhat overstated, but not false for that: life insurance is blood money.[3]

My farewell to revenge draws nigh. Retirements tend to have rituals associated with them, retirements from taking revenge no less than retirements from writing about it. In the latter there is the dinner that shoves you out the door, capping a career with a staged event in which people are constrained to say nice things, mostly false, or make a few safe ribs and roasts. Some wags in the audience cannot resist rolling their eyes and muttering hostile truths distinctly enough to be guiltily appreciated a full table or two away. In retirement from real revenge, though, there is no dinner, but there is a ritual. One went to bed, or in some places an old warrior might enter a monastery instead.[4]

This ritualized taking to bed must be marked out differently from routine going to sleep every night. This retiree, like the fool in *Lear,* goes to bed at noon, so to speak. The old avenger ostentatiously takes to bed and stays there, moping and lamenting, or he simply turns his face to the wall.[5] This ceremony, like the one of putting ashes on the Torah, with which it has a rather distinct kinship, is worth examining, for it is loaded with contrasting meanings, as it elaborately deals with emotions of grief, rage, and the frustration and shame that attend the general impotence and decline that comes with age.

The three chapters in this section will be more medieval than either biblical or modern. But bear with them: the people you will meet will grab you. The depressed oldsters and senile among them are rather grander than most. And your reward will be an explanation of one of the bizarrer rules of our own law.

TO BED IN GRIEF

What happens when an old man loses his son and must undertake to avenge him, when his duty is clear, and there are no mitigating circumstances to excuse him from the duty, unless his old age counts as an excuse? It was not an easy matter to take revenge in the days before firearms. You needed quickness, strength, endurance, and courage, or the ability to command someone who did have these qualities. An old man today can still squeeze a trigger, though he might have to get closer than he would have had to when younger to compensate for the slight tremor he has noticed over the last year that causes him to slosh his morning coffee or interferes sometimes with getting the toothpaste on the toothbrush. In saga Iceland, technologically backwards even by the standards of the time, the ax was often preferred to the sword. It was more affordable, needing less metal and skilled labor to make it. The metal did not have to be of an especially high quality, either, just good enough to smash, if not cleave, a skull. But to smash a skull, you had to get close. And the person you were trying to ax would not just stand there patiently. If he were younger, stronger, faster, meaner, you stood zero chance. So you sank into despair out of grief for your son and out of frustration for your inability to do anything about it.

Despair might be the lot of the younger avenger too, but he would not have the fortune to excuse his cowardice with old age, if cowardice were part of the picture. The world's most famous piece of literature is about how hard it is for a son to avenge a father, a father who gets to die in his sleep, no less. The ghost, it should be observed, comes back to haunt not his killer but his avenger, the primal guilt, it seems, being not murdering a father but not avenging a murdered father. A ghost needed to haunt his murderer only if he had no one among the living to avenge him. Hamlet is young, and thus the bed-taking ritual is not available to him, so he soliloquizes and goes a bit mad instead.

When an old man took to bed in these circumstances, he announced he was no longer a player in the game. He was retiring. The gesture bears resemblances to rituals of surrender: your corner throws in the towel in a boxing bout, you cry "I give" when wrestling as a kid,[6] you wave a white flag as a soldier, coming out with your hands up. But these rituals of surrender differ from the one of taking to bed, because the going-to-bed ritual was available only if you could reasonably be counted old, even if you had not been so counted up until then. Old age does not figure in those other rituals of surrender. I will examine three cases.[7]

Case 1: Kveld-Ulf

A Norwegian named Ulf gained considerable wealth as a Viking. He was also a berserk. He gave up raiding, got married, and settled down. He was well respected, a man to be reckoned with in the district. He would, however, get rather moody and unpleasant to deal with around evening time, and to the great relief of his household he regularly retired early to bed. People nicknamed him Kveld-Ulf, Evening Wolf, though he caused no one any trouble, handling his own lycanthropic urges by sleeping them off. He fathered two sons.

The eldest, Thorolf, became a retainer of King Harald Finehair. Thorolf fought superbly, and was rewarded with substantial lands and privileges in northern Norway. But he grew too popular and Harald sensed that Thorolf was already, or was surely soon to be, a threat to his power. Thorolf defied Harald's demand that he return to court to serve with the king's retainers and household men. And soon after Harald attacked and killed him.

When Kveld-Ulf heard of Thorolf's death, "he was so sorrowed by the news that he laid in his bed on account of grief and old age." His second son, Skallagrim (Bald Grim), who now did much of the farm work, went in to see him often, and "told him to pull himself together, saying, that there were other things more appropriate than just lying around uselessly in a sickbed:[8] 'better that we take revenge for Thorolf. We might be able to get a shot at some of those men who were involved in his death. And if we can't, there will be others we can hit that the king would not be pleased to lose.'"[9]

Kveld-Ulf then spoke a verse lamenting his old age. Age causes "my revenge to be slow, though I still desire it." Father and son knew there would be no getting at King Harald or any others who had actually assaulted Thorolf. No matter. Skallagrim is practical when it comes to revenge. You take whom you can get. The only qualification needed for being an eligible target is that the king would be annoyed by the loss of that man. Sometime later, Kveld-Ulf and his son, with their household men and tenants, boarded two ships, with twenty men on each, and, with old Kveld-Ulf in a berserk fury, killed a shipload of the king's men, some fifty of them. Included among the dead were two boys, the sons of King Harald's foster father, age ten and twelve, who jumped overboard trying to escape and drowned. The avengers spared "two or three, those who seemed of the lowest status," and hence not worth killing because Harald would hardly be irritated by their loss.[10] These men were sent as messengers to Harald to tell the news; we are not told how Harald treated these poor bearers of evil tidings.

Kveld-Ulf and Skallagrim, each commanding one ship, then headed for Iceland to escape Harald's reprisals. Kveld-Ulf fell ill on the voyage: "It is said of those men who are shape-changers, or those who went berserk, that when thus possessed they were so powerful that there was no resisting them, but as soon as the fit subsided they were left much weaker than usual. Such was the case with Kveld-Ulf when he regained his normal self. He felt exhausted from the energy expended in the attack, and he was so completely weakened that he lay in bed."[11] He died shortly after and was buried at sea.

Taking to bed figures rather centrally in Kveld-Ulf's biography, whether it be to grieve, to die, or to sleep at night. It is the grieving that I am most interested in here; I will return to his deathbed in chapter 12. I have claimed that taking to bed in grief is ritualized behavior, a formalized retirement from active duty; much of that is discernible from an examination of this text, but this text alone would be insufficient to establish the claim if we did not have more than a few others in a number of cultures.[12] Given my tastes I will focus on some vivid examples in the sagas and *Beowulf.* They are dense with relevance to old age, losing it, and hanging it up.

Egil's Saga is explicit that Kveld-Ulf takes to bed on hearing the news of his son's death because of *grief and old age.* The pairing suggests that the behavior would be inappropriate were he younger. Age provides the reason, or the excuse, for grieving in this fashion. Skallagrim, his son, illustrates the grieving behavior appropriate to younger men: violent and vengeful action. Styles of grieving are age coded no less than they are gender coded. Kveld-Ulf is not behaving improperly for a man his age, but his son is trying to get him to manage his grief more productively. And he is right: the old man had one more killing spree left in him. But just one; then he can retire. Skallagrim's urging his father to action instead of letting him lie passively moaning and groaning maps onto the advice Beowulf gives to old Hrothgar, the Danish king who is grieving the loss of a loyal retainer to the revenge Grendel's mother took for her son:

> Don't grieve, wise (old) man. Better it is for a person
> That he avenge his kinsman, than that he mourn much.[13]

The sentiment is clearly proverbial in these cultures, their sort of grief counseling.

Grief can readily generate depressed torpor and lamentation or violent lashing out. Grief, besides its obvious connection to sorrow, is also closely annexed to anger, rage, and frustration.[14] Nor need the loss that is grieved have been caused by a human agent for this to be true. Deaths by disease, acts of God, generated the same emotions. The church was well aware of the dangerousness of grief. Theologians blamed excessive grief because, unsurprisingly, it led to "chiding God,"[15] to cursing him, to hating him, and even to abandoning him. We saw in the previous chapter how the Jewish liturgy provided the mourner with the opportunity to let off some steam and get a hostile lick in on God in Psalm 6 before dutifully praising him in the Kaddish. The grieving person, because he might feel aggrieved, was in danger of lashing out. Thus Claudius's first words to Hamlet in act I address Hamlet's excessive display of grief. Claudius knows that excessive grief in great ones must not unwatched go. Says Walter Burkert, more chillingly than one expects from a scholar: "Death is mastered when the mourner becomes a killer."[16] Or, as in our case, gets his blood money from Metropolitan Life.

Case 2: Sturla

How do we know Kveld-Ulf's behavior is formally ritualized? The short answer is that we see the ceremony parodied in both comic and intensely tragic settings. The comic one can be briefly told, the tragic one will take a little more space. Sturla, known for his acerbic wit, and now an old man, hears of the death of his enemy, a woman named Thorbjorg. A year earlier she had lost her temper and gashed his face severely when she tried to stab out his eye in order to make him, as she said, look like the person he most resembled: the trickster Odin, the one-eyed god. She had grown frustrated with Sturla for pettifogging in a lawsuit in which Sturla's party's case was, as a legal matter, quite weak. Upon receiving news of her death, Sturla immediately took to bed:

> People asked him why he was doing so and he answered, "I have just heard some news which I consider quite distressing."

"We hardly believe that you would grieve Thorbjorg's passing," they responded.

"There's another reason why I'm suffering. I figured that there would be no lack of grounds against her and her sons while she lived, but it wouldn't look good if I continued hounding them now that she's dead."[17]

This partakes of the wit of the sick joke in every sense, for he is posturing as ill with despair, in a fit of depression, though not so ill that he cannot make it into an elaborate joke. Ironies abound: his retirement, only half a mock retirement at that, is in fact forced upon him by a common feature of male old age: the loss of intimate dealings with women.[18] His enemy is dead, and he sincerely grieves her passing, but not for charitable reasons. Sturla can make the parodied ritual sting because he is an old man, eligible to perform it without irony. Moreover, her death, though it does not deprive him of any real basis to continue his enmity with her sons, does deprive him of the delight he takes in hounding them, the motive of which was mostly to torment their mother.[19]

Old age stymies revenge not only because it weakens you but also because it kills your enemies before you can. Seeing your enemy die in the course of nature, after having lived a long life, is very imperfectly gratifying, if at all. The saga writer adds his own irony, for within two sentences Sturla is dead, though three years pass in those two sentences. His taking to bed is his last action in his saga. He had indeed retired.

Case 3: Njal

The most elaborate ironic performance of the ceremony occurs in the most complex and powerful event in the entire saga corpus, the burning of Njal and his family in their farmhouse. I cannot deal with all the nuance and the disturbing ambiguities in the action, but suffice it to say that there has been no love lost between Njal and his sons ever since, and even well before, the sons murdered Njal's beloved foster son, Hoskuld. The avengers of the foster son, led by Flosi, arrive in force at Njal's farm. Njal, his sons, and the male household members array themselves outside to meet the attackers. Njal counsels going inside to defend from there. Skarphedinn, the oldest and most formidable of the sons, advises against it. These are men, he says, who will resort to fire. But he obeys his father nonetheless, with a cold propriety to which he gives a hard ironical edge: "I do not mind pleasing my father by burning in the house with him, for I am not afraid of dying."[20]

The attackers, after meeting strong initial resistance, opt for setting the building on fire, as Skarphedinn guessed they would. Flosi goes to the door and offers Njal and his wife, Bergthora, along with the other women, servants, and children, passage out. Njal, and then Bergthora, decline: "I have no wish to go outside," said Njal, "for I am an old man now and ill-equipped to avenge my sons; and I do not want to live in shame." Bergthora too refuses: "I was given to Njal in marriage when young, and I have promised him that we would share the same fate."

Then Bergthora turns to Njal.

"What shall we do now?" asked Bergthora.
"Let us go to our bed," said Njal, "and lie down."

Their young grandson wishes to join them. Bergthora tells him to leave but he refuses. "But that is not what you promised, grandmother. You said that we should never be parted; and so it shall be, for I would much prefer to die beside you both."[21] Ever the doting grandmother, Bergthora gives in, to the uncomprehending dismay, every year, of my students.

Njal carefully has a bed prepared; he orders his steward to cover their bodies with an ox hide as he lies down with his wife and grandson. That is the last that is heard from them. Skarphedinn makes a characteristically wry remark: "'Father is going early to bed,' he said, 'And that is only natural, for he is an old man.'"

Njal is rather consciously combining three rituals into one when he lays himself down. First, he is planning a martyr's death, and by ordering the ox hide to cover them, he is improving the odds that his body will be preserved. Later, when the bodies are dug out, the preservation of Njal's body, a conventional and sure sign of sanctity, is proclaimed a miracle. The author calls attention to the managed nature of the miracle by inserting a small detail: the young grandson had inadvertently placed a finger outside the ox hide and it, unsurprisingly, had been burned off. Any miracle, it is more than hinted at, was worked by the ox hide.

Second, he and Bergthora are also reenacting their wedding ceremony, not just by going to bed but by following the precise letter of the law, which requires that a valid marriage be sealed by going to bed "in light,"[22] that is, illuminated by firelight, visibly and witnessed. This time the light is somewhat brighter and warmer than when they were first married.

Third, Njal, like Sturla, is going to bed to enact the revenge-retirement ritual, knowingly and ironically: "I am an old man now and ill-equipped to avenge my sons; and I do not want to live in shame." Whereupon he takes to bed, which, as Skarphedinn notes, is age-appropriate behavior. Njal has it every which way. His counsel to go inside in the face of the more astute tactical counsel from his son can be understood to be partly motivated, only half unconsciously, by a desire to avenge his foster son, letting the fire do the job on his own sons. If his bad advice takes down his sons and family, his clever way of managing the revenge-retirement ritual ensures that the burners will pay the price for martyring a saint.

From these three cases it is apparent that the ritual works at several levels. It can be a sincere expression of grief, an unstudied gesture of frustration, and a studied gesture of retiring. It can also be a plea for help, a request for someone to step up and help an old man in need. It should be apparent that the ritual bears many points of congruence with sitting dharna, a ritualized self-humiliation, that requires others to fulfill obligations they may have toward you. You are the age-weakened creditor, making your demand for the repayment of favors from abler, younger, more powerful people who still owe you. We will see soon that one version of the taking-to-bed ritual even engages in Irish-like fasting.

Njal's taking to bed does wonders in motivating people to avenge him and his family after they were burned to death.[23] His carefully arranged saintly martyrdom provided a rallying point to enlist supporters to their cause, who would before have been rather chary of siding with Skarphedinn and his brothers after their unprovoked murder of their father's popular foster son.

When the Christian Njal goes to bed to die a martyr, there is no discussion of forgiveness. In one familiar Christian paradigm, as we have noted, the deathbed is the place to seek forgiveness for one's sins. Christianity too thus made the deathbed a bed to which one retired from revenge, though in a rather different way from the ritual we have been discussing, in which forgiveness does not figure at all. Presumably the dying Christian, fearful that salvation would be withheld unless he forgave his enemies so that he too would be forgiven, must not only forgive the wrongs done him that he did not have the means to avenge, but also forgive those wrongs he had earlier avenged and beg forgiveness for having not forgiven them. I am not sure there is much virtue in forgiving wrongs you have suffered that you are too weak to avenge but would if you could— about as much as virtue as that chastity earned by impotence or undesirability. Nor need your deathbed forgiveness of your enemies keep your sons from attending to unfinished business after you died. Even if you do not, as David did, order hits on your deathbed, you might still bring about the same results—and perhaps not quite inadvertently, either—by being ever so forgiving.

ONLY AS OLD AS YOU FEEL

On occasion we have old men who die with their boots on, but this is usually divorced from revenge. Old warriors cannot resist one more fight: William the Marshal, the most skilled fighter of his day when younger, led a victorious charge in the second battle of Lincoln (1217), as regent for Henry III, at age seventy-one.[24] Villehardouin tells of the remarkable doge of Venice, Enrico Dandolo, completely blind and apparently over ninety, who shared the command of the notorious Fourth Crusade, which sacked

Christian Constantinople (1204) rather than engaging Muslims. Villehardouin has nothing but praise for the doge's intelligence, courage, and leadership abilities: "The Doge, . . . in spite of his age and blindness, was very wise and brave and full of energy."[25] Back in simpler and more primitive Iceland, Sighvat Sturluson, son of the witty Sturla whom we just saw taking to bed, dies in combat at age sixty-seven.[26] Advancing toward the enemy, he goes down more from exhaustion than from his wounds, though once down he is hacked to death at the explicit orders of the opposition leader. Old age did not argue for granting him quarter because as long as he bore arms he had not retired and was in the game, in the game to kill and be killed. Dying with Sighvat was a farmer, Arni. The enemy asked Arni why someone "so little and so old" was fighting. Unlike the big-time power player Sighvat, he was small fry and the suggestion is that they would spare him on account of his age. Not availing himself of a perfectly legitimate excuse, he refused to withdraw. So they killed him: "Arni Audunarson died there with great glory. . . . Arni was in his seventies."[27]

A nod in the direction of tough old coots was made in the ancient Icelandic laws, which stipulated that a man was still qualified to be an acceptable witness to a formal truce until age eighty, if, that is, he was still "capable of dealing death and defending his life and property, of using a shield and shooting from a bent bow."[28] Recall the poet Bersi the Dueler, who rises from his sickbed to take down his brother-in-law before he calls it quits. And of a certain Hrut it is said: "Hrut was in his eighties when he killed Eldgrim, and his stock went up considerably as a result."[29]

Diminutive old Arni puts the lie to the Norse proverb "The older a man gets the more cowardly (effeminate) he gets."[30] People of my profession and social class in the West prove the perspicuity of that gloomy proverb, if we grant the overly generous assumption that we had some courage when young to lose once we got older. More of us than is seemly are to be counted among those "bearded fruit-juice drinkers" and "food cranks" who so disgusted George Orwell. Such a person, he said, is "willing to cut himself off from human society in hopes of adding five years on to the life of his carcase; that is, a person out of touch with common humanity."[31] Not with present-day educated American humanity, a curmudgeon might say. The content of "common humanity" changes with the times and it is not always a change for the better. When Orwell was complaining in 1937 about food cranks, the average life expectancy in Britain was around sixty. Now our own food cranks are trying to get to ninety or more. Orwell's crankiness was of a different type, and it surely was not conducive to long life. He died at forty-six.

Historians who write on old age have consistently noted the relatively recent development of pinning retirement to a chronological age, say, sixty-five or seventy. In the ancient, medieval, and premodern worlds, there were some age-graded events, like legal majority, and old age–based excuses from certain onerous services, but there was as a general matter no set retirement age, though in medieval Iceland the law held that if you fathered a child when you were eighty, whether you could still deal death or not, that child did not count as an heir. Your children fathered by prior, more appropriate, marriages had a right to assume such miraculous events would not cut down on the size of their inheritance.[32] Generally, a worker retired when he could no longer work: when his eyes went bad if a craftsman, when his back and legs gave out if a cultivator. Women kept going until they dropped: washing, cooking, sewing, laboring in the fields, brewing and selling beer. In other words, you retired when it was clear to yourself and others not that you were old, but that you were too old.

There was thus no fixed rule that at a certain age you were out of the vengeance game. If you wanted out, you had to announce it, or you had to have it thrust upon you by others who made it clear that you no longer mattered or were no longer up to it. Arni was being told by those who killed him to back off, that his age excused him, but he preferred not to use age to justify retiring. Old age could have excused Sighvat at sixty-seven had he been less of a big-time political operator. He was still too powerful and had made too many enemies over his active career. I suspect he knew he would not be spared whether he bore arms or not and decided he might as well go down swinging, even if he was clearly out of shape and not physically up to it. No one would ever trust that even as an old man he was not going to keep running the show from his bed.

CHAPTER 11.

Paralysis of the Spirit

As we saw with Kveld-Ulf when he took to bed because of grief and old age, such retirement is only partly a throwing in of the towel, for it seems to carry with it a conditional clause: I will quit the field, I will retire, as you see me retired here in this bed, *unless* you help me. But there are much gloomier takings to bed, born of despair and frustration, where there is no help in sight, nor any contemplated. Just emptiness, a longing—though the capacity to long is itself compromised—for escape from this miserable world, not to a better world, but to a different kind of nothingness. The world and soul go empty, because the heart is too full of grief, too frustrated, utterly dispirited.

Suppose your child drowns or, even more unsettling, suppose one of your children kills another, not as Cain did Abel, intentionally, but by accident or maybe recklessly, crashing the car drunk and killing his sibling. In medieval versions of cases like these, one took to bed too, mobilizing the same ritual. At one level this is about retirement, though more in the style of a surrender with no one to surrender to, an objectless giving up. Life ceases to be worth living because of the soul-destroying frustration of having nothing or no one you can hit back at, nothing to take it out on, nothing you can do at all. Two cases of this sort have produced much commentary because they have been recorded with consummate artistry in the texts in which they appear. The second one has a reasonably happy ending. Not this one.

PUT OUT THE LIGHT

When Beowulf is an old man, having ruled for some fifty years, his kingdom is ravaged by a dragon. Before the fight he is about to undertake against it, he sits down outside the dragon lair and reminisces about his life. Having made a name for himself killing monsters in his youth, he speaks partly to embolden himself, partly to sum up his life and to say farewell to it. Doom hangs heavy. He tells of his grandfather King Hrethel, who was also his foster father from the time Beowulf turned seven. Hrethel died of despair. Embedded in Beowulf's account of Hrethel's misery is an extended simile of another old man who likewise just gives up, lies down, and awaits death. Beowulf, in contrast to these two men, will go out as he entered the poem: looking for a fight with a monster in a good cause. Beowulf's narration and especially his story of his grandfather Hrethel[1] is presented in verse so powerful that it is worth learning Old English to read it before *you* lie down to die. Its profound sadness, its dignity, its sheer sublimity in line after line would more than repay the effort.

Hrethel's life was ruined by an accident. His eldest son, Herebeald, was killed by his second son, Hæthcyn, who missed the target he was aiming at and killed his brother:

> For the eldest, unfittingly,
> A deathbed was spread by his kin's doing,
> When Hæthcyn, with an arrow from his horn-bow,
> Hit his lord and brother,

Missed the mark, and shot his kinsman,
One brother the other, with a bloody shaft.
That most grievous deed was not compensable,
Utterly dispiriting to the mind; yet thus it was
That a prince should lose his life and lie unavenged.[2]

Accidental slayings of this sort were quite common in European premodernity. Thus Hamlet's casual metaphor to Laertes to excuse his killing Polonius: "Free me so far in your most generous thoughts, / That I have shot my arrow o'er the house / And hurt my brother" (5.2.238–39). Hunting accidents were frequent. William II Rufus, king of England, died from an arrow shot by one Walter Tyrell that missed a deer but nailed William.[3] And other sports were rough. Orderic Vitalis in his *Ecclesiastical History* tells that of the seven sons of the Norman noble Giroie, five died violent deaths: two, perhaps three, of them accidental. Arnold got three ribs smashed in a friendly wrestling bout and died a few days later and Hugh was lanced accidentally by his squire when they were just horsing around.

The story of one son, Ralph the Ill-tonsured, who did not die by accident but by the benevolence of divine intervention, is worth relating because it is pertinent to the themes of retirement and how best to order one's old age in penitential preparation for death. Ralph loved knightly pursuits inappropriate for the cleric he was. When he grew older, reports Orderic, he "finally gave up the pleasures of the world . . . he took vows under Abbot Albert and humbly implored God to afflict his body with an incurable leprosy so that his soul might be cleansed from its foul sins. His prayers were answered."[4] Orderic is not trying to engage in dark-humored comedy. What counts as divine beneficence changes over time and across dispensations.

One problem with hunting accidents or serious injuries sustained in sports is that it takes a leap of faith or plenty of gullibility to believe they are accidents. Deaths often benefit someone, like heirs, or enemies who are not heirs, and it is hard not to suspect these beneficiaries of perhaps having arranged the accident. Even if they didn't arrange it, there is still cause to resent the benefits that come their way or the crocodile tears you believe they are shedding and to cast blame or hate in their direction. Their benefiting from the death is itself grounds for enmity or for doubting their causal innocence in the accident.

The unfortunate parent of the child slain by his brother is unlikely to be much consoled that it was accidental and not intentional when his son shot an arrow over the house and "hurt" his brother. The parents lose one child, probably loved now more than ever; their relations with the surviving child no doubt undergo a change too, becoming more emotionally complex than Freudian veneerings could hope to make them. Could you keep yourself from having the thought that if such a curse must befall your house it would have been better had the siblings' roles been reversed, especially if the dead son were already the favorite, as in that sentimentalized Oscar-winning film, *Ordinary* [very rich] *People,* with its obligatory final affirmation? Little imagination is required to see that there is not much consolation there. Would you engage in self-pity? How did you so anger the gods that such as this is your lot? You just might retire to bed singing a song of sorrow and die. This is what Hrethel did.

After the passage just quoted, Beowulf gives an extended simile that elaborates Hrethel's misery. He likens him to an old man who must watch his son hanged on the gallows for some crime. In imagery that makes vast emptiness seem as constricting as you will see Egil's clothing to be in the next section, the suffering of the old man is described thus:[5]

> So it is with a mournful old man
> Who must suffer his son swinging
> Young on the gallows. Then he raises
> A sorrowful song, as his son hangs there,
> A joy to the raven; and he, old, wise,
> Can offer him no aid.
> He is reminded every morning
> Of his son's journey to elsewhere; . . .

Burdened with care he gazes on his son's dwelling,
The winehall wasted, windswept the beds,
Emptied of happiness . . .
Then he takes to bed, singing his sorrow song,
One alone, for the other one gone.
To him the fields, the dwelling places,
Everything, seemed too spacious.[6]

In their day it was not uncommon to see children predecease parents, but, as noted at the beginning of this book, for some the experience was no easier for that. This old father in the simile takes to bed, "singing his sorrow song, one alone, for the other one gone." The simile fades almost imperceptibly back to old Hrethel, who "likewise" is overwhelmed by "roiling sorrow of the heart for Herebeald," the sorrow indistinguishable from frustration, and specifically the frustration of unavengeability, of losing a son and getting nothing in return, neither blood nor money.[7]

Beowulf imagines his grandfather's despair as a kind of psychological and legal locked-in syndrome. What else to do but to waste away in anguish and die:

He might not settle the feud with the slayer,
Nor might he hate that warrior,
Do him hostile deeds, though he did not love him.
Then in great sorrow, for the wound that beset him,
He gave up the joys of men, and chose God's light.[8]

Hrethel cannot "hate that warrior," his son Hæthcyn, but "he did not love him" either. This hardly means he is indifferent, neither hating nor loving. His feelings for Hæthcyn, the errant shooter, are mostly negative. The very thought disallowed the father is what haunts his mind: to "do [Hæthcyn] hostile deeds."

The word "hate" (Old English *hatian*) in the second line, however, is not primarily to be counted an emotion term in this passage. It is more a juridical and social term. Hate marks a state of being in feud with someone, of having formally hostile relations, and no feud or formal hatred is justified here. The word "love," too, is frequently employed across a variety of cultures simply to indicate alliance in political matters, a commitment not to work against the interests of the other, not the emotion that goes by the same name. But in this passage love is doing mostly emotional work, and meant subtly to contrast with the technical sense of hate as formal enmity.

Official hostility is exactly the relation Hrethel is not allowed to have with his son Hæthcyn on two counts. First, though filicide, especially among those who play power politics, is hardly unthinkable, it is not something you can legally undertake unless your son openly defies you, rebels against you. Even then, third parties will exert themselves to make peace, or do the job themselves so that the parent does not have to dirty his hands directly.[9] What is a person to do who is equally obliged both to the victim and to the killer, as the father is here? It is the primal position of Adam, unable to avenge Abel, whose blood must thus call out to the Lord. What is someone like Hrethel to do? Pay himself compensation with one hand and receive it with the other, kill one son to avenge the other? It is the problem of Hamlet one degree closer in. Can Hamlet kill his closest living male relative to avenge the person who had been his closest living male until he was murdered?

There are ways around the problem. You can outsource the revenge, like Njal did, by counseling going inside and letting Flosi burn your sons. Suppose the victim, Herebeald, was married and his wife's brothers then took revenge on Hæthcyn, because Herebeald's widow suspected that her husband's death was no accident, while old Hrethel sat back and was not quite displeased by the result. Or, more commonly, feuding cultures borrowed a page from God's book, his first book, and solved the matter by exiling the kin killer, unless the killer took it upon himself to flee the district. Such was the lot imposed on Cain, and the one that Absalom took upon himself after he had justly killed his half brother Amnon for raping his sister, Tamar.[10]

The second and more determinative consideration is that the rules change when the killing is accidental, though as I have hinted above, and as you know from your own experience, you can feel murderous hatred for the person who harms you by accident no less, and indeed sometimes rather more, than for the person who harms you intentionally. Imagine having your child run down and killed by a person texting on his phone while driving. He sacrificed your kid for LOL. The person who intends you harm is doing you an honor in comparison. Imagine your brand-new car, two days old, getting sideswiped in the grocery store parking lot. Do you not feel a vengeful urge surge within you, even if you are the type to be shopping at Whole Foods, in whose parking lot the defacing occurred? We take no consolation in chalking it up to the black humor of an Intelligent Designer or to Dumb Luck.

Early legal systems made allowances for unintentional slaying and accidents.[11] They might, for instance, provide cities of refuge for the accidental slayer to flee the avenger of the blood, as in Numbers and Deuteronomy, or halve the amount of compensation due, as in the ancient Hittite laws.[12] But because people were suspicious of accidents, it also had to be clear that there was no prior enmity, no history of hate, between the killer and his victim. In old Icelandic law and in feuding practice, the presumption was that harms were intentional and the burden was on the person seeking the benefit of the softer sanctions for accidental wrongs to prove he did not mean to cause harm. Better not laugh after you unintentionally tripped a guy. The laugh would mean you enjoyed the consequences, and that was sufficient to read intent back into what initially had been an accident.

As today, accidental harms had to be paid for; you just did not necessarily have to die for them if you paid up. And that you stood a good chance of dying if you didn't pay up was a powerful incentive to make amends. In fact, the best way to prove you did not mean the harm was to offer with alacrity to pay generous compensation. Apologizing, so easy to fake, was not acceptable unless its sincerity was confirmed by payment.

At any rate, it might be advisable to run for your life if you accidentally shot the king, or your master. Recall the sons of Giroie mentioned by Orderic Vitalis, particularly Hugh, who was killed accidentally by his squire: "[Hugh] and some of his friends stopped

near the church of St. Germain near Échauffour to amuse themselves by throwing lances; an ill-aimed shaft carelessly thrown by
his squire wounded him mortally. Great hearted as he was he called
the squire and whispered to him, 'Fly at once, for your wound will
be my death. May God have mercy on you. Fly before my brothers
discover this and slay you for it.'"[13]

Though the dominant and perhaps controlling legal rule regarding accidents was that the squire should be able to buy his way
out with compensation, the fact of the matter was, as the dying
Hugh knew, the squire was unlikely to be accorded the benefit of
the death being deemed accidental. He would, moreover, not have
sufficient assets to pay a respectable compensation.

TURN ON THE LIGHT: FASTING AGAINST ODIN

I have had occasion to mention Egil Skallagrimsson several
times. He was the precocious toddler who composed his first poem
at age three and cleaved his first skull at six, and more than a few
thereafter. He was the grandson of Kveld-Ulf, our first take-to-bed
retiree, and he inherited from his grandfather certain lupine and
berserk traits. Egil was not a moderate man; he was given to excessive indulgence in violence, drink, poetizing, hatred, and avarice.
The dust having settled from his childhood killing, he took his
mother's hint that it was wiser to kill abroad, whether in Norway or
on Viking raids in the Baltic or mercenary expeditions in England
did not matter, as long as it was not in Iceland. He made sure every
penny owed him was accounted for or someone was going to have
to pay, even if that someone was not the one who owed it. He was
not quite as particular about debts he owed others, unless it was
settling a score. Those debts he made sure to repay. When and if
he repaid kindnesses, he paid in verse, a kind of coin it was easier
for him to mint than the silver he hoarded. Given his reputation
as a poet, however, getting paid in verses by Egil was a good bar-
gain for the recipient, as long as Egil did not sneak in some snide
insults which, because of the general obscurity of skaldic verse, it
was fairly easy to do and get away with.[14]

When Egil was in his fifties, his son Bodvar drowned ferrying wood across a fjord when his boat sank in a gale. After burying Bodvar next to his own father, Skallagrim, Egil rode back home and "went straight to his bed-closet, lay himself down, and shot the bolt on the door; no one dared speak to him." Egil swelled up so much that he burst his tunic and leggings. He lay there another full day, taking no food or drink, then into a third day, and still no one dared speak to him. His wife, Asgerd, then sent for their married daughter, Thorgerd.[15] She arrived, demanded Egil open up and let her in to accompany him, she said, on the same journey to Freyja he was embarked on. Egil praised her: "You do well, daughter, by wishing to join me. You have shown me much love. How could anyone think I could wish to live with grief like this?" After some time, she managed to trick her father into drinking some milk, which he thought was water. That turns out to have been sufficient to violate the terms of the ritual so that it had to be halted. Egil was angry enough to bite through the drinking horn, but Thorgerd suggested that since this plan to die had been ruined they should stay alive long enough for him to compose a poem in memory of Bodvar: "And I will carve it on a stick, then we can die after that."[16]

Egil proceeds to compose an extraordinary poem, which he entitles *Sonatorrek,* or "Loss of Sons," justly appreciated to this day, and maybe the single most famous Old Norse poem outside the heroic Eddic corpus. The poem is complex thematically, dealing with revenge, grief, frustration, consolation, compensation, procreation, death and, self-consciously and reflexively, with the relation of poetry itself to each of those themes. It is a poem also that openly speaks of the frustration of being denied revenge. How do you kill the sea? What way is there to get even? "I did not have the strength to go against my son's killer, for anyone can see the powerlessness of an old man." It is the grief/revenge/frustration/old-age complex again. Egil complains against Odin, his patron, who has betrayed him. But in the end the poet comes to understand that Odin has compensated him, for he had already given Egil his poetic powers. With poetry comes some kind of consolation, exactly what most grief counseling and religious mourning customs mean to offer. From Odin he gets the means that allow him to contend with the god in a way that will make the god sit up and listen: "Odin, that wolf killer, has, if I look at it a certain way, given me compensation for the evil, a flawless skill."[17]

The poem itself comes to stand in the place of the son, much as purses of silver paid over to compensate for a dead kinsmen were understood to be a substitute for the victim. Egil is quite frank that compared to getting paid in flesh and blood, other forms of compensation are second best: "It is said that there is no real compensation for a dead son except raising up another one, which everyone can see fills his brother's place."[18] How biblical: God compensates Adam and Eve for the loss of Abel by providing them with Seth, a substitute whose very name means substitute (Gen. 4.25). Similarly, God also feels it fair recompense to provide Job with a new batch of children to replace Job's pre-wager progeny, killed off as part of God's bet with Satan (Job 1.18–19, 42.13). Contrast this practical fungibility of human life with our official commitment to the uniqueness and dignity of the individual. A trip to the mall, to a football game, to the airport, however, forcibly reminds one of the truth of human fungibility, though self-flattery, rather more successfully than the ideology of our sacred uniqueness, spares us thinking the same about ourselves, unless we are really in a state of despair.[19]

Much in Egil's poem maps onto the neat juxtaposition of the hostility voiced against God in Psalm 6 followed immediately by gestures of praise and obeisance in the Kaddish. Egil is fasting against Odin. Like a poor Irish creditor at the doorstep of his powerful debtor, or like the Indian creditor sitting dharna before his debtor, he refuses food and raises a lament. He is also performing the taking-to-bed ritual we have already seen, for he is retiring to his bed-closet in a formal display of grief, despairing of revenge and eligible to perform the ritual on account of his age: "Anyone can see the powerlessness of an old man."

Egil is literally exploding with grief and frustration. I am unwilling to dismiss wholly the physical symptoms—his swelling so as to burst the seams of his clothing—as so much exaggeration and medieval credulity. My skepticism is tempered by my own ability to generate symptoms within minutes of reading the warning label on medicine I have just swallowed.

Egil means at some level to starve himself to death. He is engaging in histrionics but his intentions are not false for that. He really means to die, somewhat more sincerely than we "really mean it" when we threaten our children with a punishment that they never have had nor will ever suffer. Egil's meaning to die has a longer half-life, but it still bears an expiration date set sometime before he would die of starvation. The ritual is performed in the presence of others, who are both to serve as an audience to the grand performance and then to intervene to bring it to a halt once the more intense self-violent urges have run their course. He does not go out into the trackless wastes that make up most of Iceland and lie down there, where he would either die or have to embarrass himself by thinking better of carrying the ritual to its lethal conclusion. His daughter Thorgerd plays her role expertly, managing to stop the performance without calling Egil's sincerity into question in a way that is no shame to her father. This ritual toys with death, but it is not suicidal in the manner of hara-kiri.

Still, this is Egil, a man of extremes, so that even Asgerd, his wife, who can gauge him well, is concerned enough on the third day to send for their formidable daughter.[20] But his wife may be following a cultural script too, one in which everyone knows that three days is the max and it is time to find a way to bring matters to a close. When daughter Thorgerd arrives, she immediately goes into high dramatic mode. She not only joins the performance, she takes over as its director. The trick of substituting milk for water shows us some of the strictures governing the fast. Sips of water apparently are within the rules, but food, in which category milk falls, is not. The ritual adheres to strict formalism, so that once a stricture is broken the ritual ends.

Thorgerd knows that in Egil's hands poetry is a weapon. He can chastise and insult the gods with it, memorialize his son, and memorialize himself as a person who manages to avenge himself against the most impossible odds by his sheer Odin-given talent. To be noted too is that, to get her father jump-started, Thorgerd does more than suggest he compose a poem; she also indicates she will inscribe it in runes, so that Egil will not have his composition die with his own breath. The runes themselves are magical, and Thorgerd is literate in them, a stenographer of sorts with her knife and stick. There is the faintest hint here of something like the Graeco-Roman curse tablets etched in lead, the *defixiones;* she is carving a *defixio* against Odin and the sea.[21] Did Asgerd send for Thorgerd because she was adept at runes, or did Egil make sure that his wife and all his children would be literate in runes? We do not know.

What if old Hrethel had been a poet of Egil's talents? Would the consolatory powers of skillful poetizing have provided a sovereign remedy for his grief as it did for Egil's? On the other hand, would Egil have been able to achieve the same consolation if Bodvar had not drowned in a storm but had been killed accidentally by his own brother? It does not seem so. There has to be a difference in the degree of psychological difficulty in settling accounts with the sea, no matter how much we animate it, and with knowing that one of your sons killed the other.

We see in these cases another example of the war of opposites in proverbial wisdom: does time assuage psychic pain or exacerbate it? Hrethel wastes away in frustration and sorrow; Egil fasts against Odin, composes a poem, and then gets on with his life. Consider how the law deals with the life of a complaint: it subjects it to a statute of limitations. A wrong that gives rise to a legal claim has a life. Some crimes, like murder, may, depending on the jurisdiction, live forever, but most legal claims, and surely those deemed accidents, grow old and die, though quite differently than we generally do. If a particular claim must be brought within six years or expire, it is as healthy a claim in the fifth year as it was in the first. The evidence may grow staler and frailer, but if you have preserved the evidence, and your witnesses' minds have not rotted, the claim has the same legal force from the day it arose until the stroke of twelve on the last day of year six. The claim dies of that stroke, the law presuming that your inaction is less a sign of your inability to act against the wrong done you than of your not caring enough to bother.[22]

Legal commentators disagree as to how to describe accurately the status of a claim on the wrong side of the limitations period. Some say, as I have, that the claim has died: others say, no, it still lives, but in an abode of the shades, where your claim exists still, only the remedy for it having died. The second view as a practical matter seems hairsplittingly silly. A right deprived of its remedy and thus unassertable? What good is that? But in some settings that view is psychologically apt. The image of the claim still alive but paralyzed captures in a figurative way the frustration of living with an unassertable claim, in which the very unassertability makes for obsession, for too much caring. It is a different sort of limitation that denies Egil and Hrethel; it is not that time kills their claims but that a conceptual limitation puts their harm in the domain of irremediability. That does not mean they are not consumed with vengeful desires, it is just that these cannot be discharged upon anyone or anything else. In the case of old Hrethel, unfulfillable revenge was discharged on himself. Someone had to die for Herebeald.

CODA: MME. NERONI AND AUNT FAY

Lying down, standing up, and sitting up are not just functional daily positions assumed by the human body. They also feature as moral metaphors and do symbolic work. The meaning of these bodily positions varies by age and sex. Lying down for a woman is not lying down for a man. Do women take to bed? They do in nineteenth-century novels, and often when they are young. The classic case is Mme. Neroni in Trollope's *Barchester Towers*. From her various sofas she directs much of the novel's action and might even be understood to author a good portion of it. She pretends to be crippled, and might be, but it is never made clear that she really is, or how badly so if she is. She holds men in thrall, mocks them mercilessly, and the reader too, who desperately wants to know just how badly disfigured her legs are under all that Victorian cloth.

My great-aunt Fay was a struggling actress in the early 1930s. When she could get only minor roles at the Goodman Theatre, she took to bed in her own early thirties and never really got up again, claiming her back would not allow it. Because she was beautiful, an engaging conversationalist, and unceasingly dramatic, she was wooed and won there and had two children there. Like Mme. Neroni, she had retired to bed young and beautiful to rule the roost prone, in a grand parody of how men think they want their women. Her future husband did not have to work to get her to bed; she was already there. But work he had to to try to get her out of it. She would have none of it. Eventually he came to want none of it too. How different from the ritual expounded upon in this and the preceding chapter, though one can even see in this kind of taking to bed an aspect of vengefulness.

I do not want to overstate the formalistic aspects of the revenge-retirement ritual. That it is a ritual should be clear. That it is a form of fasting against and sitting dharna should also be clear, but it is also a familiar gesture of depression and despair. No matter, for even if these old men should take to bed because they were sorely disheartened and what we would now call clinically depressed, they knew exactly how their taking to bed would be read. This retirement ritual, in certain instances, as I noted, is a discreet way of asking for help, an admission that you can surely not undertake revenge alone. But the retirement also might be absolute and final, no strings, no conditions. That is when you take to bed because you can read in everyone's eyes that that is where you belong. Not even the snake oil of the positivity psychologists prevents you from picking up on the hint. So you spare everyone further embarrassment and take yourself with barely passable politeness off to bed, though in fact you have been ordered to bed, as a child is. A request for a glass of water might buy you five minutes more and register some small resistance. But it is already past bedtime and your day is done and you are finished.

CHAPTER 12.

Yes, You Can Take It with You

Die you must; and they say you cannot take it with you. What exactly does that mean? Does it counsel you to live it up in wasteful riot in your last years? If you wait until then, more likely you will waste it in a demented haze in a nursing home, having it consumed not in riot at all, but in keeping you minimally comfortable while Death is stuck in traffic six nursing homes away. Or is it to be construed as moral advice against penny-pinching avarice, advising you rather to annuitize your assets so as to have your wealth expire the moment you do? No point in saving it for Goneril and Regan. This strategy can be adjusted to allow for modest bequests to your Cordelias, though why assume that these beloved souls will not waste the assets in ways that would eat you up with chagrin were you alive?

But you can take it with you. How you manage it depends on where you think you are heading once you die. A boat might be outfitted and you laid in it; accompanying you might be your dog, your concubine or wife, your horse (each of them throttled first), along with plenty of food and weapons, perhaps your work tools. Well-heeled women could be accompanied by slaves, their pets and jewelry, though not their husbands; in the Northlands they were provided with scales, not to see if they were sticking to their diets but because women engaged in mercantile dealings, and the world beyond, no differently from this one, was unthinkable without weighing, measuring, and meting.[1]

Think of how little we would know of the past, of Egyptian civilization, of ancient Germanic cultures, of many others, if the dead did not take it with them on their journey to the West, or to Hel, or across the sea, places more amenable than the bleak dimness of Israelite Sheol or Greek Hades. *Beowulf* opens with a funeral ship putting out to sea, the ship loaded with goods for the use of Scyld Scefing, whom it was bearing to his new world. Just such a well-furnished vessel was unearthed in 1939 at Sutton Hoo, Suffolk, which occasioned much reconsideration of what had been previously dismissed as poetic license in *Beowulf*'s descriptions of jewels, weaponry, and funereal wealth. We really only start to know about people who lived before us who did not write or build in stone if they thought of death as a state where the material you accumulated here could do you service there. We thus are likely to know more about materially rich cultures than nomadic bands, and much more about inhumators than cremators, about mummifiers than those who left their dead for scavengers, "a joy to the raven."

An economist might argue that the apparent irrationality of burying so much wealth or sending it up in a puff of smoke or sending it off with the dead on a ship might not have been irrational for society as a whole. One could posit some not-so-remote causal connection between a culture's wasteful farewells to the dead and its being able to afford such wealth destruction. The demand for well-provisioned journeys to the West spurred production, provided jobs, sent people off on raids and mercantile adventures to accumulate goods for the final festivities and for provisions for the journeys. This sounds like the usual economist's own falsely soothing positive thinking, but in this case there might be some small grain of truth to it.

I do not want to assume too much about various cultures' motives for having the dead take it with them. The living might have felt that if they did right by their dead and did not keep the corpse's gems and weapons for themselves the favor would be returned when they were corpses. But it may have been less a matter of picturing death as moving to a new subdivision than a baser motive that supported taking it with you. The dying person or the corpse might have cared more to prevent the living from enjoying his stuff than about his own being well accoutered in the next world. One wanted to continue to own, possess, and use one's property; and if death rendered that impossible, then damn if anyone else was going to. Those who were immolated on funeral pyres along with their possessions, whatever their beliefs about the land of the dead, were at least making sure that their deaths were not going to provide a windfall for grave robbers or heirs, at least as regards their prestige goods. The dead still had to trust the living to put the valuables in the blaze, but the dead, it was believed, were not without ways of enforcing their wishes in this matter.

The preservative effect of Danish bogs made sure that it was not just the wealthy and powerful who provided us with keys to unlock their lives by means of their deaths. The dead criminal and outcast, and the sacrificial victim, offered information too. Tollund Man, the best preserved of the bog people unearthed in Denmark and a familiar face in coffee-table books and on television history specials, was perfectly preserved. Preserved too was his cap and the noose around his neck, showing that he died either as a criminal or as a sacrifice and was then placed in a bog to feed the monsters there or to enlist the muck to suck him back in should he try to play the revenant and haunt his tormentors. Magically, he is with us more than two millennia later. We know exactly what he looked like, and it helps that he has a kind and serene face. Imagine the vexation of his tormentors were they to know his fame and the fellow feeling he elicits, unless, that is, they would have taken his fame to be a sign that the gods looked propitiously upon his sacrifice.

Figure 2: Tollund Man, fourth century B.C. Credit: Robin Weaver.

A recent study on "deviant burial customs" in early Anglo-Saxon England shows how people intent on humiliating the outcast and pariah ensured the wretch more solicitude than is prompted by the chieftain whose rich burial makes us think more of the artist who did the gold filigree on the brooch, the smith who made the pattern-welded blade, more of the horse, the dog, the slave buried with him, than of him. The skeletons with hands behind their backs, necks broken, beheaded, or buried face down, speak. They too take things with them, are forced to by their executioners. Many of the graves of deviant burials of women are furnished with amulets, suggesting that these were the burials of "cunning women," witches, who were to remain possessed of the tools of their profession.[2]

THE DEAD HAND IN THE FLESH

A rather unpleasant man named Hrapp (not the Hrapp we met in chapter 9), an immigrant to Iceland from the Hebrides, settled on a farm to which he gave his name, Hrappstead, in the Lax River Valley sometime in the tenth century. He bullied his neighbors and accumulated a comfortable amount of wealth. Old age finally sapped his strength and he took himself to bed. He called his wife over and said, "I have never been the sickly type, and it is most likely that this illness will end our marriage. When I am dead, I want my grave dug at the living-room door; set me in it standing upright, right at the entry, for then I will be able to watch over my farm even more carefully."[3]

Hrapp dies, and his wife does just as he asked, "for she wouldn't dare do otherwise. And as bad as it was dealing with him when he was alive, it was considerably worse now that he was dead, for he was given to 'after-walking.'" Hrapp's hauntings drive his widow away. His son stays on but soon goes crazy and dies, and the farm falls vacant. Hrapp continues to cause mischief in the neighborhood until the local chieftain, Olaf, digs him up and relocates him, which turns out to be insufficient to quiet him. Olaf finally succeeds in "laying the ghost" by exhuming him again and cremating him (in the Norse world ghosts are not aery spirits but very dense matter). And lest the ashes reassemble themselves and allow Hrapp to continue to plague the neighborhood, they are scattered at sea.[4]

The no-goodnik Hrapp might seem somewhat comical to us, and I suspect he was to them too, as long as his story was located a safe distance away. If word got out that you were buried upright at the front door or that your zombie was lodged in your house, its price would drop, its market shrink, even today. In a 1991 case, *Stambovsky v. Ackley,* a New York appeals court held that the seller had a duty to inform the purchaser that her house was occupied by poltergeists, a claim the seller did not deny. The court reasoned that the duty to inform arose because the buyer would not have been able to discover the ghosts on his own by a meticulous inspection before signing the purchase agreement. The purchase agreement was thus voided.[5]

Hrapp, unlike these shyer New York poltergeists, would have introduced himself promptly. He was deeply invested in his property. He considered it an extension of his own personhood even more intensely than political philosophers are wont to claim our property is an extension of ours. He shouldn't be faulted for that. His property should be dearer to him than ours is to us because it was scarcer. Even though Hrapp was relatively well off, his margins were slim. Let spring arrive later than usual, cattle murrain hit, a cold summer follow a late spring, and his household would find itself in desperate straits.

Hrapp, though, is not interested in taking his wealth with him when he goes. As he makes manifestly clear, he ain't going nowhere, as one of similar type might say today. Hrapp also ritualizes his taking to bed, but not to perform the revenge-retirement ritual we have discussed. His is a sickbed, which he declares to be his deathbed. His time has come, and he is making his will known. Unlike our written wills, which are meant to dispose of our property, his will is rather that his corpse be disposed in a certain way to make sure his will is carried out.

Return now to Kveld-Ulf as he lay dying at sea, enervated by the berserk fit that possessed him when he avenged his son. Kveld-Ulf "called together his crew and said to them that he considered it likely that they would soon part ways": "I have never been the sickly type, and if it turns out I die, which I think very probable, then make me a coffin and push me overboard. And it would go rather against my own expectations, if I do not get to Iceland and claim land there. Give my son [Skalla]grim my greetings when you meet him [remember, they are each commanding a different ship] and say to him, if I get there before him, though it might seem far-fetched, that he should build his home as close as possible to where I reach land."[6] That is what happened. Kveld-Ulf's coffin, a makeshift ship of sorts so that his burial mimics those of the old Germanic chieftains, does not bear him to the figurative land beyond but to a real land beyond, Iceland, a land like no other, in

the exact middle of nowhere. It is there that Kveld-Ulf will determine the location of the new family estate. His abode of the dead
becomes his living kin's new home.

Kveld-Ulf's last hours bear an uncanny resemblance to Hrapp's.
Both give instructions on their deathbeds and both make sure they
are carried out once they die, though Kveld-Ulf doesn't need to
resort to haunting to do so. The living welcome his input, aided
no doubt by the limited extent of his demand. Kveld-Ulf can afford to be more reasonable than Hrapp; he can have no powerful
proprietary feelings about a land he has never been to.

Hrapp and Kveld-Ulf are both weird. Uncanny, too, but in a
different way, is that Hrapp speaks on his deathbed as if he had
read the saga that Kveld-Ulf appears in. They both use the same
rare word to describe what they have never been: *kvellisjúkr,* which
I have rendered as "sickly type." They employ the same formula
and express the same sentiment: "I have never been the sickly type."
Both know when they are dying. Part of what is admirable about
them is their cold look at their own death. No wishful thinking
undoes their rationality, no looking on the bright side idiotizes
them in positivity smog or leads them to deny the obvious or to
fear it, and lucky too is that they did not outlive their brains. They
die in complete possession of their wits.

Kveld-Ulf, his son Skallagrim, and his grandson Egil provide
a family study in this second kind of bed-taking ritual, deathbed
taking. When it was Skallagrim's turn to grow old and "weak with
age," Egil took over the management of the farm. Skallagrim had
thus retired when he could no longer do the work. The night Skallagrim was to die, Egil and his wife are invited to a feast at another
farm. Before they set out, father and son have a talk.

Some years earlier, Egil and his brother had fought in the service
of King Athelstan of England and Egil's brother fell in battle. The
king gave Egil two chests of silver, which he specifically said were
to be paid as compensation to Skallagrim for the loss of his son.[7]
But Egil keeps a tight grip on the chests of silver:

"You've been in no hurry, Egil, to hand over the money that King Athelstan sent me. Just what are you intending to do with it?"

"So are you short of money, father? I didn't know that," Egil said. "I'll let you have the silver when I'm sure you need it, but I know you still have your hold on a chest or two of silver of your own."

"I guess you think you've already taken your share of our property. But keep in mind then that I will do just as I please with what I have in my control."[8]

Egil departs for the feast. When the rest of the household is asleep, old Skallagrim saddles up a horse, rides out with a chest of silver, and sinks it in a marsh. In the morning, the servants find him seated upright on the edge of his bed, so stiff with rigor mortis that they cannot straighten him out. Egil is sent for and he hurries back home. He goes to where Skallagrim is sitting and "took him by the shoulders and forced him down on his back. He laid him down on the seat, closed his eyes and stopped his nose and mouth. He ordered the men to take shovels and break through the south wall. When that was done, Egil gripped Skallagrim under the head, the others took his feet, and they carried him out of the house through the hole in the wall." Skallagrim is quickly ferried out to a steep ness where he is placed in a mound with his horse, his weapons and tools, "but it is not mentioned whether there was any money laid in the mound with him."[9] Even the stingy Egil does not stint his father his horse, tools, and weapons, all of which would come in handy in his new world.

Egil buries just enough with Skallagrim to keep Skallagrim from making meddlesome visits. Skallagrim was just the kind of strange character, like Hrapp, whom one would not be surprised to find walking after. He showed every indication in his first hours as a dead man that he intended to remain active. He was sitting up, eyes open. Like Hrapp, he insisted on staying upright and so his son had to wrestle him into the prone position proper to a well-behaved corpse.

No one was about to show Skallagrim the door either. That would be too risky. Doorways were magical spaces, as Hrapp well knew. Skallagrim was thus to be removed from his house through the wall, lest the newly dead man misconstrue being taken out the door as an invitation to return. They dig through the wall—Icelandic walls were built of turf—on the sunny side of the house, the side of the living; they take him out there, stiff as a board, and then block the wall back up. As with the wall, so with the corpse: block up the holes. Close his eyes, stuff his mouth and nostrils in order to control the evil eye, to prevent the spirit from getting out or getting back in. Then they bury him on a promontory, a peninsular no-man's-land, with enough ritual goods so as not to insult him. And hope.

Skallagrim lives by the talionic golden rule. As his son has held out on him, so he will hold out on his son. If Egil denied him Athelstan's silver, Skallagrim will deny Egil a rough equivalent of his inheritance, sinking it in one of the ubiquitous bottomless pits, crevices, and bogs that dot the Icelandic landscape.

Egil too grew old, and did not like it one bit. Never easy to deal with when he was strong and healthy, he did not get much easier now that he was lame, nearly deaf, and blind. He complained incessantly. The serving women mocked him. Even the greatest berserk heroes got beaten up by older kids when they were little; and if they survived until old age they were treated to the ridicule that is the lot of the old, if they got any attention at all.

Egil kept those chests of silver from King Athelstan under close watch. He occupied his time, it seems, musing about what to do with them. On one occasion, he gets an idea that tickles him to no end. It is the kind of idea most would tell for a laugh without the remotest intention of ever putting it into action. Not Egil. He tells his beloved niece Thordis, with whom he lives, that he wishes to go one last time to the Allthing (the annual assembly): "I want to take those two chests to the Law Rock when the most people are gathered there and then I will scatter the silver; I would be amazed if they divided it evenly. I bet there would be pushing and shoving; it might even lead to serious fighting. The whole assembly could end in a brawl."[10] Egil has found a way to join Professor Carstensen's happy oldsters.

In a touch of perfect realism Thordis humors the crazy old rogue by telling him it is a splendid idea, and it "will be remembered as long as people live in this land." She hastens immediately to her husband, Grim, to make sure Egil goes nowhere. Grim orders him to stay home, which leaves old Egil in a sour mood. With Grim away at the Allthing and Thordis up managing things at the sheepcotes, Egil orders two of Grim's slaves to saddle a horse for him just as people are getting ready for bed. He says he wants to go to the hot springs. He takes the chests of silver with him, and the next we see him it is morning and the household servants find him stumbling about outside the fence leading the horse: "But neither the slaves nor the chests returned."[11] Egil died a few months later. He confessed to killing the slaves but never told anyone where he hid the money.

There is no mention of any property being buried with Egil. But in a sense Egil performed his own pagan burial replete with grave goods and companions. To complete it he would only have had to jump in the bog after the silver and the slaves. He was already a dead man walking, deaf, blind, lame, demented, so in his own mind he was bringing himself to an end. His soul was with that silver.[12]

Hrapp, the weirdest of the four, still wants to use his property when dead; Kveld-Ulf wants to have one last say among the living by determining the location of his kin's new residence after he dies. One might see some greater virtue in their motives than those of Skallagrim and Egil, who are moved more by a desire to frustrate their heirs. Between the two, Skallagrim is on firmer moral ground than Egil. He is only depriving Egil of roughly the amount Egil had wrongfully withheld from him. But by the time we get to Egil, it is pure "If I can't have it then no one can." You must admit there is something strangely admirable in Kveld-Ulf and Skallagrim, in Hrapp, and even in Egil.

Aren't Egil and Skallagrim engaging in their own kind of eating, drinking, and being merry by consuming their wealth in a way that wastes it completely? They are indeed making merry; nothing gives them more pleasure than disappointing those who were expecting the wealth would become theirs. But eating, drinking, and being merry is also a form of taking it with you. One of the paradoxes of feast or famine economies of the premodern world is that what we would think of as wasteful consumption can be seen as a form of saving. At harvest time and after the autumn slaughter of the herds, you were loaded with food. You could store it and watch the rats, insects, and mildew take their share, and thieves, fire, and servants theirs, or you could feast, glut, and get fat, storing the calories that way. Vomiting was wasteful but storing the food was not risk free. The occasional regurgitation, moreover, was balanced by the constant constipation that was a natural consequence, for the wealthy at least, of a diet consisting mostly of meat and cheese. Constipation allowed for the extraction of maximum nutrients before the waste was released, either in a vision of justification by faith, in one famous case, or by resort to "physic," or by visitations of those plagues of dysentery that often meant you would not have to worry much longer one way or another about food and evacuation. If you decided to keep your animals on the hoof to kill them only when you needed to eat them, you would have to add in the cost of feeding them. It was unlikely your hay harvest could sustain more than half your herd through the winter. Eat, drink, and be merry, and if tomorrow you died, then at least you had taken it with you—as fat. Your last supper would also still be in your gut when they buried you. We actually know what Tollund Man ate for his. His stomach contents were preserved along with the rope and his cap.

THE DEAD HAND *RAPPING*

I have mentioned *King Lear* more than a few times. It is an object lesson for many objects, all of them grim, with its wanton cruelty and callousness: the good stupidly inept in the face of the motiveless malignancy of the heavens and evil people. It is a play about poor Lear losing it in every sense of the term. And what better vehicle to carry its toxicity than retirement in old age? The battle is of children against parents, the natural conflict that exists between the generation of the old and the generation that will displace them. It is the image I evoked earlier with Cronus and Saturn and us positive old folks on one side, and on the other children impatient for the property of the old, all of it, since should the old man hand over the bulk of the estate while still alive, only reserving to himself a modest annuity, the annuity comes to be resented with a passion stoked to incandescence by the advance payment. And if the young in medieval times, once they reached the age of majority, resented long-lived parents, imagine the resentments in the offing for us aged souls now, given our unseemly numbers and our pigheaded staying power.

The theme is an old one: Absalom gets impatient with David's longevity, and three centuries before that in a text from Ugarit, the son of King Keret does too. In both these cases the fathers had not formally retired but were felt by their sons, not completely incorrectly, to be neglecting their duties on account of sickness and old age. If Lear curses his daughters with horrific rhapsodic graphicness, Keret curses his son more coldly but no less effectively (the remarkable softness of David toward Absalom runs against expectations, expectations Joab made sure were not disappointed):

> May Horon smash, O my son,
> May Horon smash your head,
> Athtart-the-name-of-Baal your crown!
> May you fall down in the prime of life,
> Empty-handed and humiliated.[13]

Medieval didactic tales warn old people to avoid handing the farm over to the children, that the bonds of filial affection were not to be relied on when it ran against the children's economic interests, as I mentioned in chapter 4.[14] *Lear* is the grandest and most memorable of such cautionary tales. The cold message echoes that of the preceding section of this chapter: hold on tight with both hands until you die, and even then do not let go. That lesson was hard to act on until very recent times. Your eyes and hands grew weak; you could no longer work; there were no old-age pensions, though some very select few could buy a corody, an annuity of a sort, that would fund their board and perhaps a room in a monastery until they died.

If politics now favors the interests of the old as against the young, the common law has pretty much come to the same conclusion, but in a time when it was less economically destructive, given the smaller ratio of old to young that afflicts us. Children can be disinherited in every state (except Louisiana), though rules arising in the nineteenth century made the spouse qualify as an heir and prevented her complete disinheritance. Subject to his spouse's claim, the testator only had to meet minimal qualifications of being of sound mind when he signed the will. If he should become completely demented later, that did not affect the validity of the will. One issue the law wrestled with, however, was whether to let the dead testator play at being Hrapp, and if so for how long and to what extent.[15] As long as he willed his property outright, it would be controlled completely by the living he willed it to. The dead hand would simultaneously arise and die at the instant of the testator's death, which was the precise moment his will became effective to dispose of his property. No problem there. But what if he sought to attach strings to the property, or to keep his dead fingers in the pie, so that the person who got it found that he could not dispose of it or was required to use it in a certain way?

Except for people intent on founding dynasties and accumulating and controlling the devolution of family wealth for centuries, few thought it was a good idea to let the dead control their property forever. Times change and the uses to which a rational person might want the property put in 1168 were likely to be manifestly foolish in 1630, let alone in 2011. Yet shouldn't the beneficiaries be forced to honor at least some of the desires of the generation who sweated, suffered, fought, and maybe even died to create the wealth the youth were to get for free or, in the case of Lear's daughters, for merely having to profess unfelt love in public? How do we balance the competing interests of the living and the dead?

The common law hit upon a compromise rather generous to the

dead. A rule was crafted to set a maximum limit on how long the corpse could pull the strings. In the seventeenth century, judges came up with the Rule against Perpetuities (RAP). Perpetuities were those strings that threatened to tie up property forever with contingencies, forfeitures, or directions for devolution. This rule has been the bane of law students and lawyers for a century or two. Few seem to be able to apply it, or to draft wills and trusts without violating it. The inability of middling lawyers to understand it figured crucially in the plot of the film *Body Heat* (1981), in which a conniving black widow Kathleen Turner seduced and took advantage of the inability of William Hurt, the lawyer, to draft a disposition that would meet the requirements of the rule.

RAP has been recently reformed, which means dumbed down, even gotten rid of in some jurisdictions, supposedly to prevent it from frustrating reasonable dispositions that run afoul of the rule for some flyspeck technical violation that an insufficiently vigilant lawyer failed to notice. RAP was also reformed because it was in the interests of lawyers to do so, as it became increasingly a concern that malpractice actions would be brought by people who thought they were going to get millions from Grandpa only to find Grandpa's bequest to them had failed because Grandpa's lawyer screwed up. Before the reforms, courts bailed out inept lawyers by denying the intended beneficiary any standing to sue. It was the testator to whom the malpractice claim belonged. His lawyer was the one who had screwed up, and since the testator was dead, the lawyer was home free. When finally the courts began to grant standing to the disappointed beneficiaries to sue the lawyer who wrote the will, the judges still found ways to let the inept lawyer off the hook before it was decided finally to dumb down or get rid of the rule altogether. One notorious case, for instance, held that the lawyer who had drafted the offending clause willing $75K in 1961 dollars to the intended beneficiary was not liable to that disappointed beneficiary because the rule was too hard for a lawyer of "ordinary skill" to understand. No malpractice, just practice as usual.[16]

The common law RAP, rather than give the dead man a fixed

number of years to control the course of the property, like 50, 90, or 120 years, used a flexible formula to set the allowable limits of dead-hand control: "No interest is good unless it must vest, if at all, within a life in being plus 21 years from the date the disposition becomes effective." I am not about to burden you with a law review article on RAP,[17] though I have had no compunction about burdening you with saga characters whose names you cannot keep straight. But I do want to give you enough to understand the law's accommodations to the interests of the dead.

The rule was designed by judges thinking in terms of family wealth distribution, of letting the decedent control his property for the lives of his children and up to the age of majority of his grandchildren, at which time all strings had to dissolve or the conditions imposed be fulfilled. Once, however, you turn lawyers loose on what should be a simple rule, you find yourself in the city of Dis made up of hidden alleyways in which diabolic muggers lurk, certain to torment the dead man who thought he had left his beloved grandkids or nieces and nephews property that instead ended up in the hands of his wife-beating son-in-law.

So why is this "life in being [at the time the grant or will becomes effective] plus 21 years" period so hard to master? Because by the late eighteenth century RAP was interpreted to require "remorseless application." That meant that if you could think of any crazed possibility, no matter how improbable, that might make the strings stay attached longer than a life in being plus twenty-one years, the disposition failed and either passed to the residuary legatees of the will or, if it was the residuary clause that failed, then to the heirs via intestacy.

Suppose you will a million dollars in trust with the interest income of the million to your siblings for their lives, and then at the death of the last of your siblings, the million is to be paid over to their children, your nieces and nephews, in equal shares. At the time of your death, you are survived by your parents, who are in their nineties, and a sister and a brother and their children, your nieces and nephews. The rule requires that the interests of your siblings and their children vest—that means become unconditionally the property of the beneficiary—within the RAP period. Know too that for a gift to a class such as siblings, children, grandchildren, or nieces and nephews, it must vest within the rule period for each possible member of the class or the gift fails to all members of that class. In this example, RAP takes down the gift of a million dollars to the nieces and nephews, though the gift of income to your brother and sister is good. The million ends up passing to the University of Michigan Law School, which you named as the residuary legatee in your will.

The problem is to find a life in being, someone who is alive the moment the instrument creating the interests becomes effective, which for a will is the moment of your death, who will work to validate the interests given to the beneficiaries. The principle of remorseless application leads to the following scenario. After you die, your mother and father have another child. Call him Ishmael. Ishmael is what is referred to as an "after-born" child, born after the instrument whose validity we are trying to determine became effective. He is also an after-walker of sorts who will destroy the gift to any children he should come to have—they would be your nieces and nephews—and to the children of his siblings who were already in existence at your death. But, you say incredulously, my ninety-year-old parents are not about to do the deed of darkness, or to be fertile if they did. Sorry, for RAP purposes they are randy and fertile. That rule was settled in a case called *Jee v. Audley,* which held that as far as RAP was concerned, fertility was to be presumed for the entire course of a human's life.[18] The presumption, though far-fetched as a practical matter, is less so now, what with in-vitro fertilization, frozen eggs and sperm, than it was when the case came down in 1787.

Why does your brother Ishmael merely getting born turn out to be a dastardly deed, so unkind to your nieces and nephews? Because it means that the class of your siblings cannot work as validating lives in being at the time of your death to make your gift of a million good to their children, your nieces and nephews. Suppose a month after Ishmael is born, your parents, other brother and sister, and all their kids die in a plane crash or a car wreck or an earthquake—you can invent any means you wish to kill them off. Such lethal fantasies are part of the fun of doing RAP problems. Suppose too that, like his Melvillian namesake, Ishmael alone survives to tell the tale. Your brother Ishmael can still collect the interest that you willed to your siblings, for he necessarily would have been born within the lives of your parents, who were alive when you died. But the problem is that Ishmael may have a child, who would be your niece or nephew, and that child might not be born until twenty-two years after the tragic events that wiped out your family. The gift to that child of Ishmael is void because it would not vest within a life in being at the time of your death plus twenty-one years and that unborn child of Ishmael destroys the gift to all your nieces and nephews. Wait a minute, you say, there are tons of other people in the world who are alive at the time of my death and surely some of them will be around when Ishmael has his kid and that kid turns twenty-one. Maybe, but maybe not. What is there to say that an invasion from outer space might not kill off everyone else who was alive at your death and only one other person in addition to Ishmael survived, a nice young girl, who was born after you had died, and with whom Ishmael then coupled?

I am not making this up. The gift you made to your nieces and nephews fails precisely because of a scenario like this. But what if that does not happen, you say? Tough. The decision about the validity of the provisions is made not on what does happen, but on what might happen in the most crazed concatenation of events you can come up with.[19] You see now why reforms decided to dumb down the rule. Under the reformed rule, a gift is good now in a majority of jurisdictions if it complies with the terms of the old common law RAP or, if not, a ninety-year period of dead-hand control is substituted rather than voiding the offending provisions.[20] Damn. Why rid the law of such surreal imaginings because lawyers, who invented the rule to begin with, are incapable of understanding it? What am I to do to fill up the week I used to spend on this in my Property class, delighting in the terror it generated in all but a few of the stranger students, who took to it immediately?

Why did the common law countenance the bizarreness of such

remorseless application? The judges were concerned, it seems, that the rule period was too generous to the dead. Any modestly competent lawyer could give the dying owner powers to control his wealth for more than a century. How? Draft the clause to get a group of people among whom there are some toddlers to work as lives in being: "this trust to terminate twenty-one years after the death of the last of the babies born in Bellin Hospital the week preceding my death." So the judges set out to interpret the rule to whack the knuckles hard of the dead hand and wipe out the gift. Woe to the intended beneficiary if the testator's lawyer forgot about infinite fertility and other pitfalls of the rule known as the unborn widow, the slothful executor, or the precocious toddler (a case in which to find a RAP violation a boy had to father a child before he turned five after first getting born to a sixty-seven-year old woman named Mrs. Gaites). The reform tosses these concerns out the window by conceding an overly generous ninety years and is incapable of generating good stories to boot.

So the dead's hands do reasonably well, thank you, at least if they were wealthy and well counseled and still cared to have a say. Nor were all the dead unsocialized and selfish. In some traditions, they would be quite polite and take care to repay obligations they owed the living. A tale from the Talmud cuts against the darker grain of this chapter. The tale is part of a discussion of whether and what the dead know. The embarrassing line of Ecclesiastes 9.5—"But the dead know nothing"—is explained away as not really referring to the dead but to the living wicked, who are as if dead. The real dead know a thing or two, a belief more easily sustained when most of the dead had not lived to be old enough to have Alzheimer's and people died with more marbles than they do now: "Ze'iri deposited some money with his landlady, and while he was away visiting Rab she died. So he went after her to the cemetery and said to her, 'Where is my money?' She replied to him: 'Go and take it from under the ground, in the hole of the doorpost, in such and such a place, and tell my mother to send me my comb and my tube of eye-paint by the hand of So-and-so who is coming here tomorrow.' Does not this show that they know?"[21] The story's point is that the dead know who is going to die and when. Poor So-and-so. Though Ze'iri may be surprised his dead landlady has acquired that eerie specialized knowledge of the future, he would not be inquiring of her the whereabouts of what may have been his security deposit if he did not also expect that she retained her capacity to remember, or her moral sense, let alone her ability to carry on a conversation. She does not wish to keep from Ze'iri what is not hers, and she also expects small favors to be requited with small favors. So would Ze'iri bear the message to have her eyeliner brought to her since So-and-so is coming tomorrow anyway? She thus retains the small vanity of wishing to look presentable, though dead, a vanity that is both a motive and consequence of being properly socialized. And given that her mother is still alive, the dead landlady was still reasonably young and perhaps quite fetching. Dead hand is the wrong metaphor to capture this woman's contact with the living, or the sweetness of the tale.

PART V

Sentiments

CHAPTER 13

Owing the Dead

.

To what extent must the living respect the commitments and the wishes of the dead, or repay the debts we owe them, when they did right by us, when they sacrificed and gave and we inherited and received (and consumed) the benefits? We can, in fact, easily avoid paying these debts, as our moral sense, which demands memory and faithfulness, shrinks along with our brains; the dead have no means to compel us to pay them back. There are no Hrapps among them. My generation will pass on obligations to our descendants too, but they will be obligations of a different sort. They will simply inherit our debts, the ones incurred and never repaid. And they will have to pay them; they will have to declare real bankruptcy because of our moral bankruptcy. Living people, holding real bonds, will have their hooks in our kids and grandkids; we made our offspring cosigners of our notes, made them violate the strictures in Proverbs, even before they were *sui juris.*

Some would allege a theory of democracy that denies the dead an interest in the present. Democracy by this view empowers the present community to decide and arrange its affairs precisely as it sees fit. There is no obligation to the dead other than to maintain the very democracy they established that denied them a say once they died. Easy case if it is slave owner who still wants his say, but is it as easy when it is a soldier who fought his country's wars, whatever you thought of the war? And if we admit that the dead have some vague interests that we must consider, is our duty toward them discharged by paying lip service to their sacrifices on Memorial Day and Veterans Day, to their wisdom on Independence Day, where we pay back their thoughtfulness and courage with fireworks and parades? Cheap coin. We use somewhat better coin when we reflect on their achievements or offer prayers of remembrance, such as Yizkor services among the Jews, or visit their graves, if we find the time and the weather permits. And as we move from inhumation to cremation, cemeteries will become relics rather than a home to relics. They will cease to make demands to be visited; what then? Digital images to the rescue, watching digitalized clips of dead Dad and Mom? Airbrushed zombification, but how unfair to those who predeceased the relevant technology.

If you think I was irrationally charmed by Hrapp and Egil and their mean-spirited demands to bind the living, and in Hrapp's case to remain corporeally active among them, what would you expect me to think of the honor and deference we owe to the dead who died in battle, or fled tyranny and starved themselves to give their families a chance, who deferred the instant gratification that we take for granted? Will you dismiss me as having gone preachy, a fatuous Polonius? These dead need have done none of this out of any greater commitment to virtue than our own weak commitment; they too wanted an easier life—out of the czar's army, the pogroms, the famines—though perhaps not as easy as the one they passed on to us. They had their scoundrels and losers; they were stuck with the usual temptations of sex, drink, and pulling fast ones, and gave in enough to keep moralists busy in every generation. They were human, after all, more fully human than we are since they were missing the plastic and silicone parts, the injections, the chemical maintenance that keeps us going.

And virtue, perhaps, was easier for them, if only because certain temptations were not as readily satisfied then as they are now. They had to work harder and take greater risks to be bad. It was easier to keep your nose to the grindstone, to save, to read, to think, before the pill and credit cards, before the constant distraction of iPods, YouTube, one-click porn, before smartphones, GPS, and talking cars. Sheer necessity forced some virtue upon them, even if it was at times against their will.

But how can a Jew, for instance, not conscientiously maintain and pass on a connection to his ancestors who were murdered in countless hordes in the very decade I was born? And when the desire to finish off the remnant is still the official policy or barely unofficial policy of a third of the world? It would be cowardly not to maintain the connection, though I would not even have been able to march off like a lamb to the slaughter as too many did. I would have cringed and begged. And never would I have mustered the berserk fury of the zealots who gave the Romans all they could handle. I owe those who did, as I owe those millions who died for no reason at all.

And as an American I owe the soldiers who fought and died or risked their lives that that nation might live. I owe the president who truly changed the world. Imagine if that government of the people, by the people, and for the people perished from the earth, or had been shown incapable of fighting or winning a war fought to prove that such a polity could exist in accordance with its grandest professed principles. Play a counterfactual history forward. Western Europe would not be so free, nor would we Americans, northern or southern.[1] Lincoln was a world historical figure, like Alexander, Caesar, Paul, Genghis Khan, Luther, or Napoleon, and much kinder. Our world would look very different had he not lived, had he not had the perfect soul, had he not been perfectly pragmatic, witty, and something of a literary genius, perfectly committed, humane, cagey, cunning, and ready to kill and be killed.

We owe the dead big time, not just because they gave birth to us, but because they suffered and died for us; Jesus was not the first to die or be sacrificed for the benefit of others.[2] Even in the Christian dispensation, Christ depends on the sacrifice of Moses, whose death was no less cruel, indeed psychologically, if not physically, crueler. Jesus got called to his promised end, Moses had his dangled before him and snatched away, having to settle for a view from Pisgah on the outside looking in. Nor need we think so grandly. Many a common soldier, many a defender of family and home died for others, with no certain knowledge that their death made a difference, and they will continue to do so.

I can see your eyes rolling; mine feel like they should be. Such platitudinous pieties tend either to bore or to raise suspicions of hypocrisy, of cheap and easy moralism. I think, though, I am sincere. I am only too aware of my own propensity to go soft and romantic over people who lived long ago, not so much because I am foolish enough to think civilizations before the pacified American suburb embodied some golden age, but more because I tend to lose my moral and critical bearings the farther back I go. I find myself giving ancient and medieval moral monsters a pass partly because they generated such good stories. It is as if the violence, the atrocities, the perfidies get fictionalized merely for being old, rendered into a period piece suitable for HBO or a video game. When it is David, Sennacherib, Alexander, Marius and Sulla, Caesar, Charlemagne, Robert Guiscard, the Conqueror, I shake my head only half in horror, the other half succumbing to bemused admiration, as if these souls played a game meant for gods rather than humans, so godlike was their energy, their ability to compel respect, so free they seemed from all constraints. Can you blame Alexander for believing he was divine? Even their small-mindedness had a grandness in the amount of risk they were willing to take for a straw and the amount of misery they were willing to dish out and sometimes suffer for so little or for so much, it seemed not to matter.

Move to the twentieth century, and only the horror survives, when the cold killers were creating a world of Gulag and death camp. The Peninsular War, as Goya captured it, already two centuries old, has not gotten its moral pass yet either; it takes more time, or the fortuitous absence of a Goya to prevent the horror from remaining so graphically present. But it is not just Goya's presence, because Cromwell in Ireland or Wallenstein and other commanders in the Thirty Years' War do not yet get their moral pass. The crude woodcuts are more than enough. But before then? What of the obvious delight those Assyrian reliefs take in the torture and humiliation and mutilation of their enemies? Is it only graphic representation that can trigger my shallow moral capacity, for the vomiting lions sick unto death in depictions of rigged hunts and those cowering captives could break my heart—when, that is, I do not find myself half smiling in disbelief at the brutality of the winners.[3]

I try to curb my tendency to be overawed by the medieval and the ancient, putty in the hands of their chroniclers and tale-tellers, by insistently reminding myself that I have an obligation to them, and to the profession I am in, to get it right. But I am never quite sure I am not a pathetic Miniver Cheevy, child of scorn for being born too late, though my romanticism can be quickly cured with a small prompt of imagination. God forbid I should have lived back then; God forbid I should have lived a mere eighty years ago in Lithuania or Kiev where, if my paternal grandparents in the one case and my maternal kin in the other had not emigrated, they and theirs would have been exterminated. I am quite happy to have been born too late, not having what it takes to make a reasonable go of it in a world of good stories, the world I study for a living.

That said, I still find the wise dead considerably wiser than those we hold to be our modern-day wise men and women who, the more famous they are, the more likely they are to be charlatans. But even a wise pastor, rabbi, or priest of today, the equivalent of the village wise man, fares less well in comparison, for they would now have their wisdom compromised by the psychobabble, positivity cant, new-agey motivational-speaker drivel, and opinion polls that are no less inimical to wisdom in the low- to middle-brow range than are the academic Freudianism and Lacanianism or the faux tough-mindedness of genetic determinism and economics at the somewhat higher-brow end.

There I go lapsing into the-good-old-days tripe, even though I know that every age had its equivalent of our therapeutic and positivity imbecility; then as now people consulted mediums; plagues of prophets and soothsayers bilked innumerable fools; conmen and holy men ran healing and miracle rackets. Then as now there were people who dealt in sound bites of condensed shallowness. When it comes to folly and knavery there is nothing new under the sun. And then I must remember the danger of cherry-picking the good stuff from the past and comparing it with middling, undistinguished stuff of today. But then even laundry lists that are four thousand years old, and much of what survives are basically laundry lists, are interesting for their age alone, and for the bonds of humanity they forge, the humility they impose.

Yet, conceding all this, I feel obliged to talk up medieval people especially to combat our smug belief that smart people, excepting the ancient Greeks and Chinese, and perhaps Augustine and Aquinas, only began to exist post-Renaissance, and then in very small numbers until the Enlightenment. And really smart people, we think, only began to populate the planet in any numbers in the nineteenth century, with the likes of Faraday or Darwin, but mostly in the early twentieth with Einstein et al. From there it is a mere hundred years to the smartphone.

I tell my saga students that blood-feuding people had to be practically wiser and more cunning than we are now, if only because their margins for error were smaller, the stakes higher for them in routine social interactions and transactions. No, life and death did not hang in the balance every second; it would be romanticizing the heroic past more than it romanticizes itself to claim it did. The prosaic past, in fact, might have been even grimmer than the heroic past when it came to deadliness. Disease and lack of calories more than held their own against raiders and plundering armies when it came to making life precarious.

In any case, life hung in the balance more often for them than it does for us in the free West, considerably more so. You had to be pretty good at discerning motives in others, reading their inner states—better than we safe souls are, for sure. I marvel at the unfathomable complacency that can allow someone to walk down the sidewalk intently texting a message and thinking that if he bumps into someone or forces them unknowingly to have to give way, that he will not have to account for himself, secure that he will not suffer a much deserved beating to help him regain a modicum of manners, to assist him in the project of avoiding giving unwarranted offense to others. As Bernard Mandeville wrote in his *Fable of the Bees* (1732 edition) regarding the benefits of dueling: "Those that rail at Duelling don't consider the Benefit the Society receives from that Fashion. . . . It is strange that a Nation should grudge to see perhaps half a dozen Men sacrific'd in a Twelvemonth to obtain so valuable a Blessing, as the Politeness of Manners, . . . that is often so willing to expose, and sometimes loses as many thousands in a few Hours, without knowing whether it will do any good or not."[4] And now you must suppose I have really lost it. But Mandeville was being playful and somewhat ironic; though, as often is the case, we do half mean our violent overstatements. Only half, for given my own temper and lack of patience, I could even have managed to exasperate a positive psychologist so badly that he would have shot me at twenty paces (or I him).

IT IS FOR US THE LIVING

Return to Lincoln. We had to memorize the Gettysburg Address when I was in grade school. But as with any iconic speech, like "To be or not to be," we seldom bother to attend to its meaning. It becomes a mantra, like prayers, meant to evoke a mood more than to bear any specific propositional content. The Gettysburg Address— its brevity, the myth of its not being well received, of its being written on the back of an envelope on a train to the battlefield— is part of the Americanness of most Americans of my age. Somehow the perfect words found the perfect visage and body to compose and speak them: the sorrow and intelligence of the face, the angular gauntness, the nontrite handsomeness, the haunting gravity that was never compromised by his comic gift. Would the speech mean as much if it came from flesh and bone formed in any other way? Were we to make gods of men, or send gods down to be men, then this man should be First.

I seem to lose it when it comes to Lincoln worship. So let us nitpick a few sentences in the address, though we end up even more worshipful in the end. Lincoln manages brevity and compression while at the same time employing what appear to be wasteful words.[5] An English 101 teacher would mark him down for the wordy archaicism of rendering "eighty-seven" as "fourscore and seven." With that archaicism, though, Lincoln means to mobilize the grandeur of the King James Version's preference for making sixties and eighties threescores and fourscores. Few people in his audience would have needed a calculator to do the math or have had to Google the meaning of score to know that he was dating the founding to the Declaration, not to the Constitution. The King James Bible, its diction and rhythms, its power, was burned into their bone.

It is a phrase in the second paragraph I want to remark on. I provide the first paragraph too so the grammatical antecedents are clear:

> Fourscore and seven years ago our fathers brought forth, upon this continent, a new nation, conceived in liberty, and dedicated to the proposition that all men are created equal.
>
> Now we are engaged in a great civil war, testing whether that nation, or any nation so conceived and so dedicated, can long endure. We are met on a great battlefield of that war. We have come to dedicate a portion of that field, as a final resting place for those who here gave their lives that that nation might live. It is altogether fitting and proper that we should do this.

The repetitions of "nation," "conceived," "dedicate(d)," "great," and "field" help create an incantatory effect as well as make it crystal clear what is being referred to. Lincoln had a very good ear.[6] Half rhymes, such as endure/war, proposition/portion/proper, field/final/lives, produce unforced euphonies. The plays on words, such as when "dedicate(d)" can grammatically govern a proposition as well as a cemetery and also pick up the homophony with "dead," are without a hint of excessive artifice. So too when the "lives," a plural noun, of those dead provide the lifeblood so that the verb "live" can sustain a nation. Both "dedicate" and "live(s)" shift between concrete referents—battlefield cemetery and dead bodies—to abstracter ones—a proposition and a nation. This is already a poem in prose in its first two paragraphs, before, that is, it even gets going.

But what do we make of "or any nation so conceived and so dedicated"? Wouldn't our English 101 teacher strike it out as unnecessary, repetitive, especially in a speech this brief? Is Lincoln just putting it in for euphonious filler to help generate the incantatory effect the speech would not only come to have but already was designed to have when first delivered? I have already anticipated my justification for the appropriateness of the clause a few pages ago. Lincoln was not just speechifying, or so blinded by his own patriotism that he elevated to world-historical significance this particular battlefield in this particular war to a "great battlefield" in a "great" American civil war. He rightly sees, even foresees, what is at stake for the principle of political equality should the North lose the war. He is not exaggerating. France had botched it. The Americans, with our cancerous compromise to found the union, could also fumble it away unless that flaw in the founding were amended, the cancer excised by force, since it could not be cut out by words.

The war is great too because it was a war like no other. Railroads transported troops to the various fronts; the battlefields were growing larger as the ranges of artillery and rifles increased (thus giving a double sense to the "great" battlefield in the text of the speech). Telegraphs kept the folks back home apprised of successes and failures within less than a day of their occurrence. Photographs vividly captured the death and destruction. But because the entire American experiment in governance, its latitudinarianism, its freedom and liberty, was at stake, the stakes were surely as high or higher than they were in the Roman, even the English, the French, or the Russian civil wars. At stake was an entire way of conceiving government and citizenry. In "or any nation so conceived and so dedicated" Lincoln means to emphasize that this war was not only an American war but a war to secure a transformative kind of political and moral society available for others if, and only if, the United States could survive this test. If such a society could not win on the battlefield of this particular war, more than borders would have to be redrawn.[7] He was, I think, largely right. And those dead on the battlefield did not die in vain, because of one man, nor did he lead in vain, because of them.

CHAPTER 14.

Going Soft

With old age, you see, one of the amends one can make is not to be ashamed of having patriotic sentiments. Where but in the United States could I have had such a good life to complain about?

A good portion of the last chapter expressed gratefulness, somewhat against the pose of much of my exposition up until then. But I cannot stop with Lincoln and the Gettysburg dead. Losing it, in its early stages, makes for reflection. Not surprisingly, many of these reflections involve remembering, and thus recognizing and admitting debts incurred. As I already mentioned, "to remember" in the Hebrew Bible and in *Hamlet* is an obligational term. It means discharging debts. But so many of the people we owe are dead, dead before we could pay quit to their gifts we received. That hardly cancels the obligation.

Though an old man could take to bed to announce he was unable to pay back wrongs that were his responsibility to requite, the same ritual was not available to beg off the obligation to requite the good things he had received. In our day declaring bankruptcy works perversely as such a ritual. It strikes me as much easier to sympathize with and pardon an old blood feuder in a culture of honor and feud for throwing in the towel when he is no longer up to the physical and emotional demands of taking revenge than it is to excuse a bankrupt in a consumer culture. We can put weighty positive glosses on not paying back the bad things done us. We can call it Christian or humane or being civilized, and should our inaction or forgivingness be partly motivated by cowardice, fear is a motive we can readily sympathize with.

But what positive glosses are available to excuse not paying back debts incurred for benefits we have received? It is hard to find any; a couple of courses in economics and knowledge of business cycles and statistics need to be recruited to provide the basis for some special pleading. If in the end we decide the bankrupt is less the knave we vaguely suspect he is, it is because we declare him a fool, a victim of knavish creditors who tricked him into accepting benefits they (and he) should have known he could not repay. We thus give him a moral break at the expense of his dignity, calling him in effect a dimwit. We might be less judgmental if we simply declared him unlucky, but that is not doing him much of a favor either, because it nudges him ever closer to stamping a capital L on his forehead as a Loser, casting him thereby into the outer darkness. In any event, legal bankruptcy is not generally available to escape the obligation to repay the kindnesses of friends, family, near strangers, and the dead, though rotting memory can do much the same.

Now, with memory in decay, will you be able to recall what you owe to whom? Can you rewind and replay in order to make your accounting? Can you make accurate assessments? Memory deteriorates. Old people have been proven, as noted earlier, to generate more false memories than younger people.[1] Beware any vivid detail in an older person's account. The particulars are precisely what he can no longer dredge up, and thus are made up. Much of what we relive was never lived in the first place, it having been invented, exaggerated, or misremembered. Our pasts are subject to all kinds of wishful thinking, rationalizations that even a full-volume brain, let alone a shrinking one, is heir to. Add to the failures generated by aging, the blindness generated by self-interest when debt and obligation are involved, and you find yourself claiming that you already repaid the debts, or you think that the favors done you were really paybacks the other owed you, if you can even call what he did a favor.

Return to the obligations admitted, those you are sure you still owe, the kind word at the right time, the harsh shaming words at the right time that put you on track, all those things that, when you look back, ended up being of greater benefit to you than you ever could have realized then, or than the person doing the helpful deed ever thought he was doing.

There are favors that are meant as favors, and the doer of them reasonably expects a return favor at an appropriate time, or immediate displays of gratitude, though I still feel something more is owed to the two or three grownups who regularly picked me up hitchhiking home from high school. But most of the undischarged debts that aging memory dredges up are of the type you owe the teacher who was merely doing her job faithfully, the professor whose love of his own subject infected you; you thus feel you owe them for just being the people they were. Such things are felt as debts on the receiving end but the doer of them intended no particular favor demanding a payback. Pop psychology talks about "paying it forward," discharging the debt by doing a similar good deed to someone else. Add a dash of positive thinking and you can declare yourself off the hook, in easy self-forgiveness.

That cannot be the answer. You do not try to discharge the responsibilities that come with being a teacher to pay back your old teachers. You do it because you owe it to your students as a first-order matter, because it is your duty, your job, because you could not think of doing otherwise. You still owe all those people from way back when, but is there a way, short of hare-brained table tapping or spirit channeling, to make the payment? I will offer some suggestions, but they hardly provide a convincing answer beyond having to accept, in the end, that some debts are not possible to discharge adequately, no matter what you do. We are born debtors and die much the same.

NOSTALGIA?

Can it be that indulging in nostalgia, as I seem to have been doing in the last few pages, is a way of paying back those debts? Surely that has to be as pathetically hollow as the self-forgiveness that comes with "paying it forward."

How to classify nostalgia: is it a curse of old age, a sign of displeasure with the way things are? Would the positive-emotion crowd think it a positive emotion? Probably, given the company it often keeps with syrupy sentimentality.[2] There is something trivial about it, as a general matter, in a way that grief, guilt, anger, disgust, shame, hate, mother love, and a sense of duty are not, again as a general matter. Think of nostalgia, and you think of life insurance commercials, of oldie stations, period-piece movies, usually set in the English countryside. It is one of the key weapons in the arsenal of admen to pick your pocket.

Nostalgia, originally, was a fancy name for a particular kind of homesickness a seventeenth-century Swiss mercenary soldier might feel.[3] But it has broadened and shifted its sense. Nostalgia, unlike homesickness, cannot properly be about the recent past. Nostalgia requires enough time for a golden haze to form over the past. You feel it for the remoter past or for the mother country, and not even necessarily your own past or mother country, but the imagined one of your parents and grandparents or other people's parents and grandparents. That is why you can be understood to feel nostalgia for the music of your parents' romantic years, before you were born: we'll meet again, don't know where, don't know when. You can feel it too for times that never happened at all.

Nostalgia must usually cut across two "ages of man." I would look manifestly silly to claim to be nostalgic about middle age, even if there are things about it I already miss: like my memory, or a particular shirt that finally wore out. A person generally must be in middle or old age before he can properly be nostalgic about his own childhood, or in old age before he can be nostalgic about young adulthood. On the other hand, you can surely be nostalgic about your children's toddlerhood as soon as they reach puberty, that being such a seismic change that it makes nostalgia justifiable though only ten years have passed, and one age of man—theirs, not yours—has run its course.

Nostalgia generally involves the sense, true or not, that there was once a bright side to look on, even though when you think more precisely about it, you know you would still have plenty to complain about were you transported back then, just as you complained when you were in it. Nostalgia is not denied the pessimist. Pessimism can be quite kind to the past so as better to justify a view that things keep getting worse. The good old days is not a myth born of optimism. Should you press the pessimist, he would be more than happy to show you how awful the past was too, especially if he can ruin another's dreamy nostalgia. Nostalgia is really, he would say, nothing more than the experience of quintessential goneness with a gilding of soft melancholy, providing a sentimentalized soundtrack even to memories of the bully who beat you up, like Shmuel recalling the Polish boy who knifed him, or you recalling, with a sense of sadness for the loss, the boredom that oppressed as you rode yet again around the block on your bicycle at twilight because there was no one to play with. "The gloomiest past is dearer than the brightest present," says David Levinsky in Abraham Cahan's 1917 novel.[4]

You know you are old when you get nostalgic about the state of the academy when you were in grad school, nostalgic for professors who knew so much more than you could ever hope to, who were consummately literate, wrote with clarity, before everything collapsed in the humanities into "theory," the chief qualification of which seemed to have been hatred for your own language. Historians held out longest—they actually had to know something before they could start theorizing about it—nor did they have to apologize for telling good stories. But then they too, even some medievalists and classicists, started to cave, becoming more like New Historicists. Yet another scam. You wonder if it is a par-

ticular symptom of losing it that even though you know you are
right in these judgments, you seem to forget that some amount of
your own work qualifies for your own hate list. As to how much
qualifies, well, that is part of taking stock that is too painful to
undertake. My wife says it comprises everything after my first real
book, *Bloodtaking,* with only *Audun and the Polar Bear* and maybe
The Mystery of Courage since then receiving a pardon.

THE FEELING OF LUCKING OUT AND THANKFULNESS

The sentiment I am trying to get a fix on, and which has features
we might associate with the triteness of nostalgia, wants desperately to claim, however, something weightier for it by keeping the
notion of debt in the foreground. I want this sentiment, whatever
it is, to be imbued with a sense of unfinished business, a need to
call up the dead, the owed, and settle matters. I am, I guess, trying
to give a moral component to plain vanilla nostalgia that it does
not have. Those shades, those souls from the past I would call up
from the dead, I feel something like love for, though I might feel it
only as part of this reflective exercise. Not such a love that I would
want much more contact than that which I can have via reflection,
nor would they want such contact with me. We do not want, nor
could we have, a close relationship with everyone we feel this sense
of owing for kindnesses rendered, or for just being who they were
when they were who they were. Nor should I let myself get too
carried away here with the positive. Reflection also brings to mind
people you loathed and to whom you owe nothing good, but they
slip into the background for once. For once the good people oust
the bad from center stage, assuming, that is, you are not inventing with false memory the unpaid debts you now claim to owe in
order to prove to yourself just how deeply moral and honorable
you can be.

To the extent that taking stock focuses on particular scenes and
people, people to whom you feel indebted, you feel a suffusion of
gratefulness that morphs into a general sense of disbelief at having lucked out, which you accompany with that slow shake of the

head, a gesture you make though quite alone. Does the gesture come unbidden? Is it a sign of the sincerity of the sentiment? It is not exactly as if you mean it to be unwitnessed. We play our social roles for imagined audiences all the time, or for ourselves as our own audience. But this shake of the head, I suspect, has more primitive roots: it is a ritual of thanking the gods, God, Fortune, the Powers That Be.

The feeling of having lucked out, with its sense of disbelief, grows into something somewhat graver, with which it shares kinship: thankfulness. Thankfulness for getting to make a living reading and writing whatever I wanted. Can one be said really to hold a job if one gets paid for doing exactly what he would do if he were independently wealthy? My father could never understand it: teaching five to six hours a week, and then getting summers off and sabbaticals and leaves: "Did I hear right, they pay you your full salary? Weren't you off last year too? What can your students expect to do with this Icelandic whatever you call it?" He would sometimes say Irish, not because Iceland and Ireland only differ by one consonant or are reasonably closely situated on the map, but because he could confirm that Ireland existed, having known many Irishmen but no Icelanders. "What use would anyone put it to?" These puzzled queries would be accompanied with a shake of the head that signaled resigned disbelief. The headshake of resigned disbelief differs from the headshake of disbelief for having lucked out. The accompanying facial expression is different; if a sigh accompanies each of them, they are different sighs: my father's one of despair, mine a phew of relief.

My father felt as if his own son was a harbinger of the four horsemen. Each year he would ask again what exactly it was I got paid for, having repressed his woe at the prior year's answer. Each year I would make the same halfhearted defense: that writing is hard, especially when you know you are writing for an audience— the term does not seem quite right—of a couple of thousand if you got lucky. "Do you teach any law?" he would ask. "Yes, Property." He looked more forlorn: "But you know nothing about property; you have never taken an interest in the business." (He was in real estate development). The genuine forlornness was harder for me to endure than when he gave a contemptuous snort, which he also did on occasion.

My sincerest defense, other than the general one of learning for learning's sake, especially when it does the honorable service of keeping the genius of the dead among us, is that if he only knew how great the sagas were, he would be compelled to concede a life well spent for me, if for no one else. The sagas, he would see, were no less sublime than ancient Greek or Hebrew productions (though he would still wonder what use future lawyers would make of Greek and Hebrew), even sublimer because we expect great things from the Greeks and the Hebrew Bible. What expectations does anyone have of Iceland? What knowledge at all? Iceland's having the highest per capita rate of winning major international beauty contests by several multiples? Its active volcanoes? Its having become the object lesson in the dangers of excessive leveraging of investments?

My students ask me every now and then whether I was drawn to the sagas because of what they perceive to be my natural vengefulness or if I learned vengefulness from the sagas, a hardness they attribute less to my faux tough talk, which could fake out no one, than to my ungenerous grading curve and class attendance rules, with grade reductions for having a cell phone go off. Which was chicken, which egg? Did the sagas transform an original forgiving, loving nature into one on the lookout for slights I must pay back? My father, when I mentioned the students' question, had an answer: "No," he said, "you were difficult from the start. The sagas had nothing to do with it."

Thankfulness, no different than its baser cousin, the disbelief at lucking out, is a feeling that varies inversely with your own sense of merit. Christianity came up with the doctrine of grace in part to explain the sentiment. The feeling of thankfulness may be the best argument for why we need gods, or God, lest there be no one to thank or alive to thank, a thought that is not my own but, with decaying recall, I cannot remember where I read it or who said it. God is the surrogate recipient of those thanks, those unpaid debts owed to the dead, to those teachers, to the guy, an Icelander, who sat next to me in a seminar in my first year of grad school in 1970 and said, "You oughta read *Njal's Saga,*" which I had never heard of, and who was thus responsible for giving me my vocation, my very purpose in life.

A thanks to the gods is meant to work as a thanks to these people, and though it is repaying the debt I owe on the cheap, it still seems to me better than no acknowledgment of the obligation, or thinking I satisfy it by paying it forward with no specific dedication of a payment via memory or thankfulness.

That shake of the head for having lucked out, that feeling of extending some kind of thankfulness out somewhere into the universe, has partly a defensive motive too. As I mentioned earlier, and this qualifies as a recurring theme in this book: it is about not presuming on your luck. This kind of generalized thankfulness for all the favors, intended or unintended, all the unpaid debts that you are ratifying as owed, means you are not taking your luck for granted. Nothing is guaranteed to kill luck faster than that. Good luck is scarce, especially your own allotment of it; best to use any trick you can to economize on it. Those blessed with good luck generally are blessed with an instinct for knowing when not to press their luck. Not pressing it and thankfulness are strategies to keep the gods from going over to the enemy. Not pressing your luck is also another way of indicating the sincerity of prior occasions of thankfulness; it is a sign of knowing you have had it, if not good, then surely better than you ever expected or deserved.

Thankfulness, its precise experience, might vary with what you are thankful for. Is feeling thankful that the mortar shell that fell ten feet away turned out to be a dud the same feeling as having lucked into a well-paying job teaching Icelandic sagas? They might be closer than you think. Relief figures in both of them, though more in one case than the other. Thankfulness for your job assumes a very low baseline of what you expected a job to be, that expectation formed when you were a stock boy in the auto parts section of Shopko back in high school. Each of them, the dud or teaching sagas, involves a sense of fortunate escape. Thankfulness for benefits received is partly constituted by a sense of the harms averted, a there-but-for-the-grace-of-God recognition. Any cause for thankfulness, any cause for joy, with just a tweak and a little imagination, can be accompanied with a sigh of relief.

Once we add the gods to the experience of thankfulness, thankfulness gravitates toward conventional gratitude. Gratitude, in the distinction I am drawing, requires it be displayed to a specific person for favors rendered, or equally, for disfavors withheld. Thankfulness is more diffuse and generalized, spraying out in all directions.[5] Thankfulness leaves us wondering to whom and how it should be performed. With gratitude we know. The obligatoriness of a response is clear, felt as a burden, and not infrequently resented.[6] Ask Lear who, knowing this (which was why he asked for it), still asked for it and in one sense got what he asked for, which means he got *more* than he asked for. Like any ritualized obligation, displays of gratitude can be overplayed or underplayed, raising a suspicion that the recipient is being mocked. As in the humiliation rituals discussed earlier—displays of gratitude are a subset of humiliation rituals—one is not to inspect too closely the sincerity of the sentiment expressed or the true sentiments it is hiding.

There is a boisterous hymn Jews sing at Passover called "Dayenu," the word meaning "that would have been enough for us." It goes on for fifteen stanzas with a long refrain to each stanza. The refrain is actually only one word, *dayenu,* sung about ten times, but with the first syllable repeated many more times before letting the full word follow. Each stanza expresses gratitude for a specific thing God did for us which, if he had only done that one particular thing, would have been dayenu, more than enough. But that is manifestly false. No one believes that any but one or two of these fifteen divine gifts would have been sufficient. One preposterous example: "If he had split the Red Sea for us and not brought us through it to dry land, it would have been enough." Another is overtly sacrilegious: "If he had given us manna to eat and not given us the Sabbath, that would have been enough," for in Judaism Shabbat is deified, a female divinity on a par with the Virgin in Catholicism. Shabbat is not to be compared with gratitude for manna. Inevitably, someone at the table observes that dayenu is really said about the prayer itself. Enough already. Many families skip more than two-thirds of the verses to speed things along in order to get to the actual manna, the sumptuous dinner, for which the assembled will be truly thankful, having waited so long to get it.

Because displays of gratitude are obligatory and because it is easy to give a passable performance no matter what your internal sentiments—thus Goneril and Regan—gratitude, like remorse, is rightly suspected of being faked as often as not. As I have written elsewhere, we teach our children how to display remorse by ordering them to say "I'm sorry" *like you mean it.*[7] Gratitude too is taught by parents ordering it to be performed: "Did you say 'thank you'? Now say 'thank you.'" And thank-you notes? They are a burden to write. No one expects them to be sincere, but people do expect to receive them when they are deemed proper. Yet consider the genius of the following thank-you note, which subtly interweaves two genres: complaint and thank-you note. The combination achieves the impossible: a *sincere* thank-you note that sells perfectly its own sincerity. My youngest child, Hank, received this when he was eight from Ben, to whose birthday party he had been invited. On the front of the thank-you card is a cartoon cat, beneath which is printed, "Thanks, it was purrr-fect!" Turn to the inside and we find printed in pencil, in a style a paleographer would call the "unstudied erratic hand of an eight-year old":

> To Hank,
> Thanks
> for Dragon Rider!
> I exchanged
> it for
> some goosebumps
> books.
> I will
> enjoy them.
> > Ben

> To Hank,
> Thanks
> for Dragon Rider,
> I exchanged
> it for
> some goosebumps
> books,
> I will
> enjoy them.
>
> Ben

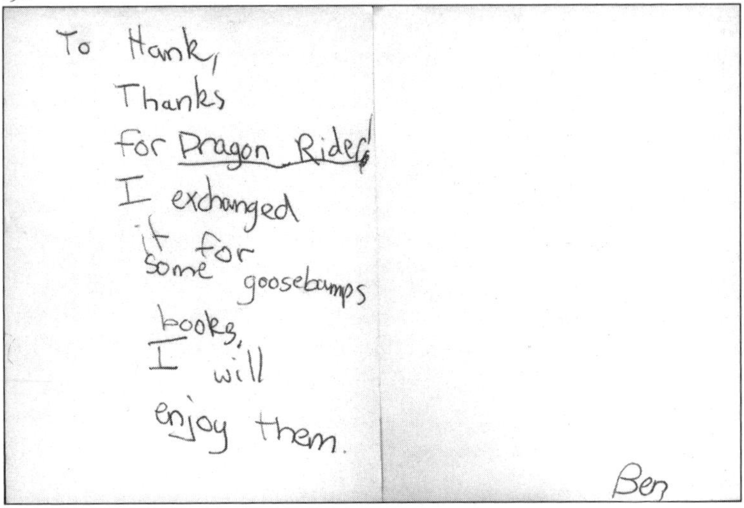

Figure 3: Thank-you note from eight-year-old, Ann Arbor, A.D. 2003.
Credit: William Ian Miller.

If displays of gratitude are often of suspect sincerity, thankfulness, in contrast, achieves sincerity with less effort, coming unbidden
as it often does, and is quite adequately and sufficiently experienced
privately. Thus the thankfulness expressed in the whews and phews
of narrow escapes, thus too the generalized sense of thankfulness
owed to the shades I can never repay with whom I started this
chapter. Only when thankfulness is demanded in formally ritualized prayers is it at risk of losing its heartfeltness.

My occasions for reflection tend to take place under two circumstances, one good, one bad, and both nighttime activities. One has
me somewhat under the influence before finally turning out the
light and conceding that I can no longer postpone the labor of
falling asleep. Reflections prompted by drink tend to be sanguine,
forgiving, wistful, bemused, bittersweet, generous, and loving.

These contrast in all respects with the 3 A.M. horrors, those in-
somniacal panics that seldom involve assessments of the deep past.
They focus on the recent past: that day's humiliations suffered

or offenses given, yesterday's unignorable instances of knowledge once had, now lost. And they focus on the immediate future: how am I going to get through the next day on no sleep, let alone deal with that class that is being ruined by one student whom everyone else hates and I do too? Can I avenge myself on him or get his fellow classmates to do it for me? I've got to take him aside. What will I say to him? What if he shoots me? At that moment I am consumed with self-loathing for such constitutional cowardice, but think nonetheless I had better take a look at Cabela's gun catalogue when the sun rises. With a soul like mine, I would have fared poorly in a saga, even more poorly in modern battle—either going mad for lack of sleep or getting shot for running away.

Says Odin, filling me with shame:

A stupid man stays awake all night
Pondering his problems;
He's worn out when the morning comes
And whatever was, still is.[8]

Odin mocks me, but he doesn't have it quite right for someone my age: "whatever was, still is" would be an improvement on my condition, for that would fix my brain at its present volume. Another day older, the smaller it gets.

CHAPTER 15.

Little Things;
or, What If?

Losing it, except when it is the result of an accident or a stroke, is a long, drawn-out slide. The losing it that is my main theme takes place in an analogue world. But the stories we like to tell are of those digital moments within the larger analogue domain, instances where the littlest thing had enormous consequences. We speak of near misses and close calls, both of which implicate an emotion I shall call the "sense of whatifness." Regret and relief are very much part of this terrain: regret for missing opportunities or for taking up ones that turned out to be mistakes, and relief, as when anticipated bad things do not happen or present discomfort and pain finally come to an end.[1]

Whatifness is frequently experienced aesthetically, it being commonly elicited in genres like tragedy, horror, detective, and action-adventure, whereas regret is elicited in these genres only when you wish you hadn't wasted your time watching the performance. Whatifness can consume us when studying political and military history. What if Pompey had been more patient and starved out Caesar at Pharsalus, as he knew he should have, instead of letting himself be pressured into battle against his better judgment by various senators? What if Joshua Lawrence Chamberlain had not held Little Round Top? What if, as Pascal wondered, Cleopatra's nose had been shorter? The entire story of Hitler's rise to power is told to prompt this sentiment, one digital on/off point after another going his way.

Digitalization means the greatest consequences hinge on the littlest of things. And depending on the point of view one may thank the dumbest luck or curse the perversest malevolent Design, "if design govern in a thing so small." I enlist James McDonough, a Vietnam vet, to capture the inscrutability of it all:

> A man in combat is exposed a thousand times. A gust of wind blows at the right moment to take the mortar round ten yards farther to explode harmlessly behind you. A tree grows for fifty years only to absorb the grenade fragment that would otherwise have entered your heart. A blade of grass, a bent branch, or an article of equipment deflects a speeding bullet enough to send it harmlessly through your flopping shirt or boneless flesh—or savagely through your brain or liver. And as you move mindlessly through the replacement system, the whim of an unseen clerk sends you to a unit in a quiet sector—or to a unit that will take its men like lambs to the slaughter.[2]

The feeling is of the presence of the uncanny: a micron, a hundredth of a second, a second of a degree, either 1 or 0, on or off, honored or disgraced, dead or alive.

NEAR MISSES AND CLOSE CALLS

The near miss and its mirror image, the close call, are intimately contingent. The slightest change in circumstance, in barometric pressure, in the distraction of a gnat, in how lucky you feel, can turn a certain hit into a near miss or into a plain old screwup. Near misses and close calls are themselves the contingencies in plots that make tragedies tragic, comedies comic, farces farcical, and history historical. The sense of what if, in others words, need not be any more an occasion for lament than one for guffaws.

Something like a near miss can play out over an extended period of time in endless reiterations, but it soon loses the experienced quality of a near miss. Such is the torment of Tantalus, who almost gets to the water, almost to the fruit, but it forever stays just beyond his grasp. Rather soon Tantalus would despair and stop trying or decide the grapes were sour. He would no longer find them tantalizing, unless part of the punishment were that he would have no memory of having failed on previous attempts. Give him a fully functioning memory and after less than an hour Tantalus would no longer think that if he had only moved a hair faster he would have snagged the plum, though he surely might come to regret—and thus experience a sense of whatifness—having cut up, roasted, and served up little Pelops, his son. That was a fault known to be characteristic of his lineage, and it seems of our present generation too.

In one form of near miss, you actually experience all the elation of having hit the mark. You in fact gain the object but fail to meet the conditions attached to retaining it. It is the Orpheus problem, whose sense of whatifness had to be excruciating, more so than Tantalus's. To feel the woe in its most tormenting way, the possession of the object must be of relatively short duration, not a length sufficient for the excitement of gaining it to have dissipated. If Orpheus's pain leaves you unmoved, then recall the emotional whiplash you sustain when your team scores an improbable go-ahead touchdown with ten seconds remaining, only to have the other side more improbably return the kickoff for the win.

A weak form of the feeling of the near miss becomes ever more frequent at the outset of losing it, at the onset of your old age. It is captured by a sensation of the "not-quite-rightness" of your diction. These neologisms for which I feel quotation marks are necessary are evidence of it. The words I am using to compose this paragraph are not quite as apt as I think they would have been had

I written it fifteen years earlier. You believe that precisely selected words once immediately did your bidding, but now are neither at your fingertips nor on the tip of your tongue. You have even used Word's thesaurus function, something you never had done in your life until a year or two ago, to see how to vary elegantly words like "matter" and "involve."

The lost words have not, though, been thrust altogether out of mind. When you hear them or read them you recognize them instantaneously and lament they were not there at your beck. It is the thingamajig- or whatchyamacallitization of your vocabulary. So despite the increasing tendency to drone on that accompanies old age, your droning will be done with sentences that are syntactically and lexically simpler than those you spoke when younger.[3]

The near miss and close call often exist in an equilibrium. Take a predator and his would-be prey. The prey, oblivious to the presence of danger, blithely approaches the point where the predator lurks, but one step from disaster he remembers he forgot to get stamps and turns on his heel and walks in the opposite direction. This is the standard suspenseful scene of horror film or of a nature documentary. We say he had a close call or we speak of a narrow escape. What was a close call to him, however, was to the disappointed predator a near miss.

The close call is usually understood to be a lucky escape from harm, the near miss an unlucky failure to attain a desired goal. The shot that rims out of the basket at the buzzer when trailing by a point is a near miss to the loser, a close call to the victor. The near miss is getting five of the six digits in Lotto; the close call is standing in the right place in line for the selections in a death camp. Close calls are the near misses of negative lotteries. We are not perfectly consistent in our usage; thus a reporter or air traffic controller can refer to two jetliners passing within a hundred feet of each other as a near miss, but to the passengers inside it was a close call. Nevertheless, the rough distinction survives as long as we do not ask it to bear too much weight.

Can near misses even take place in your sixties in the way you let yourself believe they did when you were younger? Can you get close enough to miss in that way anymore? Not if it means losing a four-hundred-meter race by a lean of the body, not if it means making a career decision, or most anything else that would matter in your biography. Your misses now are not near, for you now no longer get close when you miss. You are no longer in any games in which you are aiming to hit something, unless you golf, which mercifully I don't. If one would think himself the luckiest of mortals to make it to age eighty-five in good health with enough brain surviving to enjoy a good novel, and then die in his sleep, it would hardly qualify as a near miss if that person made it to eighty-four before falling down the stairs, lingering on for six weeks demented, and then dying.

Old age, though, does leave plenty of room for close calls. Think how common it is for an oldster almost to die or almost to kill others, as when you run the stop sign because you did not see it and narrowly miss the mother with a minivan full of kids. The old driver surviving the collision would rightly speak of his close call and so would the mother. Close calls all around in that case. Or consider the virtual close call frequently experienced by the youngish old person, with a mildly hypochondriacal cast to his soul, who thinks he might be having a heart attack because he has a modest pain in his chest while exercising or because he has gas or acid reflux. This gas attack is not in fact a close call—we are not on the western front in 1915—but, despite the ridiculousness of the anxiety, it still is experienced as a close call, with all the attendant feelings of relief when you find it was only gas. The difference is that in this virtual close call you have to feel cowardly and a fool for not having had the fortune to have suffered a face-saving heart attack. Real close calls are dates with Death in which Death decides at the last minute to stand you up or, to shift metaphors, to remove the hook from your mouth and toss you back in.

The misery of a near miss is much more potent and is subject to a much slower decay rate than are the corresponding joys of the close call, if they can be called joys. The relief that comes with the realization we just had a close call is a mixed experience. The euphoria and uplift do not last long. Once the feeling of having been lucky wears off, we start to question why we were singled out for such near disaster. It begins to have the look of a cruel joke too, as when the doctor tells you that you have terminal cancer but then calls a day later to say he was in error, that it was someone else's test. You whoop with joy.

The high does not last for long; the rebound effect of having false bad news revealed as false wears off quickly. You might soon spare a thought for that person who may have gotten your test results by mistake and who is now getting his make-up call, though not all close calls of this sort are zero-sum. There need be no one else who got false good news. The error may have been confined to your erroneous report.

A halfhearted consolation can even be had when the close call is not completely averted but only bruises you. The solace of "It could have been worse" is what we settle for. This, however, is convincing only when we can still experience relief, and this "It could have been worse" is not of the sort that made a life for itself in the death camps or was foisted on Lear's "basest beggar," who can always be deemed to have something more to lose to make his situation worse.

The pleasure that relief affords is contingent on what we take the neutral position to be. If pain or banging your head against the wall is the benchmark, then its mere cessation is pleasure, perhaps none truer. Relief, in other words, is not a simple joy; its experience demands either actual prior pain and wretchedness or probable misery just narrowly escaped. In this fallen world, relief may be rather nine points of pleasure's law.

Folk wisdom always understood that a good portion of the pleasure of sex was a species of relief. Old age, just like sex, offers a cornucopia of opportunities for the ambivalent pleasure relief offers. Today you get the joy of not having your arthritis hurt as much as yesterday; you get out of bed and experience the pleasure of not having thrown your back out while sleeping. You didn't lose your keys as you feared; they were where you left them, but you forgot where that was until happenstance brought you to the very place.

I have been assuming so far that the person who experiences the miseries of the near miss (or the relief of the close call) must be conscious not only of the miss but of its nearness at the time of the event. Suppose, however, that the consciousness of the nearness of the miss, or whether there was a miss at all, only comes years later. To the array of emotions I mentioned earlier that properly attend the near miss we might have to add wistfulness or bittersweetness or even, yet again, relief. Take the case of the person who attends a fortieth high school reunion and is told by the former class beauty (visualize the popular hunk if you prefer) that she had had a crush on him and always regretted that he had never asked her out. Back then the boy intensely desired to do so but could never muster the nerve for fear of rejection. What at sixteen was a nonevent is now revealed to have been a near miss. He just found out that two ships had passed in the night, a metaphor claiming its own special nook in the near miss/close call domain. The miss was near because only one little thing impeded its fulfillment, whether it was for her to have been more obvious or for him to have possessed a mite more courage. Is there any pleasure in finding out about an opportunity lost forty years earlier? But is there any pleasure to be reexperienced had you cashed in earlier? Or just a greater sense of loss, or perhaps, if lucky, a small basking in the pitiable glory of back slaps from the other old crippled guys who envy you? But then too, only if the beauty aged well.

RELEGATION

After a certain time, we all head downward, but the transition states are awkward, like revisiting the inverted metamorphosis of puberty in which a young butterfly enters a cocoon and emerges a caterpillar with hair in unsightly places. The process seems analogue, but there are moments and metaphors that digitalize it, making the change one that happened overnight, or in an *Augenblick,* the blink of an eye. Such is the moment when you are understood to have emerged from the cocoon. At some point on the downhill slope you cross a magical line that reclassifies you, and does not so much remake you as unmake you.

Here is an example of a certain kind of abrupt transition that can happen at any age past puberty, but is near certain to happen as part of the process of aging. It depends less on some objective defect (though there may well be one) than on an observer's smallness of spirit, a smallness that plagues most all of us, a few saints excepted, unless true love or utter indifference intervenes to prevent it. Have you ever noticed how one fleeting expression can mar a face forever, so that it can never recapture its prior attractiveness? Nice-looking people can have their status redefined by a laugh, a stumble, a look of fear or pleasure, a momentary grotesque contortion. Sometimes we seem to study faces with a will to find such marring moments.

You might blame your own lack of charity. You tax yourself for being shallow and intolerant, for having a flawed soul. Yet, there it is. There is no remedy. That other person has been forever redefined downward in your mind. You tell yourself that for a transient uglifying look to work such damage it must have revealed a deeper character flaw that was obscured either by artifice or, more likely, by your own shallow willingness to excuse moral defects if they happen to come in a good-looking or entertaining package. That disfiguring moment, you now feel, crystallizes the essence of that person's soul: you just uncovered his hideous portrait in the attic.

Little things are killers. They are of a sort with near misses, where everything hinges on a millimicron. But once missed, the miss seems to have been by a mile. You can see how this connects with aging and with the onset of losing it. You yourself become a near miss, a new immigrant to an allegorical empire of Almost. It starts with ever-so-slight, barely noticeable shifts of shape and retexturings of skin. And because they are *barely* noticeable, they are rather more intrusive for that fact, like the faint whine of a mosquito you can hear from the other side of the room as you try to fall asleep. Add to these small physical changes your failure to negotiate cultural nuances that are specifically age dependent. You think you just made a perfectly apt and hip reference to a rock-n-roll song or a movie, but the students just look blankly at you or are embarrassed for you.

Lost in our own self-centeredness, we shelter ourselves from the knowledge that our own gestures, tics, momentary grotesque expressions, repel others no less strongly than theirs do us. But when we add to this the effects of aging so that one risks being seen as inappropriately maintaining a personality or a style that no longer fits with what one looks like, one can opt for staying locked in one's study, writing books, and avoiding the world. We have been relegated, in the sense that that term bears in the European football leagues. Unlike those clubs and their supporters, who know they have been relegated and are shamed by it, our blindness to our own failings lets us pretend we are still playing in the same league we were last year.

Better figure out how to act your age. Acting your age gets harder to get a fix on, especially because it means abandoning the way you have presented yourself to the world for three or four decades. Anxieties about the cut of your personality start invading your consciousness; you fear you may be dismissed as something of a joke. This is not the broad comedy of the twenty-year lag that I discussed in the shop-window epiphany, where the differences are measured in geological ages and intergalactic distances. This dark comedy is about microgradations. At age twenty-five, I would be mystified by the clueless vanity or obliviousness of forty-year-old men who jogged with their shirts off or in a pickup basketball game would play on the skins team and not insist on a trade to the shirts. These were men who were proud of the good shape they were in, and they were in good shape, but they were forty and something about the fit of their skin to the muscle underneath it was not quite right. The price is a serious tax assessed against one's dignity or what has become, sadly, a pretense of dignity.

Yet there is a bright side. If old age is especially hard for that small group of the once attractive to come to terms with, it does great favors for the much larger group of humanity that is plain or ugly. Once deemed plain, we are now merely deemed old, with an occasional rare person who manages finally to grow into his features (this time "his" is not gender neutral) only when he is over the hill. Old age finally frees us from having to account for our lack of attractiveness, from paying any special price for it beyond what any other oldster must pay.

It has always been recognized by moralists that death is democratizing, maggots making no distinction between princes and paupers; so is old age. Imagine, too, the delight that formerly unattractive people experience at seeing that the nice-looking people who treated them with contempt are now not differentiable from themselves in the eyes of the young. Add this special treat to the loss of cognitive abilities and we may have finally stumbled on a compelling reason why old people, the greater proportion of whom were not attractive and only half of whom were in the upper half of their class when younger, might do well on those well-being questionnaires.

CHAPTER 16.

Defying Augury

Though I must have thought about it before, my first memory of facing up to mortality is of sleeping over at a friend's when I was six or so. He said a prayer before going to bed—"Now I lay me down to sleep"—ending with the couplet "If I should die before I wake / I pray the Lord my soul to take." What was a little Jew to make of this? And since Jesus did not appear in it, I could not dismiss it out of hand; it concerned me too. Nowadays, overprotective parents would condemn the prayer as child abuse, and sure enough it has been bowdlerized to accord with more modern sentiments, sentiments justified, in this instance, by our significantly friendlier child mortality rates than those that obtained when the prayer was composed.[1] I doubt Tommy was thinking as hard about what he was saying by rote as I was. He was facing death with no more thought than he said the Pledge of Allegiance to begin the school day. I did not sleep well that night. What if I should die before I waked? And what if the Lord removed my soul, which I had always confused with the spleen, and which if death came I distinctly preferred having interred with me?

That simple prayer reasserts itself with force in the conversation of people once they reach their sixties. How many times in the last year have you heard people opine that the best way to go would be in their sleep? The emphases of the childhood prayer have been altered to accord with present circumstances, but the same prayer it is, modified for late adult use: "If I should die, let it be before I wake, and if I have to pay over my soul to get this wish, then if you want it, Lord, take it; I don't care. Just make sure that when I die it's before I wake."

In the sagas even middling, unheroic types face their deaths with nonwhimpering resignation and eyes wide open. I hope to follow their example, and in a fit of positive thinking I have managed to convince myself I am not afraid to die. Still, I cannot help but worry about the means of transport I will be taking to the realm of the dead. Will it be by a stroke that does not initially kill me but lets me waste away without the ability to speak? A heart attack on the cross-country ski machine in the basement, where I might rot before a family member will think to check? Will I decay by degrees, enduring years of dementia, befouling myself while staring vacantly ahead and feeling no shame? Such an end would cancel out a lifetime of achievements, such as they are, and when you finally go, people will euphemistically say, "It was a blessing, really," when they mean, "It's about time; who would have thought he could have lasted so many years in that condition; nothing left for the family either."

If I have countenanced more magical thinking in this book than is seemly for a reasonably educated person to indulge, I must add that I find myself, like many an ancient, checking for omens, reading the portents. The omens and the portents, however, are not to be found in the sky. Comets, eclipses, or the flights of birds mean nothing. I do not cast a die, and if I knew what *urim* and *thummim* looked like, I would not consult them either. Entrails? The livers and kidneys, the hearts and spleens of sheep, goats, and chickens are mute. Not so, however, my own entrails. These I consult regularly. They burst forth with significant omens and portents, if only I could read them correctly, for study them I do. Each new pain, each untoward change in what used to be the unattended baseline of what it meant to feel embodied, carries ominous purport. Call it hypochondria if you want to humiliate me; I call it augury.

READINESS

I have spoken of the sense of whatifness, an emotion that is part of the emotional economy of the near miss and the close call. Tragedy does not require it, but whatifness often figures in tragedy gaining entry by way of omens, portents, oracles, and prophecies. Responses to oracles and omens vary: Oedipus undertakes action so as to avoid their effect; Hamlet defies them. Some, like Macbeth, are lulled into complacency by misinterpreting them. But the dominant convention is to adhere to a course of action in the face of inauspicious omens and ominous portents, thereby torturing us with whatifness. *Hamlet,* unsurprisingly, complicates the convention even as it adheres to it, here regarding the proposed fencing match with Laertes in act V:

> *Horatio:* You will lose, my lord.
> *Hamlet:* I do not think so. Since he went to France, I have been in continual practice. I shall win at the odds. Thou wouldst not think how ill all's here about my heart; but it is no matter.
> *Horatio:* Nay, good my lord.
> *Hamlet:* It is but foolery, but it is such a kind of gaingiving as would perhaps trouble a woman.
> *Horatio:* If your mind dislike anything, obey it. I will forestall their repair hither and say you are not fit.
> *Hamlet:* Not a whit. We defy augury. There is special providence in the fall of a sparrow. If it be now, 'tis not to come; if it be not to come, it will be now; if it be not now, yet it will come. The readiness is all. (5.2.205–18)

If Hamlet did not defy augury, he would be contemptible. So too Caesar and many a saga hero whose time was up. The omen, conventional as it is, fills us with that sense of alternative possibilities, of whatifness. But Shakespeare puts his portent, or hint of a portent, into a discussion of a wager on a fencing match in which odds are offered reflecting the betting line. The odds negotiated by Claudius are counted among the several irresolvable cruxes in *Hamlet.* No one quite knows what to make of them.[2] But "winning at the odds" must contemplate, as it does with the point spread in football and basketball, that you win the wager if your underdog team merely makes a closer game of it than expected. The winner did not cover the point spread, did not, in other words, "win at the odds." Hamlet says he will beat the spread if he is favored, or that Laertes will not cover the spread if he is favored.

The discussion is explicitly about managing chance. Can it be mere chance that Hamlet gets an attack of the heebie-jeebies at this moment? Discussing odds, managing and assessing risk in probabilistic terms, seems correlated with Hamlet's flutter of the heart. Like offering odds, that feeling of "something's up" is a way of readying oneself to deal with future uncertainty. How could betting, odds making, and portents and omens not go hand in hand? Feeling lucky?

Is Hamlet's flutter an omen? No soothsayer holds Hamlet with his skinny hand, no weird sisters prophesy, no sparrow falls, no cloud rains blood, no sacred chickens crow, no hawk kills an eagle. Nor is Hamlet subjected to ominous dreams, nor to a vision of his tutelary spirit in flames or covered in blood, as he might were he in a saga. The omen is Hamlet's own nerves. How naturalized the supernatural has become, in a play with a ghost at its heart, no less. And how human. The sensation Hamlet describes is one all but the coldest among us know well. This is the kind of omen a hypochondriacal old academic gets before playing basketball one last time, or that some people get the night before they must fly somewhere. No wonder Hamlet feels called upon not to heed it. It is just the kind of thing that it would be "womanly" to worry about.

Yet Hamlet is indeed troubled. If he were not, he would have said nothing. The mention of the ill about his heart alarms even the unflappable Horatio. He seems to catch Hamlet's queasiness.

Horatio knows Hamlet is no coward; even Hamlet knows that, despite his self-castigation as one. That Horatio (and Hamlet) are of a sudden finding omens where, to their minds, superstitious fools and cowards find them, means we are in the real presence of unbenign Fate.[3] In many cultures—Greek, Roman, Babylonian, and Israelite, among others—it was hardly womanly to take omens seriously. You went looking for omens when no obliging eagle was visible in the sky. You consulted the Pythia, or various reputable and official diviners who cut up animals to read their kidney and liver lobes. In cultures in which we might consider divination and omen seeking to be almost obsessive, there is no shame in lamenting bad omens, fearing them, or in taking good ones to heart. From the same Babylonian lament of the righteous man quoted earlier:

> Fearful omens beset me.
> I am got out of my house and wander outside.
> The omen organs are confused and inflamed for me every day.
> The omen of the diviner and dream priest does not explain
>   my condition.
> What is said in the street portends ill for me.
> When I lie down at night, my dream is terrifying.[4]

This righteous Babylonian lamenter was meeting the demands of a different literary genre than the one whose demands Hamlet had to meet. Unlike Hamlet, he does not have to be concerned about his reputation for courage.

If Hamlet infects Horatio with his own sense of uneasiness, he infects us with that frustrated sense of not being able to jump in and give our two cents' worth, to warn him of the plot against him, to warn him, that is, of the plot of *Hamlet*. Hamlet, you are in a tragedy, damn it—it bears your name for a reason—don't defy augury!

Once he washed up naked on the Danish shore near the end of act IV, Hamlet, by common understanding, has become reconciled to his fate, finally accepting the lousy lot he has drawn. But fatalism has not wholly captured his soul. Hamlet knows that the will, his will, has a role to play, that it can make a difference and is, in some nontrivial sense, free: you can either be ready for what Fate deals you or not. Readiness is all; and readiness, even in a Fate-governed world, means you are in complete control of your style points and can by force of will quell fear. Your cool is up to you.

Augury, however, is still necessary. Though it must be defied, it gives notice as to when you have to put your readiness into high alert. "Readiness is all" sets an impossible standard if it requires constant vigilance, sleeping with one eye open for a lifetime, because of the remote chance death might catch you at any second. You would end up darting nervously about like a chipmunk that can barely get a bite in to nourish himself before dashing for cover. Though chipmunks can tolerate, it seems, a high false-alarm rate, humans who are that jittery are sorry cases, surely not worthy of tragedy or epic. They might end up mad but not in a way worthy of song. You must budget how often you can go into a readiness-is-all mode. You restrict total readiness to those occasions when something is pretty clearly up or when you have already embarked knowingly on high-risk action. Augury tells you when you have to get ready. Defying its unpropitious prediction is one powerful way of making a commitment.

Why, though, should we believe Hamlet this time? He has a habit of making statements of commitment—The play's the thing . . . Now could I drink hot blood . . . From this time forth my thoughts be bloody—and not following through (2.2, 3.2, 4.4). But this time is different. All these other statements of commitment left him plenty of room to back out. This time he leaves himself considerably less room. This is the first statement of commitment he says to another person, rather than in soliloquy. The costs of breaking a resolution made to yourself with only yourself as witness are considerably lower than those incurred when you let someone else witness your statement. Especially when that someone is Horatio, the person you most respect in the world.

Hamlet makes his defiance of augury a decision point. He acts on his resolve, which thus confirms this point as exactly what he announced it to be: a point of no return, a declaration that this moment qualifies as now-or-never time. He is ready. So often these kinds of decisions, when recognized to be such, are attended by heebie-jeebies, portents of a kind. But as we know only too well, there are so many false positives when it comes to heebie-jeebies. They cry wolf too much. Even true believers in omens know that there are false ones and that true ones still require interpretation. So in our own way we defy them and get on the airplane, continue exercising, or walk into that ominous classroom yet again, taking our entrails to be the false prophets they usually are. And should we be so forthcoming as to give voice to how ill all's here about my heart, and then intone something about the fall of sparrows, we would look rather foolish.

When unheroic types, like most of you and certainly me, claim the present moment is a point of no return, we are often injecting phony drama into our lives or buying into the hype about the importance of which college we choose to go to, our kids got into, which major we or they selected, and that momentous decision of whether to go to law school, grad school, or become a receiver for the Green Bay Packers. There are more than a few false positives regarding the significance of these decision points. Like that moment at the fork in the road when you told yourself to take the road less traveled by, which was all the fashion, that everything pivoted on it, only to find out that the road hooked right back into the main highway after a few orange-and-white striped barrels had been negotiated.

Life-cycle milestones are accompanied with various pieties about their importance, but since nearly every person situated as I am goes through them, in retrospect and even right in the midst of them, they are experienced as little more than marking off a point on a checklist. Learning to ride a bike, check, bar mitzvah, check, driver's license, check, graduation from high school, check, go to college, check, lose virginity (things happened slower in my day), check, get married, check, kids, check, decline, check . . . the dragon comes, check's in the mail.

Though the most trivial of acts or omissions might have enormous consequences for the success, failure, or mostly middling mediocrity of our lives, such little things will not turn our lives or deaths into tragedies of perverse injustice, such as Lear's or those visited on Moses or Saul. Lear wants to be told he is loved by his children so everyone can hear it; Moses strikes a rock twice in a burst of temper; and Saul makes the mistake of not waiting for Samuel, who already was seven days late. Woe to them. For us common mortals no grand text states the cause of why one of us dies of cancer with our wits about us and another demented. Even should there be some little thing on which our fate pivots, it is unlikely we or anyone will know it for what it is or see the irony that constructs the narrative in which it comes to serve as the Irrevocably Inexpiable Deed, our Original Sin. And even should the omens be rather insistent, it is harder to ready oneself as one's brain shrinks and joints ache.

FATE TALK

The sense of what if, surely as we experience it in tragedy, epic, or saga, depends on our paying some kind of homage to the loomings and operation of some uncanny force. Call it Fate, or sweeten it with a promise of ordered benevolence and call it Providence. Or make it primordial law as Doom; or embody it in three women, as Norns, Moirai, Parcae, Fates, or as *Macbeth*'s weird sisters, who take their weirdness from the Old English word for fate: Wyrd.[5] That grand Wyrd of the eighth century metamorphosed into wrinkled hags on a Scottish heath eight hundred years later, finally bottoming out as weird stoners in an American high school. The word *Wyrd* suffered an aging process no kinder than the one we suffer. It achieved, as we will too, puerility in old age.[6]

When Hamlet invokes providence in his defying augury speech— "There is special providence in the fall of a sparrow"—he is engaging in what I call fate talk, the reference to providence rather than fate notwithstanding.[7] In Hamlet's case, fate talk was, as we saw, a way of verbalizing a commitment, publicizing it, and thus emboldening himself. By bringing fate into the picture I am not attempting to claim tragedy, or things like decline-and-falls, for such as the likes of you and me as we lose it. All who grow old decline, but very few people can be said to decline and fall in the manner of empires. To be sure, our declines lead to falls, but not of the sort that befell Pompey or Napoleon. Ours are about breaking a hip or cracking a skull on the bathroom floor.

One small problem: should it be Fate or fate talk? The uppercase elevates Fate to the heavens and makes it like a god. Lowercase fate, however, is often too small to capture the set of ideas being invoked. Keep that in mind and supply an imagined eff residing halfway between that grand Fate, commonly and not quite accurately paraded as *the* force in pagan Germanic epic and Attic tragedy on the one hand, and mere fate on the other. In any event I am not interested in a belief in something like Fate, as if it were the Germanic or Greek god, which it was not, but in how fate talk is mobilized and for what purposes.

Most people who would profess to believing that something like Fate governs human affairs do not think that Fate cannot be tricked, or do not think one could not get a leg up on it by finding out what it held in store. A belief in F/fate, like belief in God, comes in all manner of shapes, in varying levels of intensity, and with competing ideas regarding just how intrusive it, or he, is in the life of any one particular person. Fate, no less than God or the gods, was thought to sleep rather more than eight hours a day, and to play favorites.

Often we find proverbs paying lip service to the power of Fate only to confer half of its muscle on human will. Some proverbs make Fate more an appendage of will than will of Fate, thus allowing human will more areas of competence than the mere style points that Hamlet actively kept in his control when he defied augury. Consider the young Beowulf's fate talk as he describes his heroic seven-day swimming match against another youth, Breca, which Beowulf won despite having been importuned by sea serpents and predatory fish:

> Wyrd [Fate] often saves
> the unfated-to-die man, when his courage avails him.[8]

I could also translate it less literally but no less faithfully as "God helps those who help themselves" or "You make your own luck."

The narrator restates the idea about five hundred lines later, substituting God for Wyrd. Grendel, says the poet, would have killed Beowulf "if radiant God—*and the man's might*—had not prevented that fate."[9] The same proverbial sentiment can be found in classical Latin—*Fortes fortuna aduivat*[10]—which Chaucer translates accurately as "Hap helpeth hardy man alday."[11] In Genesis, notwithstanding the Lord telling her in an oracle that the older of the twins in her womb would serve the younger, Rebecca is not about to sit around passively and wait for the Lord to fulfill the oracle. She plots and implements the deception of her old blind husband and the shafting of her first born; she does all the work (25.23, 27.6–13). Oracles get fulfilled because they are read as warrants to take action to bring about what they prophesy.

Beowulf's formulation abounds in hedges. If Wyrd only "often" saves the unfated-to-die man, then when Wyrd doesn't save him, either his courage wasn't good enough or Wyrd wasn't much interested in his welfare. Not only are courage and fighting ability doing most of the work, but Wyrd seems to be sharing some inputs with another extranatural source. Thus the word *unfæge,* or unfated-to-die, one of many words that generates a good story. *Fæge,* meaning "fated to die" in Old English, survives in Modern English as *fey,* meaning fairylike or affected. Like the word Wyrd, fey suffered a considerable fall from former glory in its sense development. And by sheer accident of sound changes over the course of centuries, fey also became a homophone with a totally different word of Romance origin, Modern English *fay,* as in fairy-fay, which comes from Latin *fatum,* pl. *fata,* Latin for fate, the Fates. Both words, by purest chance, not only sound the same but their senses both partake of fate, death, and the fairy world. *Fæge* (fey), in Old English and still in modern German *feige,* also indicated unmanliness or cowardice: the link between cowardice and being marked for death was obvious to them if not always to us.[12] Add up the hedges: "Wyrd sometimes helps save a man, and then only if he is already marked as *unfæge,* as unfated-to-die, and further, only if he is one tough mother who shows no fear."

Fate talk in such proverbs, like much fate talk in other contexts,

is a way of hedging bets. Fate talk is employed to deny responsibility, to make excuses, to buy respite from blame or to shift it. Fate
talk is also put to the service of both false and sincere modesty.
When Beowulf gestures to Wyrd helping him in his battles with
sea monsters, he is in the middle of a conventional heroic boast.
These boast speeches are often performed as part of quasi-formal
contests, much in the manner of African American rapping or
the dozens. They pit two men in a brag-off, usually assisted by
considerable amounts of alcohol.[13] Yet even in these over-the-top
immodest assertions of one's own greatness, false modesty has a
part. When Beowulf pays deference to Wyrd, he is not conceding
much, but he is offering up something to placate the envy he is
provoking among those in the mead hall. False modesty's falseness
does not prevent it from gaining the reprieve it seeks from the murderous hatred envy can prompt. It is precisely the falseness of false
modesty that shows you are going out of your way to recognize
that your triumphs might be hard for others to take.[14]

Fate talk also figures prominently in the diction of complaint.
People bemoan their fate. When we invoke Fate in response to hearing of someone else's misfortune, fate talk works as a way of saying:
"Stop complaining already. It was just meant to be." Or, depending
on the tone, it can work as a rote statement of commiseration and
consolation, as in "Ah, gee, what terrible luck."

Much fate talk is a way to make complaint decorous by substituting for the tone of a niggling whine a howl of grand railing.
Some perverse solace can be found in supposing that the gods
aren't totally ignoring you. Their singling you out for pain and
harm proves you are worthy of their attention. Fate or the gods
usually do not have much interest in common people. Even in
doom-oppressed tragedy and epic, only the hero, perhaps a city,
and maybe one or two others elicit the interest of Fate. Everyone
else just goes about his business. The average person is only fated
in the sense that we all are: we are constrained by the demands of
nature to eat, sleep, excrete, ache, perhaps fornicate, and die. Most
of us are excused from Fate's operation. We—me and most of
you—are not worthy of it. It is immodest to claim that any aspect

of such lives as ours are fated. Fate ignores, in fact, whole peoples it deems of no consequence. With a bit of imagination, one can find in Calvinism's predestining pretty near everyone to damnation (and a few to election) an inspired egalitarian move. It showed that God, at least at one moment in time, took an interest in you.

By invoking fate, one pays it homage, thereby hoping to placate it, bribe it, flatter it into letting you off the hook this one time. What we might call fate cultures make fate talk obligatory, especially before actions in which the stakes are high. It may seem paradoxical to us, though hardly to them, but fate talk was how Hamlet, Beowulf, and other heroic types ended up talking about human will and its freedom and claiming no small amount of it for themselves; a culture of honor could hardly have it any other way. Acting grandly and honorably was up to you, assuming, that is, that you had been born into the class of people who were allowed to count in the first place. That department was ruled by Fate's rowdy cousin, Chance.

CHAPTER 17.

Frankly, I Do
Give a Damn

We understand "I don't give a damn," "I don't give a shit," or "I don't give a flying fuck" to be roughly synonymous except for the greater emphasis wrought by increasing vulgarity. A damn invokes matters of high value, your own soul, perhaps, and tossing it not to the winds but to hell, as if it were of no value. Shit, in contrast, invokes something of no value from the get-go, and is manifestly of this world. And a flying fuck has much less to do with fornication than with alliterative emphasis. It is flying that does the work, not fuck. It might be that rat's ass beats out flying fuck in intensity, where interestingly, instead of alliteration, it is assonance that is doing the poetic work (though I had no such intention, I am unwilling to forgo the way assonance assonates with rat's ass). All these expressions function as quasi-interjections, exclamations of which the literal content is beside the point, the point being that for the moment you see no point in further discussion. As far as you are concerned, you are declaring a matter settled, either because you have reached utter indifference, caring only to get your interlocutor to shut up (and if you are averse to swearing or do not wish to waste real invective because the stakes are just too trivial, it is a hoot you might not give) or because, quite the contrary, you are anything but indifferent and have just vehemently declared yourself committed to a course of action.

Declaring you do not give a damn can thus be a statement of bravado, a way of declaring augury defied, a way of steeling yourself to meet danger or death grandly because duty or honor demands it. In those settings a damn is surely given, as both Hamlet and Beowulf demonstrate, for they are consumed with a sense of duty, with the quality of their courage, and with their reputation for it. They care.[1]

The world of honor and grand action, as closely annexed to the tragic as it often was, gave a damn, excessively at times. Honor seemed to be always at stake. And whenever danger loomed, or life was coming to a natural end, the point was to be remembered for grand deeds, for dying well, as well as for living courageously. Nor did you get to grade yourself; that was up to the judgment of others often jealous, who were not inclined to inflate your grades. Again heed Odin:

> Cattle die, kinsmen die,
> > One day you die yourself;
> But the words of praise will not perish
> > When a man wins fair fame.[2]

But there is a hitch. Norse wisdom and the Viking sensibility are normally not so optimistic. Who says words of praise will not perish? Most have and most will. More grand deeds by more unnamed people go unrecorded than those that have been memorialized. Heroic literature evinces considerable anxiety on this score.[3] An enterprising man of heroic designs would patronize poets to make sure his tale got told; he might compose his own glories in peerless poetry, like David or Egil, or in crisp prose, like Caesar. An ancient hero really had to beat very long odds to have his deeds make it to college classes or the movies. You also stood a much better chance of being remembered if you were Roman or Greek than if you were a Balt, Pict, Maori, or Mohawk and, especially, if noble rather than common. Beowulf himself nearly didn't make it. His story survives in only one early eleventh-century manuscript and that manuscript barely survived a fire in 1731, before anyone had made a copy. By the time it was copied in the later eighteenth century, letters and whole words had flaked off the edges of the charred vellum. That qualifies in all respects as a close call for one of the grandest productions of human poetry, the manuscript nearly dying as Beowulf did, battling a fire-breathing wyrm.[4]

Heroes wanted their deeds attributed to their names; it would not have been enough that the deed be remembered but the doer be simply referred to as "a private soldier" or "a warrior" or the "one Norwegian" who single-handedly held the bridge at the battle of Stamford Bridge in 1066 so that the remnants of the defeated Norwegian force could escape. His deeds too came within one leaf of calfskin from oblivion, for they are preserved in only one of the seven major surviving manuscripts of the Anglo-Saxon Chronicle.[5]

The chances of deeds being remembered ultimately depended on their being written down, so forget about most all preliterate peoples' grand deeds, unless they managed to have been kept alive in oral tales until they got written down. Nor did getting written guarantee anything. Remembrance depended on writing on a surface that endured, like stone, or, if on parchment or papyrus, then on being copied, and then on the copies surviving mold, bookworms, invasions, fires, religious fervor, peasant uprisings, political censorship, pious revisions, and indifference. If the writing made it through this grim triage, there was no guarantee that anyone would or could read it, unless by chance a Rosetta stone had been carved, and if carved, then discovered.

At any rate, to get read today, a random eleventh-century manuscript probably has to beat odds no longer than a new academic book written on that manuscript has to beat. When there were few books or scrolls, each was more likely to get read in its own day than a book is now (even adjusting for the increase in population and literacy), when thousands of new titles appear every month, and hundreds of thousands of old ones become available every couple of years on the Internet, and books must compete with a multitude of other means of escape from having to be too much alone with our own thoughts. The language you are writing in is still spoken too, and half the world is fluent in that language, and still you lose. The field is too full. Infinite amounts of writing lead to the same dead end as no writing. Superabundance and rarity, each in its own way, end at the edge of oblivion.

The dim prospect of remembrance is what wisdom literature finds perhaps the unkindest cut of all, for what's the point of glory or deeds worthy of praise if there is no remembrance of grand deeds or of great writing (Eccles. 2.16). And yet everyone, from a small-town mayor to a big CEO to a blow-dried-haired senator to a moronic celebrity to a naive professor publishing his first or last book fantasizes he has made it into the Book of Remembrance.

Vanity. No one captures better the absurd anxiety of being remembered for "making it" than a twelfth-century chronicler named Henry of Huntingdon, an archdeacon, whose twist on the commonplaces about the evanescence of fame and glory deserves to be read and remembered by more than the few medievalists who know of it. For those few others who by chance have read this far, I pass on Henry's words:

> This is the year which holds the writer. The 35th year of the reign of the glorious and invincible Henry, king of the English [Henry I, 1100–1135]. The 69th year from the arrival in England, in our own time, of the supreme Norman race. The 703rd year from the coming of the English into England. The 2,265th year from the coming of the Britons to settle in the same island. The 5,317th year from the beginning of the world. The year of grace 1135.
>
> This, then, is the year from which the writer of the *History* wished his age to be reckoned by posterity. . . . Already one millennium has passed since the Lord's incarnation. We are leading our lives, or—to put it more accurately—we are

holding back death, in what is the 135th year of the second millennium.

Let us, however, think about what has become of those who lived in the first millennium around this time, around the 135th year. In those days, of course, Antoninus ruled Rome with his brother Lucius Aurelius, and Pius the Roman was pope. Lucius, who was of British birth, ruled this island, and not long after this time, while these emperors were still in power, he was the first of the British to become a Christian, and through him the whole of Britain was converted to faith in Christ. For this he is worthy of eternal record.

But who were the other people who lived throughout the countries of the world at that time? Let our present kings and dukes, tyrants and princes, church leaders and earls, commanders and governors, magistrates and sheriffs, warlike and strong men—let them tell me: who were in command and held office at that time? And you, admirable Bishop Alexander, to whom I have dedicated our history, tell me what you know of the bishops of that time.

I ask myself: tell me, Henry, author of this *History,* tell me, who were the archdeacons of that time? What does it matter whether they were individually noble or ignoble, renowned or unknown, praiseworthy or disreputable, exalted or cast down, wise or foolish? If any of them undertook some labor for the sake of praise and glory, when now no record of him survives any more than of his horse or his ass, why then did the wretch torment his spirit in vain? What benefit was it to them, who came to this?

Now I speak to you who will be living in the third millennium, around the 135th year. Consider us, who at this moment seem to be renowned, because miserable creatures, we think highly of ourselves. Reflect, I say, on what has become of us.[6]

But for the lack of twenty-four years, Henry is pointedly addressing you and me. And he nails it. How many have heard of Henry of

Huntingdon, the author of a chronicle—*Historia Anglorum*—especially important for the reigns of Henry I and Stephen of England? Henry, the author, would probably enjoy the irony of being mildly refuted by the fact that nearly a thousand years later he is still being read; he even found himself assigned in a class one of my daughters took in college. This passage knocked her off her feet. He might also be surprised to learn that the Briton king Lucius who "was the first of the British to become a Christian, and through him the whole of Britain was converted to faith in Christ" and who "for this . . . is worthy of eternal record" is purely legendary. He never lived; his eternal record is a lie, not that that makes much difference, for here we are mentioning him.

Other ironies are consciously intended by Henry, and they are subtle. The exacting care with which he situates himself in time by throwing various numbers of years at the reader exposes the vanity of thinking your time is a special time. He hints too, almost blasphemously, that there will be no Second Coming. He anticipates, with the year 1000 having come and gone with no appearance, the same for the year 2000. The number of years will just keep mounting, swamping the events of previous years in more and more clutter, and will continue to do so.

And he taunts those men of ambition with an academic's revenge: you men of power depend on us nerdy scholars, or there will be no remembrance of you, and even should we write about you, you guys are not studious enough to inform yourself about what we write. Can you name the person who occupied your position before you? How far back? Henry is doing a variation on Ecclesiastes' terser "There is no remembrance of former things; neither shall there be any remembrance of things that are to come with those that shall come after" (1.11)—but he makes it new under the sun. And he gave enough of a damn to write it down so that just maybe some people would take heed of it, and perhaps praise its author, whose name he makes sure is part of the text, so that if read, he is not lumped in with that grand writer Anonymous, author of some of the greatest and most important writing that humanity has produced: "tell me, Henry, author of this *History, tell me.*"

PART VI

Redemption
from the Pasture?

CHAPTER 18.

Going through
All These Things Twice

I have not yet been put out to pasture or farmed out, but the time is drawing near when I will be. The motorcycle my family mocks me for riding might launch me into a real pasture, making it the pasture of my passing, not one for metaphorical grazing. I should apologize for mentioning the motorcycle. It is 1,800 cc too. A colleague ridiculed me for "the infinite regress of excuse making" to justify bringing it up, "about as cool as having a penile implant and announcing it to the world." But I cannot help being proud of the bike—such feelings have a will of their own—and my one excuse is that I did not take it up in middle or even old age; I have been addicted to the damn things since I was twenty, insecure in my masculinity right from the start, though then my reflexes were fast enough to make for close calls rather than organ donation. Still, I have begun ruminating as if I were grazing in the pasture already. And there flashes upon my inward eye reconstructions of my past, which morph into musings on what I might have done differently.

Would I do it over if I could, would I do it over if I *should?* Are do-overs and redos allowed? Are they possible? Would it be a curse or a blessing if they were? What if the past is not quite irrevocable? What if I got a second chance? Would I take it?

Recall too that by one clichéd but apt metaphorical capturing of *senium,* that is, of old, old age, we are unwound, back to infancy, fitted with diapers, preverbal, unable to walk. So there are unwinds, but they are not preludes to redos.[1]

THE FRAGILITY OF IRREVOCABILITY

One aspect of irrevocability explicitly faces the future by trying to make present commitments to restrict it, to lock in a course of action in the face of temptations to deviate, the kind we touched on when Hamlet defied augury. But resolutions and promises, though we declare them irrevocable, are often provided with escape clauses and come with varying levels of "really meaning it." Insurance and prenuptial agreements, the mere existence of divorce laws, for example, work against irrevocability's grain by hedging bets.

The second aspect of irrevocability is about the degree of done-ness of the past. In an obvious and uninteresting sense the past is irrevocable. The physics we live by does not allow for uncausing an event that has already occurred. Nonetheless, the past is less a done deal than we might want to think; it is subject to all kinds of forgetting, misremembering, reinterpretation, reinventing, and denial. History is not just written but constantly rewritten, which is hardly shocking news. In our own lives, we can remedy past errors, just as we can screw up past successes, or redefine whether they were successes or screwups, but can we turn the clock back or unwind events so that as an official matter they never occurred? Can we erase time, and if so under what circumstances and how thoroughly? The question seems silly, but in our put-it-all-behind-us culture, entire erasures of the past are held to be a wise coping with something called adversity. These untruth-and-self-reconciliation-commissions aside, such forgettings make practical sense in more than just our own little lives; sometimes they are politically and practically necessary. Æthelred the Unready, in a truce with the Viking fleet in 994, agreed that "all killings and all plundering and all the harms which were done before this truce was made, all of them shall be set aside, and no one shall avenge them or demand compensation for them."[2] A person who lost his family and cows to Viking axes or slavers might not be able to forget so easily, but as a legal matter forgetfulness was thrust upon him.

Forgiveness following penitence does not qualify as an erasure of the past. Absolution requires a full remembering of debts incurred and that they be formally recognized as having happened, with responsibility for them accepted; only then are they forgiven or formally deemed satisfied. Moreover, in some traditions, a judgment of the sincerity of present repentance is held in abeyance and can be proved to have been sincere only if the wrongdoer refrains from future offense.[3] In other words, though we might say forgive and forget, let bygones be bygones, the forgetting is conditional, a fiction; and the quality of the earlier repentance can be finally determined only at the wrongdoer's death. A once-forgiven offender is treated as a repeat offender, a backslider, and not as a first-time offender, should he offend again.

Unless the offense is expunged. Expungement purports to erase the past. Should a person whose offense has been expunged be asked if he has ever been arrested and convicted of a particular offense he is allowed to answer *truthfully,* "No." Expungement is more than just forgiving; it is also forgetting. But not all expungements are forgiving, though the expunged events are forgotten. For instance, consider whether God's creation in Genesis 1 was his first world. Do we know that it was not a redo? Might he have wiped out entire prior worlds for some offense or on a whim? Theologians and biblical interpreters took the issue on. Try as one might, it was next to impossible not to devise backstories to Genesis 1. And there are some grand efforts in the genre: the first two books of *Paradise Lost,* for example. If the angels could rebel in heaven, war and fall before day one with no real scriptural warrant, why not wonder further what God was doing before this creation, in the same way people might wonder what was happening before the Big Bang.[4]

Philo of Alexandria (d. A.D. 50) and St. Augustine (d. 430), among others, argued that the very notion of "before" made no sense to God, for whom all just *is*.[5] Augustine says he will not answer, as others have answered, those who ask, "What was God doing before he made heaven and earth?" Those others answered thus: "He was preparing hells for people who inquire into profundities."[6] The only way to answer such a question is to declare by fiat that it is a nonquestion, one meriting an eternity of beatings in the woodshed. God plays by a different physics than he gave to humanity, except for the few theoretical physicists he placed among us. But Augustine liked the joke well enough to reproduce it, and despite his philosophy, he too wonders.

The ancient rabbis are not as philosophically adept as Augustine, almost willfully. Philosophical thinking smacked of going Greek, a temptation the dominant currents of Christianity could not resist, but which the stubborn rabbis, representatives of a stiff-necked people, could resist with ease, creating their own very different interpretive world. Their style, hard to describe except by sampling it as we did in the discussion of fasting rituals and what the dead know, could at times be surreal. To the uninitiated (like myself), it looks like free association, absolutely bonkers. Even the initiated whom I have consulted confess that it looks that way to them now and then. That is part of its charm.

Was "in the beginning" really the beginning, asked the rabbis? Or was God going back to the starting blocks after a false start, trying to get it right this time, with the record of previous attempts, failures, and false starts expunged? Like the student who carefully hides how much he studies, had God been secretly practicing and training so he could be held in awe as a pure natural?[7] One Jewish sage said the Genesis text still bore traces of earlier worlds. R. Abbahu, in a discussion of the verse "and there was evening and there was morning" (1.3) of the first day of creation comments thus: "On the basis of that formulation [specifying that evening already had been designated; 'and there *was*' already evening] we learn that the Holy One, blessed be He, had been engaged in creating worlds and destroying them prior to the moment at which He created this one. Then He said, 'This is the one that pleases me, but those did not please me.'"[8]

If you think "there *was evening*" does not provide much of a hook on which to hang prior worlds, God himself seemed to provide more circumstantial evidence for the proposition. He nearly destroyed this world and had to covenant to restrain himself from ever employing water again to do the same. Sodom and Gomorrah in a smaller sequel got to experience the destructiveness of his fire. God seemed to have barely suppressible urges to kick in his sandcastles when they didn't turn out to his liking.

On other occasions he threatened to turn the clock back, regretting having favored the children of Israel, who repeatedly failed to heed his commands, who cut deals with other gods and even with other versions of himself that he did not approve of (thus the golden calf). The most bloodcurdling unwinding appears as the conclusion to the litany of harrowing curses that appears in Deuteronomy 28.14–68. This is what will happen to God's chosen people if we fail to "remember" the covenant: "And the Lord will bring you back in ships to Egypt, a journey which I promised that you should never make again; and there you shall offer yourselves for sale to your enemies as male and female slaves, but no man will buy you" (28.68, RSV). Should the people not keep the commandments, the curse will unwind the exodus, the liberation, and all prior covenants and promises. Back to Egypt it will be, in slave ships. And never again will you see the road to freedom. But this unwind has a twist, for there will be no restoration of you to your prior slavery. You will actually hope to be made slaves again. In slavery, unless condemned to the mines, which is little more than the cruelest of death sentences, there is food, enough to keep you working, enough to keep you sufficiently attractive for sex, or healthy enough, if a woman, to be a wet nurse. In slavery there is an admission that you are worth the keep to someone. This curse, however, renders you completely worthless. You will be on display in the slave market, but no one will buy you, no matter what the discount. Do not indulge in thinking that your worthlessness frees you from slavery. Freedom from slavery means moving *up* out of enslavement, up out of Egypt. You are condemned to going *down* to Egypt land, down lower than a slave in Egypt, a total loss of whatever value you might have had, condemned to annihilation, to nonbeing, to nothingness. The clock just got set back to zero. You just got uncreated.

No wonder the rabbis found warrant in the text for God having made and destroyed prior worlds. He was as imaginative and poetical a destroyer as he was a creator. Indeed, he takes his template for destruction from his template for construction. By unwinding the latter, playing the reel backward, we get back to Egypt, back to zero, back to *tohu v-vohu* (the "formlessness and void" of Gen. 1.2).[9]

The book of Genesis itself is characterized by redos, rebeginnings, repeats. No sooner does God rest from the six-day creation of chapter 1 than we see him back at work in an entirely different account of creation in chapter 2, doing it again. Covenants are repeated, reperformed, as if the prior ones had not taken place or were forgotten or, more charitably, were felt to require frequent ratification by redoing. God covenants with Abraham in Genesis 15 by passing between the halves of a cleaved heifer, goat, and ram. In the ancient Mediterranean world, contracts were consummated in blood and body parts; God felt he too had to follow the rules and seal a covenant in blood and severed flesh.[10] A mere two chapters later the covenant is redone as if it had never before been performed. It is as if the world had Alzheimer's. The blood and sliced-up flesh are still there, but this time it is Abraham who plays the heifer; he is circumcised to seal the deal, his losing "it" being a way of making the commitment serious, putting up part of himself as hostage, with the implication that the rest would be forfeit should he fail to keep up his end of the deal. And one of the provisions of the contract was that it was to be performed every generation for every male baby, a self-replicating covenant. Thus the renewal of the covenant with Abraham, with Isaac, and with Jacob.

Fundamental legal questions lurk beneath the text. To what extent does an heir succeed to the legal personhood of his father? Is he a perfect continuation of his father's legal personhood, so that all rights granted to and all duties assumed by the father pass to the son automatically at the father's death? It seems there is some anxiety on this score and that is why the covenants are reperformed, so that Isaac knows, without doubt, that he is bound in his own right as well as by succession to his father's position. But it may well be that God too must reperform the covenant for the same reason Isaac must. He might not be quite the same God as the one that covenanted with Abraham.[11] The covenants with Isaac and with Jacob in effect qualify each as a first-time enactment between two somewhat different parties than the one between God and Abraham. Just to make sure all is clearly defined we perform again what was before deemed an irrevocable covenant, in order not only to bind Isaac to the duties of his father but also to bind the God of Isaac to the duties of the God of Abraham.[12] We might claim less dramatically that these redos are really only reminders, but then remember what we have noted about the obligational aspect, often bloody, of remembering.

Perhaps, though, the most remarkable redo of creation, for English speakers, at least, is one that escaped the notice of the secular public and it happened in our lifetime: the "In the beginning" formulation of the first words of the Bible, the *In principio,* was in 1985 rejected in the new translation of the Jewish Publication Society's version, and the high and mid-Protestant New Revised Standard Version partly followed suit in 1989. They accepted the medieval Jewish commentator Rashi's philology of the Hebrew word *be'reshit,* the first word of the Bible, as referring not to a particular moment, to a point in time, but to an already ongoing process, with much stuff already preexisting the formal first act of creation, the *Fiat lux,* Let there be light. Thus JPS: "When God began to create heaven and earth—the earth being unformed and void . . . God said, 'Let there be light'"; and the NRSV: "In the beginning *when* God created the heavens and the earth, the earth was a formless void." It boggles my mind that such a significant redoing of the Jewish and Christian foundation myth was not front-page news, especially given the ammunition it would provide those who want to war with creationists. Getting the Hebrew right so as to get the English right is not a trivial matter.[13]

One would like to think of irrevocability as adamantine; friable, fragile crystal is more like it. A good portion of human legal and social relations suggests that people never quite believe in the irrevocability of what is claimed and intended to be irrevocable. Ancient treaties, medieval charters, and childhood pacts are peppered with bloodcurdling anathemas to ensure that what is declared irrevocable—namely, the treaty, charter, or pact—will stay that way. Do not dare change my words, my decrees, my laws, says Hammurabi as he concludes his law code with a lengthy litany of curses should anyone dare to.

The aspect of irrevocability that deals with the doneness of the past converges with that aspect of irrevocability that attempts to lock in present commitments in the future. Thus we redo, reperform, renew that which was done supposedly once and for all. Redos of covenants are ways of pushing past commitments forward. That which is established must not only be repaired but be reestablished, or rededicated, as Lincoln called for at Gettysburg.

We entertain, it seems, an ineradicable belief that if irrevocability (or durability) is actually achieved it is not likely to be a feature of good things: contrast eternal damnation with an orgasm. Beauty, health, peace are transient, and pleasure cloys if it lasts too long. Good times may roll, but they roll to an end usually by the time you wake up the next day, if not sooner. If they roll longer than that, we call it a bubble, its very duration proving it to have been an illusion. On the other hand, the undesired tends to be long-lived and nonillusory. To get a bubble never to pop one must get to heaven, but entry is restricted, the location is disputed and, unless you are Enoch or Elijah, you have to die first. Nor is it clear that once you get there your stay cannot be terminated. You might misbehave or get ideas and be cast down. Why should a soul who makes it to heaven not succumb to the temptation Lucifer, an angel, no less, could not resist?

As a practical matter, people expect things to be irrevocable only for a time. They give irrevocability a half-life or a termination date. Irrevocable agreements are thus required to be renewed or reaffirmed in periodic rituals often specially set aside for that purpose, to remind the parties that irrevocability is still in order and has been extended. When not explicitly provided for, terminal dates are implicitly supplied. Irrevocability has a short time horizon when you believe the world is about to end soon. The assumption behind the New Covenant of Christianity was that it would not need to be irrevocable for long (1 Pet. 2.9–10; Exod. 19.6). More practically, in feud and politics, people were willing to settle for a good-enough irrevocability. A covenant or treaty was deemed effective if it held up for a reasonable period of time before being breached, reasonableness being a function of the agreement yielding some worthy mutual benefit.

Saga people made settlements that purported to be irrevocable, but which in the saga idiom brought "quiet (peace) for a while." But peace for a while was still peace, while it lasted. If anathemas and the pretense of irrevocability made a person think twice before violating a commitment, that was better than having no second thoughts. Besides, only an idiot did not prepare for the possibility of a solemn commitment being broken. That is why hostages were exchanged or women were given or taken in marriage, itself a form of hostage exchange. That is why today more people, even of modest means, are writing prenuptial agreements prior to vowing that only death will part them, knowing that such an irrevocable commitment must be discounted by a 50 percent divorce rate. Peace agreements that endured did not last because of the treaty's anathemas and claimed irrevocability but because after a while the parties no longer needed a treaty. Either they had become one people or one or both of the parties had ceased to matter or to exist.

DAILY DO-OVERS

I am one solitary soul, losing it, not very happy about it, going the way of all flesh, anticipating being put out to pasture as I shuffle toward retirement. I have managed somehow to make it an occasion for invoking gods, Fate, Chaos, anathemas, royal decrees and divine covenants, apocalypse, irrevocability, immutability, and for calling in heroes of saga, Bible, and epic. Oh, come on! The entire universe mobilized and then unwound, made and remade, because I can no longer pull up a name or a fact, or run without blowing a tendon, or wipe out on the ice without having to think: the hip this time?

Not all do-overs or unwindings are punitive or apocalyptic. Do-overs are often a good thing, though the people drowned in the flood and those inhabiting God's possible prior destroyed worlds might wish to differ. Those who got around prohibitions on divorce by annulment liked the idea of undoing past irrevocable commitments. Think how many small-stakes do-overs occur during the course of routine conversation and allow us to remedy prospectively errors we see coming that we thus prevent, or allow us to gather better our thoughts as we struggle to hold the floor. Thus the frequent stammer of repeating the first word of a sentence: I, I was wondering.[14]

These kinds of petty do-overs do not erase the first false start; they just make it a false start, of no consequence and often not even noticed. Even so, they can become tic-like, or an affectation, as in the Oxbridge stammer; or at another undesired extreme they can become a true disability and brand the unfortunate person a stutterer, which happens when these false starts occur not only at the beginning of a sentence but also at the beginning of words that are not also a beginning of a sentence or clause. Though a speaker may mean nothing by these minor restarts, the listener, at times, imbues them with meaning. Start-overs of that sort, we suspect, hold clues to character, to motives, to matters of competence and confidence. They share with cosmetic makeovers, which are also do-overs of a sort, the unfortunate capacity to give off information that does a person no favors.

Of like triviality to these minor restarts of a sentence is the false start at the beginning of a race. The offender gets a do-over, a second chance. His recent past is not completely erased, for he gets only one more chance. Should he jump the gun a second time he is disqualified; if he does not, his false start is erased from the world of happenings. In some competitions a stricter group-punishment rule obtains. After the first false start, the next false starter is disqualified even though that is his first false start. One turning back of the clock is all that is allowed.

In other sports, a play can count for naught; the clock is reset, and the time it took drops into a black hole. A player might have had a career-ending injury on that play. The effects of resetting the clock will not cure him of his ruptured tendons, but in the world of the game those seconds never happened. One of the many differences between American football and European football (soccer) is that one allows for unwinding time and the other just adds it on.

Do-overs, however, also invite abuse. Consider how much of children's play is taken up with fighting over whether a turn counted or not. Watch ten-year-old boys play football and the game seems only notionally to be football. The real game is one of complaint and argumentation. If a turn did not reasonably accomplish its desired aim, or the opponent's did, it is claimed that it did not count. Every move, every point, is eligible for "further review" and must survive the demand for a do-over of one of the parties, even a demand to rewrite particular rules of the game.[15]

The habit dies hard and is equally a feature of solo contests. You flip a coin to see if you will keep working or watch a movie. When the puritanical coin gives the undesired result, you either declare the flip wasn't an authentic full-fledged flip, the coin having kind of stumbled out of your hand, or you change the rules and declare it is two out of three. Already from the mouths of babes, long before they have ever heard a word about forgiveness of sins or of worlds created and destroyed or of giving a scoundrel a second chance, the idea of a do-over is there in embryo, not as a mobilization of fellow feeling and generosity of spirit, not as a sign of moral development, but rather the contrary, as a naked assertion of self-interest and a tantrum against the "just having happened." The reasons offered— I was not ready, you were out of bounds, you already took your turn—make only the barest claim to pass as reasons.

Any pretense of reason can be dispensed with completely: a four-year-old offers none when you see he is about to lose it in the way kids lose it should he not get to redo the move you carefully set up for him. He could have brought the game to the end you desperately desired so you could get back to work by jumping those three kings you offered him on a silver platter. You even hinted broadly at your blunder and the opportunity it offered. Nope, he did not see it. And you could not resist indulging your Schadenfreude at the expense of your own four-year-old under the transparent guise of giving him helpful instruction by pointing out his missed opportunity. Woe unto you. You hasten to remedy your mistake by letting him have a do-over, which without batting an eye he accepts, and then feels triumphant for winning. He has fully erased the prior missed turn as ever having occurred. His pleasure in his triumph is not tainted one jot.

Disputes about do-overs take place in more than just kids' games. Should two sides to a dispute agree that time should be set back, then picking the date for the restart could lead to dangerous bickering. The most famous and immeasurably costly example is the price paid to determine the year to fix the title to property that had since changed its ownership several times between Catholic and Protestant claimants in the Holy Roman Empire. 1552? 1555? 1621? 1627? Or any of several other proposed start times. It took a couple of wars before 1618, then about the first twenty years of the Thirty Years' War, finally to set how far back the unwind would go.

IN MY END IS MY BEGINNING

Between God's destruction of whole prior worlds at one end and kids' games at the other, there is a middle ground in which the law has some purchase, where something akin to an erasure or unwinding of time takes place. Consider the consequences of giving title to property retrospective force.

When a person trespasses on another's land and stays there for the period of the statute of limitations governing the legal claim to kick him off, the trespasser will acquire title to the land the moment the limitations period is reached. He is said to have ad-versely possessed the land: adverse, that is, to the person who had the superior right to the property at the time of the trespass. That now former owner comes to discover that his land has become irrevocably unrecoverable. It is no longer his. By a simple operation of the statute of limitations and the mere passage of time, title has shifted. Even if the prior owner had paid a million dollars for it, he sees not one red cent. The once trespasser is now the owner, having got the land for free in one sense, for the price of his occupying it in another. Should the former owner try to reenter the land to take it back, he is now a trespasser and the law will compel him to leave. Nothing offends my first-year students more. The more lawyerly among them, however, immediately begin to plan to get themselves some vacation land on the cheap in the northern part of the state.

Here is what engages our present theme: the title shift does not purport to date the forced transfer of title at the moment the clock strikes twelve on the prior owner's right to eject the trespasser. Once that clock strikes twelve, the now successful adverse possessor is deemed to have held his title from the moment he first trespassed ten years earlier, assuming that is the length of the statute of limitations on the original owner's claim to eject the trespasser. The adverse possessor's newly granted title is said to "relate back" to the time of his initial trespass. By fiat, the past is transformed. Prior to the clock striking twelve, the dispossessed owner was still the owner of the land, the adverse possessor a trespasser and wrongdoer. At the stroke of midnight a new history is written. The successful adverse possessor is now understood to have been the owner for those ten years. Borrowing from T. S. Eliot, who borrowed from Mary Queen of Scots, we might say: "In my end is my beginning."[16]

What is the effect of transporting the new title of the adverse possessor back ten years in time? It can mean some good things for the new owner and some bad things. The good thing is that it means that should the dispossessed former owner sue for the rental value of the land for, say, the past five years, those years still being well within the limitations period, he would not recover a cent. The effect of relation-back doctrine is to stamp the date of the continuing ten years of wrong done the prior owner with the date the adverse possessor first entered, and on that date the clock has run. The bad thing is that our new owner can be looked to for subdivision assessments if these are in arrears. But suppose the dispossessed former owner had been paying them all along; in more than a few jurisdictions, tough luck for the doubly done-in former owner.

Relation-back doctrine of a different sort is a risk of growing old, a risk not even avoided by death. Your reputation is reevaluated in your dotage if your dotage lasts too long. If you had a glorious past it may become tainted by your embarrassingly long life. You end up remembered for your doddering vacancy, not even seen as the shell of your former self, for your former self is now redefined in light of the drooling present. People who only knew *of* you assume you have been dead for years and thus with them your reputation is still safe. But those who know and still feel obliged to visit you have to work hard not to have the present reality color their memories of the former you as someone "destined for misfortune."

Herodotus presents a discussion between Solon and Croesus, who is reputed the wealthiest man alive in their world, on happiness. The question is when the determination is to be made as to whether a life has been a happy one. Must we wait until we die before we can judge whether ours was a happy life? "Until he is dead, keep the word happy in reserve. Till then, he is not happy, but only lucky," says Solon.[17] Solon's point is that until our end we do not know how to calculate a fair average quality for our life or how to grade our middle, or even our beginning. But Solon is being too generous. We cannot make the judgment at death either; death does not lock in a reputation. And you need not have any skeletons in your closet to be at risk. What if ten years after you die it turns out that your son is a serial killer, your daughter a positive psychologist, your grandchildren drug addicts and in prison? You are not safe; your virtue, your life, will be reevaluated, and if the "dead know," as our Talmudic tale supposed they did, then in Sheol there is no relaxing, no satisfaction in a life once thought well lived if you have spawned a line of losers. Your children and grandchildren can get your blood declared bad or get you blamed for your neglect of them.[18] (Remember those checker games you hurried them through so you could get back to work?)

Nor need the risk be merely reputational. Would you grant that Priam had a happy life or any number of comfortably assimilated Jews in Germany in 1929, once we know how they ended? There is no great lesson to be drawn here except that our end is not as well defined as we might like to think, and neither are our middles, because our ends, though functionally concluded before death should we live too long, are in an evaluative sense not concluded in death. Relation-back doctrine subjects our beginnings to redefinition. Joy at the birth of baby Adolf, mewling Mao, puking Pol Pot, or Joseph later Stalin was premature.[19]

THE SHOW MUST GO ON

If child's play is the stuff of endless claims for do-overs, if much of regret and remorse lead to wishes for do-overs, if the pretense of do-overs helps sustain some idea of forgiveness, there are, in contrast, those counter-situations of once embarked, embarked for good. No turning back even if you want to, no starting over even if the start is blatantly false. The smallest step forward means you must continue, like falling off a cliff or being born. There is no crawling back in the womb for a second try or going back to the starting blocks if you change your mind once you have leapt off the Empire State Building. Such too is the high school musical. The show must go on because it gave rise to the saying itself. The saying marks a commitment to provide a middle and an end once anything that qualifies as a beginning has occurred. This allows for outright cancellations but not for packing it in once embarked.

Theater commonly provides metaphors for life. Erving Goffman showed just how extraordinarily fecund these metaphors could be, not by making life one big play but by breaking it down into thousands of plays of short duration, each with its own beginning, middle, and end.[20] The last play we will star in and still be physically present for will be our funeral, which has a beginning, middle, and end and will not last more than an hour, not counting the lying-in-state part, especially if we have outlived anyone who feels obliged to attend. As with the last cognitively impaired years of our lives, we will have no sense of blowing our part because we will have no sense. If the undertaker plays his part competently, it should go according to convention. But glitches do occur. The pallbearers can drop the casket. A former mistress might throw herself on the coffin, while the widow merely tries to weep politely, feeling quite pleased she mustered any tears at all, or perhaps she too is demented and has no clue who has died or what that means. No matter, you must be lowered into the ground and the show brought to its bargained-for conclusion.

Some rituals fail upon the first mistake and end right there, as when Egil was tricked into breaking his death fast; others, like the school play, must limp to a conclusion even though three of the players forgot their lines and another got the giggles, which infected half the chorus. That is a miserable solution, but apparently the optimal one. Think of the figure skater who wipes out in the Olympics on her first jump and then on her second too, but keeps getting up and goes on with the show. Should she quit after the first or second fall, she will be blamed for having a bad attitude and cause the audience excruciating embarrassment. If she goes on with the show, however, the embarrassment is equally excruciating. Her continuing, however, is the preferred outcome—in fact, the necessary outcome—because the point of the show is, after all, to feel the suspense of whether there will be falls and then to suffer the square root of the mortification you think the performer surely has to feel when they occur. The fall and the getting up, the shame and discomfort, *is* the show: to see the humiliation and feel exquisite embarrassment in Olympic figure skating is prime primetime material.[21]

CODA

Referee (scared): We'll replay it if you want.
Avon Barksdale: Do-over? You talkin' do-over? That ain't the way the game played. Ain't no do-overs.[22]

Avon had just lost a $100K bet to Proposition Joe; a foul could have been called on the last play but the ref did not see it that way. The ref is rightly scared for his life, this being a hoop game between the projects of East and West Baltimore, and he offers to put time back on the clock, to replay the final seconds of the game. Avon will have none of it. Do-overs ain't the way the game is played. Taking the do-over offered would look like whining, and there are rules! Ain't the way the game played.

What would you do if the prospect of do-overs was granted you? Would you be able to pass on the deal, like Avon? Could you refuse a second chance at the opportunities you soon came to regret you had not grabbed? Would you not desire a second shot to redeem your prior cowardices, to amend the wrongs you were guilty of, to acquire the knowledge you turned your back on?

Not on your life. What makes you think you have learned any lessons, or that your character somehow has so altered that you would make better decisions the second time around, that you would carpe the diem, that you wouldn't commit the same sins, show the same weakness of will and spirit, live exactly as you had before, maybe even worse? The person eager for redos might rather be looking for a repeat of the pleasures, especially the sinful ones, now that age has forced default virtue upon him, and this time he will make sure to pack Viagra for the trip back in time.

Jesus silently concedes this risk by making "born again" mean a spiritual makeover, not a turning back of the clock. The obvious-ness to us that Jesus was speaking figurally, however, was not read-ily apparent to Nicodemus, the man he was disputing with. Given some of the claims Jesus is heard to make in the Gospel of John, we can with some justice pardon Nicodemus for taking Jesus's "born again" literally and thus responding incredulously: "Can a man be born when he is old? Can he enter the second time into his mother's womb?" (John 3.3–7).

The person wanting his youth back, with an eternity of repeats, comeliness restored, all neurons firing and nether regions function-ing, would be caught up in a version of what Buddhists and Hindus understand as punishment, a judgment concurred in by the puer senex, twenty-four-year-old Bob Dylan, who was already "patiently waiting to find out what price / you have to pay to get out of going through all these things twice."[23] Do-overs, in that script, are what suffering is, what hell itself means. Best to accept the one shot we have and keep it at that, nor seek to prolong it excessively either. Old age can thus offer the modest pleasure of the feeling, suggested earlier, of having gotten through it all, akin to the pleasure of no longer banging your head against the wall.

Suppose, though, you got to do the do-over in Eden or in your safe neighborhood in Ann Arbor? Nope. Why do you think Eve ate of the apple? Because it was the only scarce item in the Garden, and hence the only thing of value. It was the only thing that could prompt any interest. Everything else was for the having at zero cost, life itself was cost free and thus meaningless, each day the same and an eternity of them. The snake was merely pointing out the obvious. She ate it to escape the movie *Groundhog Day* to which she had been condemned. Only upon escaping Eden can it be lamented as having been Paradise. Inside the walls, it was prison, and you could not get out of it even by dying. She took it upon herself to start the show that has to go on and that mercifully, by bringing death and toil into the world, gave life a middle and an end and thus some meaning.

CHAPTER 19.

Do Not Go Gentle:
A Valediction

Losing it in the sense of a general decline of abilities is about seepage and slippage, slow, inexorable decay, that steady shrinkage of the brain already under way in your early thirties. But when I lose it in rage, when I lose my patience with the vapidity of the positivity effect and socioemotional whatever it was, or when I lapse into jeremiads fulminating against our inability as a people to defer any gratification, against our blithe betrayal of the generations who built the nation, thus also betraying the generations who will come after us, sinking two centuries of achievement into a slough of debt in less than a decade, images of seepage or leakage don't capture the feel of it. Something more apocalyptic is demanded: avenging angels, justice delivered on the flesh of knaves and fools, war trumpets, and all that. You call as witnesses Jeremiah, Job, Timon of Athens, Jonathan Swift. You think of yourself as Lear on the heath in the storm, mad, and surely more sinned against than sinning.

The unflattering view of old age of ancient and enduring pedigree, you will recall, made it a time of meanness and irascibility or, given a slightly more benign cast, a time of grumpiness and curmudgeonliness. But neither grumpiness nor irascibility, in its common wings-clipped sense of irritability, has much to do with rage. Irritability seems more a last tango of mental acuity, of apt impatience with professorial pomposity, insipid optimism and positive thinking, routine charlatanism, common venality, public intellectuals, and smartphones. It is proof, or so you think, that in a significant way your sense of hearing is better than it ever was: for hearing is the sense on which annoyance thrives. I can discern perfectly the playlist leaking from the headphones of the person sitting three rows behind me on the airplane. Ambient conversation in an airport, the ever-blaring CNN—each is a separate dripping faucet forcing attention upon itself, and wearing a permanently hostile look on my face, directed now at this person, now at that, only underscores my impotence.

You old fool, Miller. Claiming perceptual acuity is only further proof of your losing it. It is your own vapid optimism, your own desperate wishful thinking, your own succumbing to the positivity effect that makes you think that your irritability is a function of acuity, of continuing finely honed engagement with the world. Like any optimist, you have suppressed relevant truth that is inconvenient. Your sense of hearing, which a few sentences ago you insisted was acuter than ever, as evidenced by its alertness to the annoying and irritable, cannot be chalked up to retained or improved aural sensitivity. What you mistook for acuteness of hearing is really proof of the breakdown of one of the most important executive functions of your shrinking brain: the capacity to inhibit or filter out the distracting, the irrelevant, the *noise*. Your hearing isn't better; it is that your ability to attend to a task is worse, worse than it ever was.[1]

So rail against old age, like Yeats, who insisted, rather delusionally, on a divide between the true him and false old age, which he thought of as something more like a soup stain on his tie:

What shall I do with this absurdity
O heart, O troubled heart—this caricature,
Decrepit age that has been tied to me
As to a dog's tail?[2]

Or like Dylan Thomas exhorting his dying father to rage against death. Raging in apocalyptic fury is a sign of life, a sign of still caring. As Thomas would have it, it is also a moral obligation:

Old age *should* burn and rave at close of day;
Rage, rage against the dying of the light.[3]

His father needs the rousing of his poet son, not unlike that provided by Skallagrim to get old Kveld-Ulf out of bed to kill one more time. Erupting in rage is just what Thomas's dying father cannot do; he is more like the old man in *Beowulf* who dies because his world has emptied itself of any meaning. Lose it, lose it—do not go gentle into that good night—rages the poet to get his father to lose it in that recent sense of the metaphor by railing against the other sense of the metaphor, the metaphor of decline: lose it as a remonstrance against losing it.

But then consider T. S. Eliot in *Little Gidding,* where one of the three "gifts reserved for age" is "the conscious impotence of rage / At human folly." Both Thomas and Eliot associate rage with old age. They differ, however, rather mightily on rage's virtue and on exactly what should prompt it. One is for raging at impotence, the other comes to recognize the impotence of rage. The first feels it is a way to go down with guns blazing against the dying of the light, grand but pointless, grand *because* pointless; the other just finds it pointless.

GOING OUT IN STYLE

As a student of one portion of heroic literature, I never tire of stories of people who face death in ways that are sublimely grand (and equally powerful stories of prudence and cunning where one puts the other to the choice of how to face death). These grand deaths set a standard few can match—they pretty much require dying in battle or in persecutions or in attempting to rescue or in some high-stakes political game to qualify. Nor can the grandness be dismissed as mere fictional exaggeration. The accounts accompanying the granting of Victoria Crosses and Medals of Honor, the detailed martyrdoms of the likes of Sts. Perpetua and Blandina show real humans outdoing even the grandest fiction. Being too accomplished a hero, however, might mean that you avoid grand death. The hazard of never losing is that you end up living long enough to lose it, as happened to Egil: blind, demented, crippled, and cold. Yet he too manages to go out in style, if you are willing to grant style points to a blind old man who managed to kill two slaves so they could not reveal where he hid his silver.

In earlier times, in most honor societies and also in religious communities, one spent a lifetime training for dying well. In the late Middle Ages, a popular manual appeared on the *ars moriendi,* the art of dying, written for ordinary Christians to help them maintain piety in the face of the temptations Death dangled before the soul still clinging to its fast-declining aching body. Despair, fear, pain, or bitterness might take the soul down by leading it to curse God or by simply finding him beside the point. These temptations mapped onto the standard negative characteristics imputed to irascible old age. To prepare for a good death, one needed to mobilize courage, patience, magnanimity, toughness, faith, which were exactly the virtues old age was likely to have stolen from the old soul. It took training, a lifetime of training, so as not to lose it in your final scene. The risk of botching it remained high nonetheless.[4] And you manifestly could not play the part well if you were demented.

Criminals were judged on how they faced the hangman, deposed kings and queens on how they faced the block. Fearless defiance and dignified penitence could appeal to the crowd, but cringing and signs of fear had them whooping for your death. An inept king like Charles I met his death with dignity, thus redeeming himself in the eyes of many and shaming more than a few in the crowd who had attended intending to exult in his beheading. And when an aristocratic warrior trembled and caved before the executioner, a lifetime of battlefield glory was erased. Says Adam Smith confirming the dubious power of "relation-back doctrine": "If he should . . . be led out to a public execution, and there shed one single tear upon the scaffold, he would disgrace himself for ever in the opinion of all the gallant and generous part of mankind. . . . His behaviour would affect them with shame rather than with sorrow; and the dishonour which he had thus brought upon himself would appear to them the most lamentable circumstance in his misfortune. How did it disgrace the memory of the intrepid Duke of Biron, who had so often braved death in the field, that he wept upon the scaffold!"[5]

One way to prepare for going out in style was to make sure you said what qualified as famous last words. Famous last words are not available to everyone, only to people of sufficient standing to have their last words attended to. The genre of famous last words put a burden on the dying famous person to say something worthy of being remembered. Sometimes just being famous and saying last words meant they would be famous even if devoid of wit. Sometimes they were attributed to you by legend as something you would or should have said had you thought to say it.

Perhaps the best performance in the genre, oft told and hard to believe given the number of bullets he took in a matter of seconds, many to the head, is accorded to Pancho Villa: "Don't let it end like this, tell them I said something." He gets credit for making a superb joke at the expense of the art of dying and its demand for famous last words. That kind of witticism, however, was not what he intended at all. He was playing it straight, anguished that he had bungled his end by not coming up with, or having precomposed and then delivered, some pithy statement meeting the conventions of the genre.

"Are you guys ready? Let's roll." There is good authority for that having been said by Todd Beamer, a passenger on United flight 93, September 11, 2001. The words are not without some wit in their effectively linking civilian resolve to warrior virtue, this time not in the context of a corporate merger or leveraged buyout, or some other pathetically unheroic context in which men in suits think themselves worthy of martial metaphors, but to take back an airplane by taking it down. The words are of Hamlet-like commitment, the readiness being all. These are justly famous words because they were not mere words but the sign of an irrevocable commitment for stakes about as high as they can get. This is a commitment to go down with all guns blazing. Not for personal glory, but because greater love hath no man . . .

What of old people? Glorious death is well-nigh impossible in pacified times. The best we can hope for is a good death. A good death in our day refers to two very different kinds of death. One is the one I alluded to earlier as the adult version of the "If I die before I wake" prayer: to die in our sleep. That death is good because it makes no demands on our courage or on any other virtue, no facing pain or fear. It is deemed good because it ensures against going out disgracefully by eliminating the option of going out in style.

The other kind of good death requires that "good" bear a moral sense, something more than merely being a synonym for lucky. It requires knowing that you are dying and showing grace in the face of that knowledge. Such a death is not the going out in style that wins Medals of Honor or Victoria Crosses—it is not about sacrifice—but it does share with heroic death the mastering of fear. It need not mean being fearless; one can still be afraid. It is about how you stare the fear down or send it packing or put on a good show in spite of it, maybe even joking about it. One can simply be serene, provided the serenity is fully sentient. Or one can rage. You know (from beyond the grave) you did it up right when others envy you for it and wonder if they will have what it takes to die that way.

No one style qualified for this kind of good death, but it was a goal for everyone to manage to die well by their code. Suffer a cowardly death in an honor culture and an otherwise honorable life was redefined downward. Tearful penance could qualify as good, but Christianity had to fight against a deep honor-based sense that showing fear, even in the face of hell, was cowardly. The tears were to be of contrition, of sorrow for sin, not of fear. Death occurred as a live performance for people up until as recently as fifty years ago in the West, not as it does now when it takes place in a haze out of sight, unless you live in really mean streets or are in certain lines of work. Make dying a performance before an audience and the demands for a good show will again become insistent. Unfortunately, death is often messy, and life does not play fair, often letting us stick around too long to have wits enough to die well. We need another prayer of the if-I-die-before-I-wake sort for those who want to go out "good": let me die before I am demented, before I lose too much "it," let me die truly awake to the world and to those I am leaving. The chances keep getting slimmer for more and more of us.

The book of Genesis preserves the good deaths of Jacob and Joseph, dying in the fullness of their years, both in full possession of their wits, blessing their families, the generations of their offspring gathered before them. Jacob's last words contain detailed commands regarding his burial: "And when Jacob had made an end of commanding his sons, he gathered up his feet into the bed, and yielded up the ghost, and was gathered unto his people" (49.33).

That was counted a good death then, and it would be counted one now. But Jacob's death leaves his sons, except for Joseph, more in fear than in sorrow. "And when Joseph's brethren saw that their father was dead, they said, 'Joseph will peradventure hate us, and will certainly requite us all the evil which we did unto him.' And they sent a messenger unto Joseph, saying, 'Thy father did command before he died, saying, "So shall ye say unto Joseph, Forgive, I pray thee now, the trespass of thy brethren, and their sin; for they did unto thee evil": and now, we pray thee, forgive the trespass of the servants of the God of thy father'" (50.15–7.) Think back to David, who goes out in style with perhaps too many wits about him, physically wasted as he is, commissioning hits on two people he could not pay back in his lifetime. Did the dying Jacob really order Joseph to spare his brothers without Joseph there to hear the command? If Jacob commanded this, would these brothers not have urged him also to give the order directly to Joseph? The text leaves it open, but only by a crack. Every indication is that the brothers are making up Jacob's command; they are rather making a ritualized request for pardon by putting it in the form of a fictive command issued by their father. None of them has the courage to inform Joseph of this paternal command to his face, where the fiction of it would be even more readily discernible or be subjected to cross-examination.

Jacob is the arch trickster of the Bible, an Odyssean type who, like Odysseus, is also a champion wrestler, a sport in which guile can compensate for certain deficits in strength. One should never trust Jacob as far as one can throw him (even God could not throw him in a wrestling match). This is the Jacob who years earlier felt no compunction about having his mother set up his father to steal from his brother. Moreover, this is the Jacob who seems to have set up the young Joseph, his favorite son, by sending him off to seek his brothers in Shechem. Jacob was no better pleased with Joseph's presumptuousness than his brothers were: "When [Joseph] told [the dream] to his father and to his brothers, his father rebuked him, and said to him, 'What is this dream that you have dreamed? Shall I and your mother and your brothers indeed come to bow ourselves to the ground before you?' And his brothers were jealous of him, *but his father kept the saying in mind*" (Gen. 37.10–11, RSV; emphasis added). Within one short verse Jacob sends Joseph on an errand to his brothers who are tending the family flocks in Shechem, never to return. What must those brothers have thought when they saw the hated Joseph coming toward them, *sent to them by their father?* Is there not some reasonable basis for them to take this as a paternal warrant to kill him? If so, Reuben did not have the nerve to follow through, but they made sure to send their father a bloody token, with a cover story that looks like a coded message that his order had been obeyed.[6] Going too far? Perhaps, but then remember it is Jacob we are dealing with.

Just as it is not beneath Jacob to be somewhat advertently negligent in the errands he sends his favorite son on, or to be rather careless of his own twin brother's well-being, it is also not unthinkable that he might "forget" to command Joseph to forgive his brothers. Not to worry: like the Christian idea of the "fortunate fall" from Eden that thus made Christ necessary, Joseph has his brothers to thank, not kill, for his fortunate sale into slavery. Sell me into bondage again, please. Joseph is second in command of the world's superpower, perhaps even more powerful than Pharaoh.

Old Jacob, I would not be surprised, left it up to Joseph as to how to settle matters with his brothers; there was no parental command. In fact, Jacob's silence on the matter was a license for Joseph to kill, just as his brothers feared. In ancient Israel, dying full of years could make for a good death and going out in real style; it could be filled with lethal possibility for more than just the dying head of household. No slave strangled to accompany his master, nothing so innocently generous, just making sure scores were settled.

MAKING UP TO DIE

Making up can mean peaceful reconciliation or inventing a tale or it can mean putting on makeup, a particular style of feminine readying oneself with eyeliner, lipstick, colors and creams, with more than latent possibility of being carried out with grand effect. The estimable Jezebel, that arch villainess, goes out in style, the readiness being all.[7] It would be hard to match her for cool.

The setting is the reign of King Joram, the son of Ahab and Jezebel, the second son of theirs to rule after Ahab's death in battle twelve years earlier. The prophet Elisha, the same bald man with whom we opened this book, he who called in the bears to eliminate forty-two insufficiently respectful youngsters, is no friend of the house of Ahab. He commissions a young follower of his to anoint Jehu, one of the higher-ranking officers in Joram's army. The message was not lost on Jehu, who wasted no time in cashing in on Elisha's blessing. He rode furiously to Jezreel, where Joram was encamped.

With Joram was Ahaziah, king of Judah. Jehu made short work of both, and to finish up the coup headed for Jezebel: "When Jehu came to Jezreel, Jezebel heard of it; and she painted her eyes, and adorned her head, and looked out of the window. And as Jehu entered the gate, she said, 'Is it peace, you Zimri, murderer of your master?' And he lifted up his face to the window, and said, 'Who is on my side? Who?' Two or three eunuchs looked out at him. He said, 'Throw her down.' So they threw her down; and some of her blood spattered on the wall and on the horses, and they trampled on her" (2 Kings 9.30–33, RSV). Defenestrations became a signature form of political action among the Czechs starting in the fifteenth century, but Jezebel qualifies as the first authority figure that I know of to be deposed by having been chucked out a window.

Before she is betrayed by her own servants, who hope to spare themselves being included in Jehu's ruthless extermination of anyone qualifying as a member of the house of Ahab, she puts on her eyeliner and fixes her hair to look her best for her final scene, Norma Desmond before her time.[8]

The manifest cool of making herself up could not be better presented. She is a woman of steel, with a high IQ. The insulting greeting to Jehu defies simple translation. Calling Jehu a Zimri is her coinage. Zimri, like Jehu, was one of the top commanders in the army of Israel, forty-four years earlier. Like Jehu, he betrayed and assassinated his king and set himself up in his place. Zimri, however, ruled only seven days before Omri, father of Ahab, with the backing of the army surrounded Zimri. Seeing that all was lost, Zimri burned down the palace he was holed up in and perished in the flames. By calling Jehu Zimri, Jezebel mocks Jehu as a traitor, an assassin of his king, and curses him with the prospects of a similarly short reign. She also refuses to address Jehu by title or name, but only by her own mocking epithet. She plays it with perfect aplomb. No fear, no begging, no trying to cut a deal, just scornful defiance in the face of death.

Jezebel's opening question, "Is it peace?" is ironic and rhetorical. She knows the answer before asking. *Hashalom,* "Is it peace?" has already been asked (and answered) three times in earlier verses in the same chapter: two times by messengers King Joram sends to ask it of Jehu, and once by Joram himself, after his messengers chose to defect to Jehu at Jehu's not-so-gentle suggestion that they had better do so. Jehu's answer was an arrow between the shoulders of the fleeing Joram. By the time Jezebel asks "Is it peace?" it has become an ironic refrain, more evidence, if any were needed, of the literary sophistication of the author(s) of the text. When Jezebel says hashalom to Jehu, it is no longer a question and probably is best translated as the conventional greeting it had already become: "So how's it going, you piece of shit [i.e., 'Zimri']?"

Some commentators with considerable tone-deafness argue that Jezebel made herself up hoping to be sexually enticing enough to save her life for service as a concubine.[9] Strange tactics then to greet your killer with derision and a curse. The author(s) of the biblical text have no desire to do the hated Jezebel any favors, but she manages to extort homage from them with her cool fearlessness nonetheless.

The text thus hastens to make amends for having glorified her. Not enough that the horses trample her but several more verses luxuriate in the gore and make sure her corpse is mutilated beyond recognition:

> Then [Jehu] went in and ate and drank; and he said, "See now to this cursed woman, and bury her; for she is a king's daughter." But when they went to bury her, they found no more of her than the skull and the feet and the palms of her hands. When they came back and told him, he said, "This is the word of the Lord, which he spoke by his servant Elijah the Tishbite, 'In the territory of Jezreel the dogs shall eat the flesh of Jezebel; and the corpse of Jezebel shall be as dung upon the face of the field in the territory of Jezreel, so that no one can say, "This is Jezebel."'" (9.34–37)

Unlike the dead landlady of the Talmud whom we met earlier, there will be no point in Jezebel asking that her eyeliner be sent to her grave. She has no grave; not enough of her is left to be identifiable, and presumably her hands will not be within reach of her skull dunging the field to apply eyeliner to the holes that were her eyes. Jehu's momentary afterthought to bury her honorably is prevented by Yahweh.

Jezebel was not young when she died, though it is hard to give her a precise age. She died at the end of her son Joram's reign. If she married Ahab in the first year of his reign, that would add up

Figure 4: King Jehu of Israel groveling, face to the ground,
before Shalmaneser III of Assyria. Credit: Steven G. Johnson.

to about thirty-two years as queen and queen mother. She could
have been anywhere from twelve to twenty-five when she married.
She was probably in her fifties when she was killed. Not a young
woman, but showing not the smallest sign of losing it, even though
every part of her was detached from and lost to the rest. Scattered
and devoured as she had been, there was not enough of her in
Sheol to take much solace some years later in seeing Jehu grovel,
nose to the ground, before the Assyrian king, Shalmaneser III,
who immortalized Jehu's humiliation in stone for all to see on the
Black Obelisk in the British Museum.

THE END

I entertain fantasies of going out in style, but the fantasy requires that I not lose much more of "it" than I already have. How
is an academic to go out in style anyway? Keep writing books, ever
weaker, but just keep at it, whether they be published or not? Give
it all up and become a suicide bomber at some cultural studies

conference? Drink myself to death? There might be a kind of honor in that were I Dylan Thomas and had done so by age thirty-nine, or Hank Williams, who managed it by twenty-nine. But at my age? I am not one for keeping a stiff upper lip, nor do I play in high-stakes games so as to go out in feeble imitation of Jezebel or David. The best, I suppose, would be, like Jacob and Joseph, to die with sufficient wits remaining fully to appreciate the experience, in the presence of my family, my children and their children, should they ever get around to having them, and confirm that they are already blessed, so my blessing would merely be a ratification, a redo of a covenant that God or the gods have partly performed but cannot be trusted to keep performing. Make a few ironical remarks, to prove I have not lost it all, and then draw up my feet and breathe my last.

♪♫ "Always Look on the Bright Side of Life"

When this book was well into the editing process, I was treated to an experience worth the telling. I was spending Thanksgiving with my mother in Green Bay. The rest of the family had left for home on Saturday. I stayed on for two more days. On Sunday, killing time until the Packer game in Atlanta was to begin, I was pedaling the exercise bike in the TV room, the timer set for twenty minutes. The last thing I remember was seeing thirteen minutes left. An hour later I was in the emergency room. No, I did not faint or have a heart attack. And no, this addendum is not the first installment of a death blog; hell, I got half my mother's genes.

The neurologist on duty called it transient global amnesia (TGA). I fulfilled the checklist of precipitating causes and vulnerabilities: a history of migraine, jet lag (I had flown in Thursday from Scotland), aerobic exercise and, of course, my age. I cannot tell you much about the experience, obviously; global amnesia will do that, though four or five snapshots survived those couple of hours. My mother is the source for most of this.

Apparently having wandered out before the game started, I wandered back into the TV room, not knowing I had wandered out, when the game was already in the second quarter. My mother assumed I must have been watching upstairs, for it was unthinkable that I would miss the kickoff. She soon discerned, however, that something was not right when I asked how we had gotten to the ten-yard line, though I had watched the entire drive. I felt no confusion or disorientation. I knew who I was, where I was; all my motor functions were in order. Everything *before* thirteen minutes to go on the bike was available to me.

But I had lost the ability to add to my past from that thirteen-minute mark forward. I lived instead encapsulated in a bubble of presentness of ten to fifteen seconds' duration. Once ten seconds fell off the back end, it disappeared into a black hole. To borrow another metaphor, nothing was being written to my brain's hard drive. So there was no such thing as a touchdown drive. A play happened and then passed into oblivion. Then the next play, but I did not see it as "next." It was an entirely new event with no connection to anything before it. There was no "before."

But how did my mother get me to go to the ER? I am quite stubborn about agreeing to do things I do not want to do. How did I gain the awareness that something was not right? I think it was this: I looked at the bike and had absolutely no clue whether I had done my twenty minutes. I felt no sense of duty done, which is the small reward of finishing, nor was I tormented by that feeling of physical and moral failure for not having done my twenty minutes. Something akin to the exasperating frustration of blanking I discussed in chapter 2 must have penetrated my consciousness.

I did get a CAT scan out of it. No tumors, no signs of stroke, which was what my mother thought had occurred, just the normal shrinking of the brain in a person my age. There were two more aspects of the experience that I must mention, one merciful, one cruel. The merciful one is that because my world had its tail clipped, that it had only a ten- to fifteen-second extension backward, I did not have sufficient perspective to suffer the humiliation, or experience the comedy, of my eighty-nine-year-old mom taking her sixty-five-year-old son to the doctor. The cruel thing is that I came to my senses just as the Packers lost in the last second, which I got to witness because no hospital in Green Bay would not make the game available to someone who might be breathing his last. It is the local form of extreme unction.

Here's the rub: could writing *Losing It* have figured in any part of the causal chain, or so have angered the gods as to have made it more likely that I would get transient global amnesia than if I had not written this book? Was I being punished for exaggerating how much "it" I had lost, or for obsessing overmuch on the bits of "it" I had lost? I can hear those Arbiters of Fate saying: "So, Miller, your brain shrinks like everyone else's, you forget people's names and sometimes what you got up to do, and though most people don't forget Norse words, they forget something similar, and you think that merits a book? You ain't seen nothing yet. Here's a preview of some coming attractions, if your motorcycle wills you live so long. How about we make every exaggerated statement you've made about yourself in this book TRUE?"

True for three hours. The literature on TGA says one episode makes another no more likely than if you had never had one, but then TGA has all kinds of friends and relations who may wish to pay me a visit and who may not be so well mannered as to leave in three hours. TGA's idiot cousin, the positivity effect, itself a kind of amnesia, has evidently infected me, for I am delighted this happened. Temporary global amnesia gave me a new story to tell and a proper way to end my tale. Finally. Though never trust such promises from the aged, especially when it comes to talking about their health. Today, after I had barely completed a sentence in conversation, that same colleague who had a year earlier relayed the student's "cute old man" remark to me, cut me off: "Do you want me," said she, "to let you know when you are repeating yourself? Or would you prefer I let it slide?"

ACKNOWLEDGMENTS

I have been blessed with colleagues, friends, and family whom I can also count among the teachers that I dedicated this book to. Don Herzog, John Hudson, Kyle Logue, Richard Primus, and Mark West took the time to read the entire manuscript in its first draft. I also stole an idea or two from Bess Miller, Katja Škrubej, and Steve White and a dozen or so from Eva Miller, who provided me with more apt texts from the ancient Near Eastern world than I could possibly use, and more than a few which I did. Thanks to my colleague Ellen Katz for providing the last line of the addendum. As usual, a special thanks to an even harsher critic, my wife, Kathy Koehler, who does her best to save me from my excesses. It is for you to judge the extent of her success. Last, I want to remember my old friend Barbara Packer from grad school days, famed among her fellows for having the perfect mind, coupling wit and humor with what seemed to be infinite knowledge, and possessing a sweet soul to boot. She died December 16, 2010, at sixty-three, of ovarian cancer, with every bit of her extraordinary wits about her, the cancer not daring to commit that sacrilege, though it had felt free to invade every other vital organ.

INTRODUCTION: STRIKING OUT

1. *Oxford English Dictionary,* s.v. "lose," v.1, draft additions, May 2003, available in an updated online version.
2. *Oxford English Dictionary,* s.v. "lose," v.1, 3.b (mind, sixteenth century), 3.d (patience, from early seventeenth century); s.v. "head," n.1, 56, citing Chaucer, *Knight's Tale,* v. 1707.
3. For the text of the fifteenth-century morality play *Everyman,* see http:// quod.lib.umich.edu/cgi/t/text/text-idx?c=cme;cc=cme;view=toc;idno= Everyman.
4. The cult of positive thinking rightly drove Barbara Ehrenreich to a book-length polemic; see *Bright-Sided,* especially ch. 6, in which she treats positive psychology. I restrict myself mostly to a few jabs at the positive psychology of old age. A sober reflection on aging is promised by Susan Jacoby, *Never Say Die: The Myth and Marketing of the New Old Age* (forthcoming), whose core themes apparently are adumbrated in an op-ed piece in the *New York Times,* December 31, 2010. I expect a spate of books in the genre, given the number of us aging boomers.
5. I generally quote from the King James's version of the Bible, but on occasion from the Revised Standard Version (RSV), as here, or the Jewish Publication Society version (JPS) when it makes the point more accurately.

6. John of Trevisa's translation of *Bartholomaeus Anglicus: De proprietatib[us] re[rum], Early English Books Online,* reel position: image 94 of 522, *Liber* 6, c. 1; cited in Aers, "The Christian Practice of Growing Old"; also see Burrow, *The Ages of Man,* 88–89. The *Middle English Dictionary* glosses "hevy" in this passage as meaning annoyed, troubled, vexed, s.v. "hevi," 5a. As to "wery of hym," the sense is "bored by him"; see *Middle English Dictionary,* s.v. "weri," adj., 2b.

7. Thane makes this point convincingly in her "Social Histories of Old Age."

8. *Oxford English Dictionary,* s.v. "teen," n.2. On the ages of man in addition to Burrow, *The Ages of Man,* see Dove, *The Perfect Age of Man's Life;* Sears, *The Ages of Man.*

9. Burrow, *The Ages of Man,* 34.

10. See Shahar, *Growing Old in the Middle Ages,* 15–17.

11. Parkin, *Old Age in the Roman World,* 20–21.

12. See Cutler, Whitelaw, and Beattie, *American Perceptions of Aging,* 17. Incredibly, 9 percent of those over seventy-five thought themselves young.

13. AARP is an acronym for the American Association of Retired Persons; the acronym is now the organization's official name.

14. Coale and Demeny, *Regional Model Life Tables,* 658, "Model South, Level 3, Female"; for males the numbers are as usual slightly less generous, but only slightly, a year less expectancy at twenty and forty.

15. Thane, "Social Histories of Old Age," 95, gives estimates in England for the seventeenth century and notes local variation depending on rates of mobility of the young.

16. See Shahar, *Growing Old in the Middle Ages,* 25–26; Rosenthal, *Old Age in Late Medieval England,* 104–34; in Iceland a person over seventy was excused from fasting (*Grágás* Ia.35; see also text at ch. 10, n. 28).

CHAPTER I. THE YOU BEHIND YOUR EYES IS OUT OF DATE

1. John of Trevisa, *Early English Books Online,* reel position: image 94 of 522, *Liber* 6, c.1.

2. See Bynum, *The Resurrection of the Body,* 98–99, 122n15. Augustine was inconsistent about whether we would come back with our thirty-year-old form. If your body was deformed, then you were to get a better one (ibid., 29, 98n144); also see Burrow, *The Ages of Man,* 104. See further ch. 4, n. 18.

3. See Bynum, *The Resurrection of the Body,* who cites Origen: our resurrected bodies will be without age or sex (67); Aphrahat: that body which is laid in earth, that very body shall rise again (73); and Ephraim: we all rise as adults (76).

4. See Aers's reading of *Pearl* in "The Self Mourning." The poem adopts much of the idiom of love poetry, which cannot help but put the two-year-old into a older, more marriageable body. Among us it is the other way around: the language of love turns the beloved from an adult into a "babe" (mostly female) or "baby" (male or female). The *Pearl*-poet, however, embodies his metaphorical pearl as a woman, elegantly dressed, not as a toddler, even though she is not bearing her resurrected body, for which she must wait until Doomsday.

5. See text at ch. 3, n. 7.

6. As Mary Dove, in her book on "the perfect age" in the ages-of-man traditions, rightly observes: "It has always been easier to die in one's prime (or, in the language of earlier generations, in the perfection of one's age) than to be perceived to be living it" (*The Perfect Age of Man's Life,* 3).

7. The ability to pick up the microseconds of difference in the onset of voicing that allows one to distinguish pill from Bill, cod from God, tick from dick, decreases with age; see discussion in Burke and Shafto, "Language and Aging," 387, citing Strouse et al., "Temporal Processing in the Aging Auditory System." See also Tremblay, Piskosz, and Souza, "Aging Alters the Neural Representation of Speech Cues," 1865: "Results show that older adults had more difficulty than younger listeners discriminating voice-onset contrasts. In addition, these same speech stimuli evoked abnormal neural responses in older adults."

8. As an example of work of this sort, see Featherstone and Hepworth, "Images of Aging: Cultural Representations of Later Life." Notice "later life" as a euphemism for old age. See also Rowe and Kahn, *Successful Aging,* which advocates staying spunky, thinking positively, and then dropping dead quickly when thinking positively finally succumbs to reality.

9. I have this from a colleague who found this out visiting a relative in a nursing home. The academic literature on this issue is divided. Some demented people cannot self-recognize in mirrors or recent photos; some can. With Hehman, German, and Klein, "Impaired Self-Recognition," compare Fazio and Mitchell, "Persistence of Self."

10. Seneca, epistle 12, I.65–67; discussed in Parkin, *Old Age in the Roman World,* 69–70.

11. La Rochefoucauld, *Maxims,* no. 458.

CHAPTER 2. CAN YOU RECALL WHAT YOU HAD FOR DINNER, CRONUS?

1. Burkert, *Homo Necans,* 46, argues that the conflict between generations is dramatized in initiation rituals where the new entrant, the first-born, is the sacrificial victim, often substituted for by an animal to represent him: cf. Isaac and the ram. See further text at ch. 9, n. 19.

2. The whole culture of getting your goods now without a thought to paying for them later, the entire international financial disaster of 2008 that ominously continues as I write, the increasing national debt can be blamed, with tongue barely in cheek, on the sexual revolution. When I was in high school and the first year or two of college, it took months of effort, struggles in cars, devious stratagems, and you still came up short, if you came up at all. All changed utterly with the ready availability of the pill in about 1967. Some small thrill in the chase survived in the new regime, but instead of training for marathons, you now sauntered through a wind sprint or two. As our post-pill expectations regarding sex, so too our expectations regarding cars, houses, vacations, pensions, etc.

3. See Kramer and Madden, "Attention."

4. *Pirkei Avot,* 3.9. The passage is variously translated in English, from the harsh "Scripture regards him as having forfeited his life" or "is endangering his life" to the more lenient "regards him as if he were guilty against himself." The study that is being interrupted is of Scripture or the Mishnah.

5. James, *Psychology,* 417.

6. For convenient summaries of the psych research on memory decline, see Hoyer and Verhaeghen, "Memory Aging"; also Thornton and Light, "Language Comprehension and Production in Normal Aging," 264; Burke and Shafto, "Language and Aging," 397–99.

7. For arguments that failures in attention should be linked to declines or failures in working memory, see, e.g., McVay and Kane, "Conducting the Train of Thought." But it may be that working memory is suffering from the effects of declines in general processing speed and failures of inhibitory mechanisms, rather than failures in memory per se; see MacDonald and Christiansen, "Reassessing Working Memory"; and Kramer and Madden, "Attention."

8. For a provocatively informative article exploring the relation between cognitive development in early life and its decline and unwinding from mid- to late life, with a suitably guarded view that still manages to give real punch to the notion of old age as a second childhood, see Craik and Bialystok, "Lifespan Cognitive Development."

9. I am not alone; this is one of the many failures in cognition that provably

attend old age; see Einstein et al., "Prospective Memory and Aging"; McDaniel et al. "Aging and Maintaining Intentions."

10. James, *Psychology,* 163. Recent studies have expanded on James's insight regarding tip of the tongue experiences, or TOT: "In the throes of TOT, a person can produce semantic and grammatical information about the TOT target, but only partial information about the phonology of the word" and then "older adults rate word finding failures as a cognitive problem that is most frequent, most affected by aging and the most annoying" (Burke and Shafto, "Language and Aging," 399, citing the relevant studies); also see Thornton and Light, "Language Comprehension and Production in Normal Aging," 264–66. TOT, unsurprisingly, has been shown to be more frequent in the old than in the young.

11. See Nietzsche's classic observations on forgetting in *Genealogy of Morals,* 2.1: "Forgetting is no mere *vis inertiae* as the superficial imagine; it is rather an active and in the strictest sense positive faculty of repression." Well, yes and no: the ability to inhibit intrusive thoughts, to forget them for the nonce is clearly a positive faculty when it works to exclude the irrelevant from interfering with a present task, but there is little value to forgetting when what you have forgotten is precisely what is needed to carry out the present task.

12. Conversation with Professor Doug Kahn, who is ten years older than I am.

CHAPTER 3. SHRINK WRAP

1. Park and Reuter-Lorenz, "The Adaptive Brain," 21.1; and Willis, Schaie, and Martin, "Cognitive Plasticity," 317: "Constraints and limits on plasticity . . . become more evident with increasing age. At the neural level, there are constraints due to degradation of the neural structure (brain atrophy, number of neurons, and synaptic density)."

2. Raz, Rodrigue, and Acker, "Hypertension and the Brain."

3. Working memory begins its decline in the early thirties, slowly at first; Park and Payer, "Working Memory." Episodic memory does even worse, peaking at between twenty-five to thirty years of age, then beginning its steady decline. Craik and Bialystok, "Lifespan Cognitive Development," 576.

4. See Labouvie-Vief, "Dynamic Integration Theory," summarizing the research.

5. Germans must bear some of the blame; see the work of Paul Baltes cited below, n. 8, and in ch. 5, n. 3.

6. See Ehrenreich's discussion in *Bright-Sided,* ch. 6.

7. For celebratory accounts of Carstensen's work and work following in her vein, see Blanchard-Fields and Kalinauskas, "Theoretical Perspectives"; Kryla-Lighthall and Mather, "The Role of Cognitive Control"; more measured is Zarit, "A Good Old Age." Hers is not the only special pleading in which wishful thinking suborns what otherwise is claimed to be science; see further below ch. 5, n. 3. Moreover, the economists have gotten into measuring well-being and happiness, and they too purport to show that oldsters are a happy bunch. In a recent article in the *Economist* (December 18, 2010: http://www.economist.com/node/17722567?Story_ID=17722567) summarizing this research, various explanations were offered, but not the obvious one: that cognitive decline undoes the capacity for thinking very well, for seeing the truth. Or, as I discuss at various points in the text (esp. ch. 15), such well-being is not very well analyzed. It confuses happiness or well-being with what might better be described as relief.

8. Carstensen, Mikels, and Mather, "Aging and the Intersection of Cognition, Motivation, and Emotion." See also Carstensen, Isaacowitz, and Charles, "Taking Time Seriously"; and Carstensen and Mikels, "At the Intersection of Emotion and Cognition." Carstensen sees her work as extending Baltes's; she writes, "Socioemotional selectivity theory also complements well the model of selective optimization with compensation (SOC)," citing Baltes and Baltes, "Psychological Perspectives on Successful Aging"; Baltes and Carstensen, "The Process of Successful Ageing"; Baltes, "On the Incomplete Architecture of Human Ontogeny (Carstensen, Isaacowitz, and Charles, "Taking Time Seriously," 175).

9. Carstensen, Mikels, and Mather, "Aging and the Intersection of Cognition, Motivation, and Emotion," 347.

10. Ibid., 346.

11. See Timothy Bright, *A Treatise of Melancholy* (1586): "Sometime it falleth out, that melancholie men are found verie wittie and quickly discerne. . . . They be indefatigable [in exercise of their wittes]: which maketh them seeme to haue that of a naturall readinesse" (126); for modern confirmation, see Taylor and Brown, "Illusion and Well-being."

12. This ancient wisdom has been renamed for proper use by academics as "negativity bias"; see Rozin and Royzman, "Negativity Bias." Rozin's early work on disgust remains the best experimental psychological work on that emotion; my own foray into disgust was much indebted to his work.

13. Contrary to Carstensen is the wiser and apter work of Barbara Myerhoff working with old Jews, *Number Our Days,* discussed in part in ch. 7.

CHAPTER 4. OLD VIEWS OF OLD AGE

1. See Parkin, *Old Age in the Roman World;* Shahar, *Growing Old in the Middle Ages;* Rosenthal, *Old Age in Late Medieval England;* Burrow, *The Ages of Man;* Dove, *The Perfect Age of Man's Life;* Thane, "Social Histories of Old Age"; Sears, *The Ages of Man;* and Barbara Harvey's masterful *Living and Dying in England, 1100–1540,* 179–209.

2. The negative view also provides the baseline for the defense of old age Plato puts in the mouth of Cephalus as a time to be relished for being freed from annoying sexual passions: *Republic,* I.329.

3. This same Cato famously did not believe in allowing his slaves' old age to cut into his bottom line. He advocated selling them off, along with the sick ones. Cato, *On Agriculture (De agri cultura),* c. 2.7.

4. See the discussion in Parkin, *Old Age in the Roman World,* 67–68; Cicero has Cato give examples of old men who stayed active publicly and are praised for doing so; *De senectute* 6.

5. See Shahar, *Growing Old in the Middle Ages,* 54–59; see Aers, "The Christian Practice of Growing Old," for his sensitive reading of Will's confrontation with Elde in *Piers Plowman.*

6. See Juvenal, satire 10; see discussion in Parkin, *Old Age in the Roman World,* 80–84. Most of the same vices, with additions, can be found in Innocent III's *De contemptu mundi,* 1.11 (late twelfth century). One poetic genre features an old man warning a thoughtless youth by using vivid displays of his own physical decay to make his point. An especially good example is Oswald von Wolkenstein's *Ich Sich und Hör,* which is printed and discussed in Jones, "The 'Signs of Old Age.'"

7. Cicero, *De senectute* 7.

8. *Rhetoric,* 1389b.

9. *Alcestis,* vv. 669–72.

10. Shakespeare makes partial amends for his and Hamlet's cruel treatment of Polonius by bringing him back in the form of the honorable oldster Gonzalo in *The Tempest.*

11. See Burrow, *The Ages of Man,* 13, 21. He shows that mapping the humors onto a four-ages-of-man grid produced varied results. In some grids it was melancholy that figured as the humor of old age, not phlegm.

12. *Byrhtferth's Enchiridion,* 1.1.132. Byrhtferth of Ramsey died c. 1020. The *Oxford English Dictionary* does not relate Old English *snoflig* to Modern English *snuffly,* but it is rather remarkable that onomatopoeia would produce the proper modern reflex of the Old English form.

13. Maimonides, *Mishneh Torah,* bk. 14, Sanhedrin 1.2.3: "Neither a very aged man nor a eunuch is appointed to any Sanhedrin, since they are apt to be

wanting in tenderness; nor is one who is childless appointed, because a member of the Sanhedrin must be a person who is sympathetic"; noted in Shahar, *Growing Old in the Middle Ages,* 3.

14. On deviant graves, see text at ch. 12, n. 2; not all old wise women were objects of fear, some were just dismissed as senile and mocked, even though their dementia was perceived to give them certain prophetic powers; see the case of Sæunn in *Njal's Saga,* ch. 124. On menopause, see Shahar, *Growing Old in the Middle Ages,* 43–44, citing *De secretis mulierum* of Pseudo-Albertus Magnus.

15. For a parade of horribles, of sons and nephews leaving fathers and uncles destitute, even kicking poor beseeching Dad in the face, see Gerald of Wales, *Speculum duorum,* I.10–17, II.125–27. See R. M. Smith, "Ageing and Well-being in Early Modern England," 68.

16. Bynum, *Jesus as Mother.*

17. He did make a cameo appearance as the "Ancient of Days" in the latest book of the Hebrew Bible, Daniel 7.9–10, where he still, nonetheless, bears the markers of a Semitic storm god.

18. Thomas then offers as a proof text Eph. 4.13 quoted in the text at ch. 1, n. 2; *Summa theologiæ,* 3.46.9 ad 4; discussed in Aers, "The Christian Practice of Growing Old," 44.

19. See Burrow, *The Ages of Man,* 22, 32, 44–45.

20. Thus the !Kung bushmen who care for their old people very well, will, it is reported, give an assist to death for those who can no longer transport themselves; Lee, *The Dobe Ju/'hoansi,* 102.

21. Seneca, epistle 58, I.405–7, quoted in part in Parkin, *Old Age in the Roman World,* 70–71, and oft cited.

CHAPTER 5. OLDER, YES, BUT WISER?

1. Whether the observed increase in bilateral mobilization of the frontal lobes in older adults is compensatory or itself part of the mechanism of decline is debated in the literature; Craik and Bialystok, "Lifespan Cognitive Development," 563. If in childhood we see the increasing localization of cognitive functions to specific locations in the brain, as we age we see the slide back to what Craik and Bialystok call "dedifferentiation."

2. Rabbitt et al., "Age-Associated Losses of Brain Volume," 3.

3. When this book was in press a slew of notices appeared in the popular press referencing work by academic psychologists, like the following: "Brain Slowdown Is the Source of Elderly Wisdom," http://psychcentral.com/news/2010/06/25/brain-slowdown-is-the-source-of-elderly-wisdom/15103

.html; and in *Newsweek:* http://www.newsweek.com/2010/06/18/this-is-your-brain-aging.html. Earlier work in the psychology of wisdom is associated with Paul Baltes and his students. Wisdom was coded and quantified according to several criteria, somewhat broader than merely looking before you leap, as in the work just cited, but yielding questionable results. Baltes and his students discovered, by their criteria of wisdom, that clinical psychologists proved wiser than anyone. If this does not make you laugh, it should make you weep. The results did prompt some embarrassment, though not enough for these researchers to revise the criteria; they note generously, however, that "if there is a psychological bias to our conception of wisdom, this does not prevent nonpsychologists from being among the top performers." See Baltes et al., "People Nominated as Wise"; and Smith, Staudinger, and Baltes, "Occupational Settings Facilitating Wisdom-Related Knowledge."

4. This is true in societies generally classified as gerontocracies—see Linton, "Age and Sex Categories," cited in Parkin, *Old Age in the Roman World,* 3—and clearly in accord with the bulk of evidence. That the popes were old says very little about the treatment of old people who were not popes. See the extended discussions by Rosenthal, *Old Age in Late Medieval England;* Shahar, *Growing Old in the Middle Ages;* and Harvey, *Living and Dying in England, 1100–1540.*

5. This may be why Sarah laughs when the angels/Yahweh announce she will bear a child, even though she is long past menopause. The miracle will not be just her fertility but also Abraham's potency. The biblical text is clear that it was no less a miracle for Abraham to do the deed than for her to conceive: "Now Abraham and Sarah were old and well stricken in age; and it ceased to be with Sarah after the manner of women. Therefore Sarah laughed within herself, saying, After I am waxed old shall I have pleasure, *my lord being old also?*" (Gen. 18.11–12; emphasis added).

6. On sexual intercourse with a young, attractive woman prescribed as a medical treatment, see Peter of Spain, Version A, 225–27, in Wack, *Lovesickness in the Middle Ages,* 261, treatise Bona Fortuna, vv. 140. The curative aspects of such, with an eye to the young rather than the old, are still invoked in the idiom "What he (she) needs is a good lay."

7. Jean de Meun, *Romaunt de la Rose,* vv. 12541–14546; Mme Merle is of the type in *Portrait of a Lady.* A well-meaning version is the Nurse in *Romeo and Juliet.* See Mieszkowski, "Old Age and Medieval Misogyny"; on the duenna, see Mieszkowski's *Medieval Go-betweens,* 9–78. Also see Pratt, "De Vetula." With the duenna compare the old hag of folklore who is transformed into a beautiful young woman, as in Chaucer's *Wyf of Bath's*

Tale. Her transformation might be not just a male fantasy but a female one too. Chaucer suspected the same.

8. Wilmot, "The Disabled Debauchee," vv. 33–48, in *The Complete Poems.*

9. *Iliad,* 2.372; he also provides good advice to his son on chariot-racing strategy: 23.306–48.

10. Ibid., 4.318–25, 7.132–60, 11.669–762.

11. Aristotle, *Rhetoric,* 1378b. Along with Carstensen, sample the work of one of the leading proponents of positive emotions, Professor Barbara Fredrickson, director of the Positive Emotions and Psychophysiology Lab at the University of North Carolina, Chapel Hill; see http://www.unc.edu/peplab/. Consult her book *Positivity,* or find out for yourself what your "positivity ratio" is by taking the online positivity self-test at http://www.positivityratio.com/single.php. I will let it rest at that, having obviously no positive feelings about this kind of work whatsoever. The whole idea of "positive" in this suspect science is unexamined and pretty much contentless. Mostly it seems to mean nothing more than feeling good. What about the appropriateness of feeling good? Sometimes feeling bad is morally required, probably even more morally necessary than feeling good.

12. Studies show the greater propensity of older adults to rely more on appearances and stereotypes than do the young. Even researchers dedicated to the positivity effect find old age to be a time of advancing intolerance and greater stubbornness; see Blanchard-Fields and Kalinauskas, "Theoretical Perspectives," 262–63.

13. Hardy, *Complete Poems,* no. 660.

14. Contrast Myerhoff's discussion in her ethnography of a Jewish senior center where the women dominate, and not just in numbers: *Number Our Days,* 241–68.

15. *On the Sublime,* 9.13–15, attributed to the otherwise unknown Longinus, and usually dated to the late first century A.D.: "The *Odyssey* for the most part consists of narrative, as is characteristic of old age. Accordingly, in the *Odyssey* Homer may be likened to a sinking sun, whose grandeur remains without its intensity."

16. The same proverb with more circumstance can be found in *The Law Code of Manu,* 2.154: "Eminence does not come from age, grey hairs, wealth, or kin. For Brahmins, seniority depends on knowledge, for Ksatryias on valour, and for Vaisyas on grain and wealth; for Sudras alone it depends on age. A man does not become a 'senior' simply because his hair has turned grey. Gods call a man with Vedic learning a 'senior,' even though he may be young" (35).

17. Daughters are not mentioned, though King Lemuel's mother teaches him wisdom: Prov. 31.

18. Even Baltes's studies on wisdom revealed no great correlation of wisdom and age once adolescence was passed; see n. 3 in this chapter. The *Babylonian Talmud,* Berakoth 27b-28a, records that Eleazar b. Azariah, who because of his great wisdom was chosen to be head of the Academy at age eighteen, was blessed with a miraculous partial whitening of his hair and beard overnight so he would be taken seriously; *Babylonian Talmud* (Soncino ed.), http://www.come-and-hear.com/berakoth/berakoth_28 .html. Thanks to Richard Primus for calling this story to my attention.

19. See Curtius, *European Literature,* 98–105; Burrow, *The Ages of Man,* 95–109; enough saints play against this type to establish a competing type: the sinner whose calling comes later, in the style of Paul and Augustine.

20. "Thurghout the Juerie / This litel child, as he cam to and fro / Ful murily than wolde he synge and crie / O Alma redemptoris everemo." *Prioresse's Tale,* vv. 551–54.

21. *Egil's Saga,* chs. 38, 40. The saga is usually dated to the third decade of the thirteenth century, describing events that purportedly took place in the tenth century. The most recent English translation maintains the chapter divisions of the standard Íslenzk fornrit edition until halfway through ch. 56. For chapters after ch. 56, I will provide both numbers, the Íslenzk fornrit number first.

22. Burrow, *The Ages of Man,* 145.

23. Kempe, *Book of Margery Kempe,* ll. 1407–9. I have translated the Middle English, which is accessible in any event. The pilgrims at various times make plans to ditch Margery because of her insufferable weeping.

24. Infancy Gospel of St. Thomas, in M. R. James, *Apocryphal New Testament,* Greek B-text, 4.1. Irish saints' lives were unapologetic about the vengefulness of their precocious youngsters headed for sainthood. See, among many examples, *Life of Berach,* c. 8, in Plummer, *Bethada Náem Nérenn,* 2.25–26.

25. Curtius, *European Literature,* 94.

26. Cited in Burrow, *The Ages of Man,* 147, now readily accessible at http://www .umm.maine.edu/faculty/necastro/drama/ntown/21_christ_and_doctors .html, *Christ Disputes with the Scholars in the Temple,* vv. 221–24.

27. From Jacobus de Varagine, "Life of St. Nicholas"(c. 1275).

CHAPTER 6. THE DARK SIDE OF WISDOM

1. *Battle of Maldon,* vv. 87, 97, 140–41; slaughter-wolves = *wælwulfas.* The *wæl* in wælwulfas is cognate with Old Norse *valr,* as in Valhalla and Valkyrie, with the *val* meaning slain: Valhalla is the hall of those killed in battle, and Valkyries are those who choose the battle dead.

2. See Herzog, *Cunning;* Miller, "Deceit in War and Trade."

3. Also Prov. 21.23: "Whoso keepeth his mouth and his tongue keepeth his soul from troubles"; or from the *Dead Sea Scrolls* this small fragment (4Q412): "Put a lock on your lips and protecting doors to your tongue."

4. *Hávamál* 27.

5. See too Cicero, *De senectute* 4, where Fabius is celebrated.

6. Murray, "Confession Before 1215," 55.

7. *Hávamál* 7.

8. "The Instruction of Ptahhotep," v. 618, in Lichtheim, *Ancient Egyptian Literature,* 75. The book of Proverbs is heavily indebted to the Egyptian wisdom literature.

9. *Hávamál* 16.

10. 2 Sam. 19.32–40.

11. 2 Sam. 16.5–8, 19.22–24.

12. As regards being "in the know," consider the "wisdom" of the Mafia wise guy. It hardly involves acuity of mind. It is more a way of carrying himself, a way of indicating that he is in with the right guys, is *in* a certain kind of *know.*

13. Solomon does not even care to disguise from Shimei that the new grounds are a pretext, but it is the letter, not the spirit, that governs oaths: 1 Kings 2.42–44.

14. Amasa and Joab's mothers were sisters. David was keeping the chief military office in the family, so to speak.

15. I must confess to finding this speech one of the sublimest of many sublime moments in the Hebrew Bible. Joab has the tough cool of my favorite character in literature: Skarphedinn Njalsson of *Njal's Saga.*

16. For Benaiah's exploits, one of David's heroic thirty, see 2 Sam. 23.20–23.

17. Solomon suggests that any violation of the Tabernacle is on Joab's head for his taunting them to kill him at the altar: "And the king said unto him, 'Do *as he [Joab] hath said,* and fall upon him.'" But Joab has no authority to waive the Lord's rights regarding the altar.

18. See text at ch. 5, n. 3.

CHAPTER 7. *HOMO QUERELUS* (MAN THE COMPLAINER)

1. Bernardino, *Opera,* vol. 7, sermo 16, cited in Shahar, "Old Age in the High and Late Middle Ages," 50. Bernardino repeats an observation already found in Cicero, *De senectute* 2, though Bernardino gives it a bit more zest, and Plato has Cephalus complain about those old men who complain of their debilities (*Republic,* I.329). See also the passage from Euripides' *Al-*

cestis in ch. 4. The commonplace is frequently encountered: "Al we wilniþ to ben old, Wy is eld ihatid? (MS Harley 913, f54v, *The Kildare Poems,* early fourteenth century).

2. Ursula Dronke's apt coinage in "The Role of Sexual Themes," 11.

3. Viaticum, 1.20, in Wack, *Lovesickness in the Middle Ages,* 191, v. 47.

4. Alfred, §60, Liebermann, *Gesetze,* 1.83; *Leges Henrici Primi,* §93.19, 296. Also the *Leis Willemi,* §11.1, Liebermann, *Gesetze,* 1.501.

5. Michalowski, *Letters from Early Mesopotamia,* 47–48, no. 63, Sargonic period, 2200 B.C..

6. Wente, *Letters from Ancient Egypt,* 216, no. 352.

7. Pardee, *The Context of Scripture,* 3.113, no. 38.

8. Rosenberg, "Complaint Discourse." This delightful article describes the culture of pervasive complaint among the Bushmen, where complaining is mobilized to maintain the rough egalitarianism of the culture. A hunter brings in a kill; you, the recipient of the meat, complain about how long it took him, the puniness of the portion he gave you, etc. He complains about how small the animal is, how bad a shot he is. The anxiety for the recipient is being reduced to a debtor, the anxiety for the hunter is being thought to be getting too full of himself and ending up the object of everyone's venomous envy.

9. *The Amarna Letters* are conventionally abbreviated EA, for El Amarna. EA 124, 137.

10. Dostoyevsky, *Notes from the Underground,* 1.4. Groans and moans, like so many markers of supposed inner states, can often represent contrasting sentiments. Groans and moans mark pleasure too, not just sexual, but for a good scratching of the ears, if you are a dog, or the back, if you are human. Tears, smiles, laughter, flushing, blanching, trembling, and stares can readily indicate antithetical internal states. Underground Man's claim is harsher. Even when the toothache is real, he argues, the groans are registering a species of pleasure.

11. In the Jewish liturgy Lamentations 5.16, represents the primal oy.

12. Lambert, "The Poem of the Righteous Sufferer," in *Babylonian Wisdom Literature,* 33, vv. 43–46, dated on stylistic grounds to the Cassite period, 1500–1200 B.C..

13. Jesus is giving the Aramaic rendering of the Hebrew of Ps. 22.1.

14. Cited in Gluckman, "Moral Crises," 23.

15. Myerhoff, *Number Our Days,* xv, 7; similarly Cahan, *The Rise of David Levinsky,* 153.

16. Myerhoff, *Number Our Days,* 60.

17. Ibid., 56–57.

18. Ibid., 110.
19. See Shklar, *Ordinary Vices,* 49.
20. *Grettir's Saga,* ch. 47.
21. Levi, *Survival in Auschwitz,* 73. I discuss this in a different context in *The Mystery of Courage,* 208.
22. Adam Smith, *Theory of Moral Sentiments,* 1.2.5–3.1.

CHAPTER 8. OLD SAINTS, OLD KILLERS, AND MORE COMPLAINTS

1. Murray, *Reason and Society in the Middle Ages,* 372. More than thirty years after its publication this book still dazzles and provokes in the most fruitful of ways.
2. Any good pirate/merchant quickly discerned what was of value to the people he plundered, for then it would also be of value to him, providing him with an immediate market for sale. Illiterate Vikings could thus become booksellers. Some ten years after Anskar lost his books, we find an English nobleman named Alfred and his wife, Wærburh, donating books to Christ Church in Canterbury that they had purchased or ransomed from "the heathen army with our pure money, that was with pure gold." Whitelock, *English Historical Documents,* 539–40, no. 98.
3. *Vita Anskarii,* ch. 16.
4. Ibid., ch. 26.
5. Ibid., ch. 40.
6. Ibid.
7. There are the roses and violets of red martyrdom and the lilies of white martyrdom. Anskar's martyrdom, such as it is, would be white. Jerome, letter 108 (A.D. 404) to Eustochium, on her mother Paula's death, §32; English translation available at *Christian Classics Ethereal Library:* http://www.ccel.org/ccel/schaff/npnf206.v.CVIII.html.
8. "and which, *he thought,* had been promised him (et sibi repromissum *putabat*) . . . for it cannot be proved that this was promised as he himself interpreted the word martyrdom"; *Vita Anskarii,* ch. 42.
9. Adam of Bremen, *History of the Archbishops,* 2.60.
10. *Vita Anskarii,* ch. 35.
11. Ibid.
12. Even the most intensely self-mortifying saints were not averse to complaining. St. Anthony, after suffering the torments of demons, complained not at all during the agony, but no sooner does the Divine make its presence felt than Anthony complains: "But Anthony . . . getting his breath again, and being freed from pain, besought the vision which had appeared to him,

saying, 'Where wert thou? Why didst thou not appear at the beginning to make my pains to cease?'" *Athanasius: The Life of St. Antony,*I.10, *Early English Church Texts:* http://www.earlychurchtexts.com/main/athanasius/vita_antonii_01.shtml.

13. *Laxdæla saga,* ch. 28.

14. *Landnámabók,* S 16. Glum (his name is not cognate with Modern English *glum;* the name has a long vowel and is a poetic word for "bear") does not exclude himself from the ambit of his prayer, which is a crucial part of its pure generous simplicity.

CHAPTER 9. COMPLAINING AGAINST THE MOST HIGH

1. More formally known as obeisance formulae but thus termed by Schniedewind and Hunt, jocularly importing "flopping formula" from theoretical physics but eminently suitable for the Near Eastern epistolary style; see *A Primer on Ugaritic,* 44.

2. EA 195.

3. See also Pss. 30, 88.11–12.

4. E.g., Ps. 22.6–8.

5. Similarly, this Hittite prayer (c. 1300 B.C.) issues a pointed reminder that the gods themselves will die of starvation if they do not stop the plague: "O gods, What is this that you have done? You have allowed a plague into Hatti, and the whole of Hatti is dying. No one prepares for you the offering bread and the libation anymore. The plowmen who used to work the fallow fields of the gods have died, so they do not work or reap the fields of the gods. The grinding women who used to make the offering bread for the gods have died, so they do not make the gods' offering bread any longer." "Mursili's Hymn and Prayer to the Sun-Goddess of Arinna" (CTH 376.A), §6, Singer, *Hittite Prayers,* 52.

6. Tachanun, a couple of pages long, is said most weekdays but is suspended on certain holidays. Psalm 6 also figures prominently in Christian penitential devotion, it being the first of the seven penitential psalms.

7. See fig. 4 in ch. 19 for Jehu groveling, nose to the dirt.

8. The Mourner's Kaddish, mostly in Aramaic, with the last couple of lines in Hebrew, is as follows. Its most surprising feature is that there is not a mention of the dead person or of death:

> Magnified and sanctified be God's great name in the world which He created according to His will. May he establish His kingdom during our lifetime and during the lifetime of Israel. Let us say, Amen.
>
> May God's great name be blessed forever and ever.

Blessed, glorified, honored and extolled, adored and acclaimed
be the name of the Holy One, though God is beyond all praises and
songs of adoration which can be uttered. Let us say, Amen.

May there be peace and life for all of us and for all Israel. Let us
say, Amen.

Let He who makes peace in the heavens, grant peace to all of us
and to all Israel. Let us say, Amen.

9. For my take on praise and flattery, see *Faking It,* ch. 8.
10. Chazan, *European Jewry,* 255–56.
11. See also variously those Psalms in which the psalmist contends with God:
Pss. 13, 25, 42, 43, 44, 73, 74, 80, 89.
12. See Weinfeld, "Covenant Terminology," 193. So too in the Hebrew Bible
the notion of forgetting does not so much reference the mental state of
forgetfulness as mark a covenant violation, especially in cases of apostasy
and idolatry; e.g., Judg. 3.7, also Ps. 44.18 (Eng. 44.17); Weinfeld, "Covenant Terminology," 197.
13. See my discussion of remembrance in *Hamlet* in *Eye for an Eye,* 95–99.
14. This passage is in the Mishneh. The Talmud is made up of the Mishneh, a
compendium of the oral rabbinic law, compiled roughly between the first
century B.C. and A.D. 200, and the Gemara, which is a commentary on
the Mishneh and was developed over the next three hundred years. The
former is mostly in Hebrew, the latter in Aramaic.
15. *Ta'anit* 15A, Steinsaltz, *The Talmud,* 3.
16. Ibid., 5. The prayer to be recited is the Amidah, to this day the central
prayer of the liturgy. It is said while standing, which is what Amidah
means; see also *Faking It,* 68–72, for an extended discussion of pretending to say this prayer. It varies in length, depending on additions made
for special days. For the fasts decreed to bring rain special blessings are
inserted. One of these mentions Abraham on Moriah and hence references
the sacrifice of Isaac, for which see the discussion that follows in the text.
17. *Ta'anit* 16A, Steinsaltz, *The Talmud,* 16.
18. Ibid.
19. The view that Isaac was slaughtered on Moriah, contrary to the literal biblical
text, has a long history, detailed impeccably by Shalom Spiegel in *The Last
Trial.* The ashes of Isaac were already understood to be nonmetaphorical
in the first generation of commentators known as the Amoraim, c. A.D. 200.
Other traditions argue that the ram that was substituted for Isaac was a pet
bellwether named Isaac; see Ginzberg, *The Legends of the Jews,* 252n245.
20. Rabbi Steinsaltz (*The Talmud,* 16) has a long note showing that the ashes
as Isaac's is the accepted interpretation.

21. Maine, *Lectures,* 39–40. Sitting dharna is of ancient pedigree. Thus *The Law Code of Manu,* 8.49, p. 126. The means employed by the low to assert claims against the mighty or to resist their claims are discussed by Baumgartner, "Social Control from Below"; and by Scott, *Domination and the Arts of Resistance.*

22. *Ancient Laws of Ireland,* 1.113.

23. So too Terence McSwiney, lord mayor of Cork, who starved himself in Brixton prison in 1920 after a seventy-four-day hunger strike.

24. *Njal's Saga,* ch. 88. I am following Magnusson/Pálsson's translation for *Njal's Saga;* otherwise, *Hávamál* excepted, Old Norse translations are mine. *Njal's Saga* was written in the latter decades of the thirteenth century; its action takes place between roughly 970 and 1015. See also *Grettir's Saga,* ch. 45; *Ljósvetninga saga,* ch. 18; *Vatnsdæla saga,* ch. 24.

25. Cited in Little, *Benedictine Maledictions,* 161. I am much indebted to Little's book. See also Geary, "Humiliation of Saints."

26. Babel, *Collected Stories,* 3–7.

27. The creditor may have his son or servant do the sitting, or he may confine his own son and threaten to kill him. Jolly, *Hindu Law and Custom,* 318–19.

28. *Ta'anit* 16A, Steinsaltz, *The Talmud,* 19–20.

29. Apparently there is a rule about sitting dharna against the Persian king: "for none might enter into the king's gate clothed with sackcloth." Esther hastens to send Mordecai proper raiment.

30. See also Job 7.1–2, 11, which uses the image of a hireling trying to collect his wages unjustly withheld, as he sits dharna-like in squalor crying out unto (and against) the Lord:

> Has not man a hard service upon earth,
> and are not his days like the days of a hireling?
> Like a slave who longs for the shadow,
> and like a hireling who looks for his wages. . . .
> Therefore I will not restrain my mouth;
> I will speak in the anguish of my spirit;
> I will complain in the bitterness of my soul. (RSV)

31. Reality TV seems to suggest our capacities for Schadenfreude in another's loss of dignity are near inexhaustible, at least when the humiliation is not taking place in our physical presence.

32. "Kum" is an epithet meaning something like brother or friend, which presumes the state of relations that has yet to be agreed to by the victim's brother. It adds a dollop more coerciveness to the ritual.

33. From Durham, *Some Tribal Origins, Laws and Customs of the Balkans,* 89–90, quoted in Boehm, *Blood Revenge,* 134. Compare a similar cere-

mony among the mountain Jews of Dagestan in which the family of the killer had to kiss the dust from the feet of their victim's kin at the scene of reconciliation; see Blady, *Jewish Communities,* ch. 6.

34. Little, *Benedictine Maledictions.*

35. *Ta'anit* 16A 2–4, Steinsaltz, *The Talmud,* 16.

36. Little, *Benedictine Maledictions,* 135, citing the *Miracula S. Aigulfi,* ch. 4.

37. Ibid., 237.

38. Jolly, *Hindu Law and Custom,* 319.

39. Gregory of Tours, *The History of the Franks,* 5.18; see also the flop of William the Conqueror before Ealdred, archbishop of York; van Caenegem, *English Lawsuits,* no. 1, 1.1, also no. 139, 1.111. Moses does the same at the outset of the Korah rebellion (Num. 16.4).

40. This point is made by Rosenwein, *To Be the Neighbor of Saint Peter,* 135.

41. Unless the lord was *compelled* to play the beggar. See Whitman's discussion of legislation passed in 1790 to change the rule regarding payment of the *cens,* a nominal tax in *ancien regime* France, which was to have been brought to the lord as a sign of respect and subordination by his free tenants. The new legislation forced the lord to have to go collect the cens no differently than were he an ordinary creditor; he had to seek out his debtor. The lord, after a fashion, was forced to sit dharna upon his now not so lowly debtor. "The Seigneurs Descend to the Rank of Creditors."

42. Appian, *The Civil Wars,* 2.15. The Latin idiom for to put on mourning garb, rendered in the passage as "miserable clothing"—indeed, Cicero's own phrase for his behavior—is *vestem mutare,* simply to change clothes. This is clearly a euphemism. Euphemism often suggests the presence of taboo or the sacred; see Cicero, *Letters to Atticus,* 3.15.5.

43. See Maine, *Lectures,* 40: "What would follow if the creditor simply allowed the debtor to starve? Undoubtedly the Hindoo supposes that some supernatural penalty would follow; indeed, he generally gives definiteness to it by retaining a Brahmin to starve himself vicariously, and no Hindoo doubts what would come of causing a Brahmin's death." Along with professional self-abnegators consider those extreme cults of self-abnegation, the Cynics, and certain Shiva worshipers, among other "renouncers" in India. See Ingalls, "Cynics and Pasupatas."

44. See my *Anatomy of Disgust,* 157–61, and the bibliographical references there.

45. *Ta'anit* 19A, Steinsaltz, *The Talmud,* 66–67. The charmed circle finds its way into Irish and Hindu debt-collection practices very much of the sitting dharna type: I will not leave this circle until you pay what you owe. Jolly, *Hindu Law and Custom,* 319, mentions an ancient Indian custom of

drawing a circle, this time around the debtor, which if the debt is not paid the debtor cannot step outside. Honi was hardly a humble man and his lack of humility has been rewarded by an enormous bibliography devoted to his drawing this circle and his successful bearding of God; see most recently the discussion in Stone, "Rabbinic Legal Magic."

46. The Gemara indicates Honi has some biblical warrant for waiting out God in this fashion; see Habakkuk 2.1: "I will stand on my watch, Take up my station at the post, And wait to see what He will say to me, What He will reply to my complaint." *Ta'anit* 23A, Steinsaltz, *The Talmud,* 116. See Stone, "Rabbinic Legal Magic," 107, discussing a midrash on the Hab. passage.

CHAPTER 10. GIVING UP SMOTING FOR GOOD

1. These lines are not in William Goldman's book (1973) but were added to the screenplay (1987), which he also wrote. This chapter's title might be lost on anyone younger than fifty-five; the phrase I am quoting comes from Allan Sherman's send-up of "Greensleeves," "The Ballad of Sir Greenbaum" (*My Son the Folksinger,* 1962).

2. Burnett, *Revenge,* xvi–xvii.

3. See Zelizer, *Morals and Markets,* 46, on legislative resistance in the nineteenth century to the legality of life insurance on the grounds that is was blood money.

4. Retiring to a monastery *ad succurrendum* to end an active career of killing and plundering need not have been undertaken in old age. For an old illiterate warrior who cannot give up his old ways in the cloister and who instead beats and kills the monks, see the comic epic of Guillaume d'Orange, *Moniage Guillaume,* "William in the Monastery," in Ferrante, *Guillaume d'Orange,* 281–307.

5. As with the final demoralization of Henry II, when he found that even his favorite son John had turned against him; also see Hezekiah, Isa. 38.2.

6. Worse than having to say "I give" was being forced to say "uncle," the absurdity of which added even more humiliation and disgrace to the defeat.

7. See my *Humiliation,* 106–7, where I treat a couple of these cases in the context of emotion display.

8. The term used for bed here, *kör,* seems to have a more technical, almost legal meaning than the usual term, *rekkja,* used in the previous sentence of the passage. On the possible Indo-European significance of *kör,* see Oliver, "Sick-Maintenance in Anglo-Saxon Law."

9. *Egil's Saga,* ch. 24.

10. Ibid., ch. 27.
11. Ibid.
12. See, e.g., n. 5 above and 1 Macc. 6.5–8.
13. Ne sorga, snotor guma.   Selre bið æghwæm
    þæt he his freond wrece,   þonne he fela murne (vv. 1384–85).
    Translations are mine.
14. The anthropological citation classic on the connection of grief, anger, and revenge is Rosaldo, *Knowledge and Passion.*
15. See Wehlau, "'Seeds of Sorrow,'" 2–3.
16. Burkert, *Homo Necans,* 53, discussing Achilles heaping bloody corpses of animals and humans to accompany Patroklos to Hades.
17. *Sturlu saga,* ch. 36.
18. Sturla earlier made a joke to this effect within seconds of Thorbjorg having stabbed him: "'Let's all sit down, and discuss a settlement. No one needs to lose their temper over this because women have various ways of pursuing love; Thorbjorg and I have long been close friends.' He held his hand to his face, the blood flowing down his cheek" (ch. 30).
19. Another old codger, who had been a notorious Viking in his youth, tries to get a killing done from bed. Like Sturla, somewhat less comically (and perhaps inadvertently), he makes a joke of the ritual; *Thorstein the Staff-Struck.* The classic example of an old man taking to bed in the saga corpus is Havard in *Hávarðar saga Ísfirðings;* old and lame, his son slain, he stays in bed for three years until roused by the goading of his wife. Revenge rejuvenates him and he seems to grow younger the more he kills, going rather postal, against the usual saga norm. The saga can be seen as a parodic pushing to the extreme of the taking-to-bed ritual.
20. *Njal's Saga,* ch. 128.
21. Ibid., ch. 129.
22. *Grágás* II.66.
23. In case 1, Kveld-Ulf, in some part of his consciousness, may have known that taking to bed would irritate his louring son Skallagrim to action.
24. *History of William Marshal,* vol. 2, vv. 16643ff.
25. Villehardouin, *The Conquest of Constantinople,* ch. 16, p. 122. Villehardouin was an eyewitness to most of the events he describes, and was often in the presence of Dandolo. Earlier, ch. 9, p. 71: "Let me tell you here of an outstanding deed of valour. The doge of Venice, although an old man and completely blind, stood at the bow of his galley, with the banner of Saint Mark unfurled before. He cried out to his men to put him on shore, or else he himself would deal with them as they deserved. They obeyed him promptly."

26. For other Icelandic examples, see Ármann Jakobsson, "The Specter of Old Age."
27. *Íslendinga saga,* ch. 138.
28. *Grágás* II.305.
29. See also above n. 19; *Laxdœla saga,* ch. 37.
30. See *Hrafnkel,* ch. 8, Pálsson trans., ch. 17; cf. *Víga-Glúms saga,* ch. 18.
31. Orwell, *The Road to Wigan Pier,* 174–75.
32. *Grágás* Ia.224, 246, II.68.

CHAPTER 11. PARALYSIS OF THE SPIRIT

1. The passage has been ably commented on, most recently from a legal perspective, by Jurasinski, *Ancient Privileges,* 113–48. Ruth Wehlau in "'Seeds of Sorrow'" has a sensitive treatment of it, comparing it with Egil's *Sonatorrek;* Joseph Harris, "Beowulf's Last Words" discusses the speech as an instance of a "death song," a genre he identifies and whose formal criteria he sets out. Linda Georgianna's "King Hrethel's Sorrow and the Limits of Heroic Action in *Beowulf,*" is often cited and widely praised. It has much to recommend it in its close attention to various verses, but its core thesis is flawed. It claims that the whole episode is meant to subvert the heroic ethic in a sea of contradiction. But her view of the heroic, as Harris points out, is a straw man. The sagas, and the best epics, face up to the fact, like any legal and moral system has to, that there are cases in which there are no easy answers. That they knew there were hard cases does not mean they thought their ethic any more absurd than we might think ours is because it generates hard cases in which competing norms clash. The heroic ethic is not subverted; they accept, with intelligent awareness, that human moral and ethical systems, no matter how constituted, will not always have satisfying answers for the rich variety of problems people must face.

2. Wæs þam yldestan   ungedefelice
   mæges dædum   morþorbed stred,
   syððan hyne Hæthcyn   of hornbogan,
   his freawine   flane geswencte,
   miste mercelses   ond his mæg ofscet,
   broðor oðerne   blodigan gare.
   þæt wæs feohleas gefeoht,   fyrenum gesyngad,
   hreðre hygemeðe;   sceolde hwæðre swa þeah
   æðeling unwrecen   ealdres linnan. (vv. 2435–43)

3. See William of Malmesbury, *Gesta regum Anglorum,* 4.333.

4. Orderic, *The Ecclesiastical History,* 3.2.29–31: one died of a poisoned apple, another by a fit of madness "in the flower of youth, for he had raided the land of the church of Lisieux."

5. See Wehlau, "'Seeds of Sorrow,'" 9–11.

6. Swa bið geomorlic   gomelum ceorle
  to gebidanne,   þæt his byre ride
  giong on galgan,   þonne he gyd wrece,
  sarigne sang,   þonne his sunu hangað
  hrefne to hroðre,   ond he him helpe ne mæg
  eald ond infrod   ænige gefremman,
  symble bið gemyndgad   morna gehwylce
  eaforan ellorsið;   . . .
  Gesyhð sorhcearig   on his suna bure
  winsele westne,   windge reste,
  reotge berofene;   . . .
  Gewiteð þonne on sealman,   sorhleoð gæleð
  an æfter anum;   þuhte him eall to rum,
  wongas ond wicstede. (vv. 2444–51a, 2455–57a, 2460–62a)

7. See too the *Iliad,* 13.659, for a father weeping for his son dead in battle, and to add to the despair "no man-price came his way."

8.   wihte ne meahte
  on ðam feorhbonan   fæghðe gebetan;
  no ðy ær he þone heaðorinc   hatian ne meahte
  laðum dædum,   þeah him leof ne wæs.
  He ða mid þære sorhge,   þe him sio sar belamp,
  gumdream ofgeaf,   godes leoht geceas. (vv. 2464b–69)

9. Peter the Great had his eldest son Alexi done in. Though David ordered that Absalom be spared, Joab thought David should be following the second course. In Joab's estimation David was too soft on this matter to think clearly.

10. The classic anthropological article on killing within the kin group is Schapera, "The Sin of Cain," which shows that even intentional kin killing could be dealt with rather leniently, and in any event rarely by killing the killer.

11. For a fully argued account see my *Bloodtaking,* ch. 2; and *Faking It,* ch. 7, some of whose conclusions I reproduce here. On liability for accidental kin killing addressing this *Beowulf* passage, see Jurasinski's discussion in *Ancient Privileges.*

12. Hittite Laws, §1, 3, in Roth, *Law Collections from Mesopotamia.*

13. See above n. 4. See too the account of Abbot Wulfstan of Gloucester, c. 1090, who pleads with five brothers of a man killed by accident to accept the

proffered compensation from the killer. Wulfstan prostrates himself before the angry brothers, begging them to accept money for their dead brother. To no avail. See van Caenegem, *English Lawsuits,* no. 139, 1.111.

14. For an ostensible praise poem composed to redeem his own head that can also be read as a satire of its recipient, see *Egil's Saga,* ch. 60 (61); for his annoyance at having to pay a verse in compensation for a bejeweled shield, see ch. 78 (81).

15. Thorgerd is one tough customer; she plays a prominent role in *Laxdæla saga,* chs. 52–53, 55, where she involves herself vigorously in avenging one of her sons by making sure her other sons do not get cold feet.

16. *Egil's Saga,* ch. 78 (79).

17. Ibid., st. 9, st. 22, st. 23b–24a.

18. Ibid., st. 17. For an insightful reading of the poem, see Wehlau, "'Seeds of Sorrow,'" 12–16.

19. See my *Eye for an Eye,* 93; Daube, *Studies in Biblical Law,* 116.

20. Egil is one of those wild men who needs to have someone play the role of his manager. In Iceland they are women: his niece and wife, primarily. In Norway it is his friend Arinbjorn.

21. On defixiones see Faraone, "Agonistic Context of Early Greek Binding Spells."

22. Dukeminier et al., *Property,* 112–15; on limitations and *usucapion* see the brief but elegant discussion in Maine, *Ancient Law,* 8.284–88.

CHAPTER 12. YES, YOU CAN TAKE IT WITH YOU

1. See Stalsberg, "Women as Actors in North European Viking Age Trade" on scales in female graves; see generally the discussion in Bauschatz, *The Well and the Tree,* 33–57, discussing "house" as well as "vehicle" burials.

2. Reynolds, *Anglo-Saxon Deviant Burial Customs,* 72–74.

3. *Laxdæla saga,* ch. 17.

4. Ibid.; for a different angle on Olaf's laying the ghost of Hrapp, see Sayers, "The Alien and Alienated as Unquiet Dead," 245–47.

5. 572 N.Y.S. 2d 672.

6. *Egil's Saga,* ch. 27

7. Egil is given other compensation specifically designated for the loss of a brother; ibid., ch. 55. Notice that the compensation comes not from the killers but from the person in whose service the person died. The king recognized he owed compensation because he was the beneficiary of the soldier's sacrifice and thus owed a return gift; the king could also be seen to have been part of the causal chain that cost the soldier his life.

8. Ibid., ch. 58 (59).

9. Ibid.

10. Ibid., ch. 85 (88).

11. Ibid.

12. Egil's grave might have been unmarked. The penultimate chapter of the saga mentions that Egil was disinterred and reburied in a churchyard after Iceland had converted, but his bones are attributed to him not because they were dug up from a place known to be Egil's grave but because of their size and because his skull withstood an ax blow meant to test its unusual thickness. Ibid., ch. 86 (89).

13. Wyatt, "The Story of King Keret," 1.16.vi .55. Horon is a god.

14. See Shahar, *Growing Old in the Middle Ages,* 88–97.

15. The metaphor of the dead hand plays both sides of the fence. In modern law, the way I have been using it, the dead hand refers to the control the prior owner still wields from the grave. Not until the seventeenth century does the *Oxford English Dictionary* record it used in that sense, its modern sense. But in the thirteenth-century statutes of Mortmain (dead hand) restricting transfers of property to the church, it was not the donor but the recipient, the church, whose immortal corporate hand was the killer hand.

16. *Lucas v. Hamm,* 56 Cal. 2d 583; 364 P.2d 685.

17. See Leach, "Perpetuities in a Nutshell"; this law review article has a just claim to being perhaps the most read of that unfortunate genre.

18. Court of Chancery, 1787; 1 Cox 324, 29 Eng. Rep. 1186.

19. One of the RAP reforms adopted in a number of states instituted "a wait and see" approach to determine if subsequent events actually turned out to violate the rule. The reform was overly friendly to the dead hand and to lawyers, for now a final determination of the validity of a will might not be able to be made for as long as a century after the death of the testator.

20. See the Uniform Statutory Rule against Perpetuities, now the rule in a majority of states, e.g., Michigan Compiled Laws, §§ 554.71–4; the English Law Commission goes further, recommending abolition of the common law rule, to be replaced by a 125-year period of dead-hand control; see Dukeminier et al., 265n32.

21. *Babylonian Talmud* (Soncino ed.), Berakoth 18b, http://www.come-and-hear.com/berakoth/berakoth_18.html. As in the case of Hrapp, the doorpost or the threshold takes on special significance. Presumably the household spirits lodged there guard the money.

CHAPTER 13. OWING THE DEAD

1. See H. G. Pitt, *Abraham Lincoln,* an homage by a Brit who makes the point of how important to European freedom and democracy Lincoln was.

2. On the obligation to remember the dead, or the wish to be remembered by the living, see Margalit, *The Ethics of Memory.*

3. On the violence in Assyrian reliefs, especially regarding the lion hunts, see the account, with an academic Freudian cast to it, in Bersani and Dutoit, *The Forms of Violence,* esp. 24–66. See, e.g., among many, the picture of the vomiting lion, sick unto death, at http://demo.mdid.org/media/get/3924/ne-200_img0027/11770/full/.

4. Mandeville, *The Fable of the Bees,* remark R, 1.219–20.

5. See Wills, *Lincoln at Gettysburg,* 53, on the style of generalization and condensation in the address.

6. Lincoln's genius as a writer is oft celebrated. Most recently see Gopnik's *Angels and Ages.* Gary Wills's treatment of the address remains unsurpassed.

7. The high stakes of the American Civil War for English democracy and democracy in general was recognized by non-Americans at the time. See Charles Darwin, letter 3766 to Asa Gray, October 16, 1862, quoted in part in Gopnik, *Angels and Ages,* 134, at http://www.darwinproject.ac.uk/home.

CHAPTER 14. GOING SOFT

1. McDaniel, Einstein, and Jacoby, "New Considerations in Aging and Memory," 275–77; see ch. 2, n. 9; ch. 3, n. 3.

2. See Margalit, *The Ethics of Memory,* 62, who claims that sentimentality is an "essential element" of nostalgia, which is not counted in nostalgia's favor: "We should be suspicious of sentimentalists" (33).

3. Dames, *Amnesiac Selves,* 28–29. My hasty account of a folk nostalgia ignores the discussion of nostalgia in postmodern literary theory. An overview with suitable bibliography, perhaps tolerable to a medievalist, can be found in Trilling, *Aesthetics of Nostalgia,* 5, where it might baffle one to find that "nostalgia . . . must be understood in a dialectical relationship to history: as it attempts to reconstruct the lost past in the present moment, its manipulation of material events into aesthetic objects turns the present into history, thereby reifying the separation between present and past." I am not sure if I know what that means, or if I buy what I do understand it to say.

4. Cahan, *The Rise of David Levinsky,* 526.

5. Gratefulness pretty much coincides with thankfulness, but both are distinguished from gratitude in the ways I am suggesting; they tend to be diffuse

as to their intended object, whereas gratitude is focused on an identifiable benefactor.

6. With the rose-colored glasses that characterize the genre, Fredrickson lists gratitude as a positive emotion; see Fredrickson, "Gratitude." Gratitude may well be experienced positively by the person to whom it is directed, but obviously that person is not the one experiencing gratitude. It is often thought of as a bitter, or at best a highly ambivalent, experience because it assumes the inferiority and indebtedness of the person having to display it; see the classic observation by Hobbes on the counterfeited love, but really secret hatred, of those who receive greater benefits from one we think our equal than there is hope to requite (*Leviathan,* I.11). See too Seneca's epistle 19, *Moral Epistles,* I.131.

7. *Faking It,* 77–95.

8. *Hávamál* 23, Terry translation. The last line of the stanza is stronger than she renders it; literally: "and everything is as miserable as it was."

CHAPTER 15. LITTLE THINGS; OR, WHAT IF?

1. Although I had intended to paste in a previously published article, "Near Misses," and make a few changes to link it better with the themes of this book, in fact very little of it survives. It fell victim to that sick feeling I discussed earlier that one experiences when revisiting one's prior work.

2. McDonough, *Platoon Leader,* 15.

3. Studies show that old people simplify the syntax of their spoken sentences. They also have trouble following and producing left-branching sentences and tend to avoid them. Burke and Shafto, "Language and Aging," 381, 421.

CHAPTER 16. DEFYING AUGURY

1. The prayer existed in its standard form in the eighteenth century, American and Protestant in origin. The final lines are now usually altered banally, but mercifully, thus: "May angels watch me through the night / And wake me with the morning light."

2. See Jenkins's edition, 561–63.

3. The sense of something's up or the lesser sense of having a hunch has been shown to be a necessary part of so-called rational decision making. Thus Damasio, with neuroscience, backs Hume's purposely provocative adage: "Reason is, and ought only to be the slave of the passions, and can never pretend to any other office than to serve and obey them." Hume, *Treatise,*

2.3.3; see Damasio, *Descartes' Error.*

4. Lambert, "The Poem of the Righteous Sufferer," in *Babylonian Wisdom Literature,* 33, vv. 49–54.

5. The Old Norse cognate of Old English *Wyrd* is *Urð;* the initial W was lost in many positions in Old Norse where it would appear in the other Germanic languages. Urð was the name of one of the Norns, or Fates, she representing the past. Scholars have debated the question of how Christianized Wyrd was, thus moving it more toward Providence or Fortuna; see Frakes, *The Fate of Fortune in the Early Middle Ages.* Nothing hinges on that here, though consider this near-blasphemous line from an Old English charm: Þrymmas syndan Cristes myccle / Wyrd byð swiðost (The powers of Christ are great / Wyrd is strongest); see Deskis, *Beowulf and the Medieval Proverb Tradition,* 70–71.

6. I discuss fate, luck, and tutelary spirits in *Audun and the Polar Bear,* 73ff. See the nice discussion by Raphals, "Fate, Fortune, Chance and Luck in Chinese and Greek," esp. 537–38.

7. People were apt to mix up Providence and Fate despite Christian and Jewish theologians and philosophers undertaking considerable effort to distinguish them. I do not mean to distinguish here among related notions like Fortune, Fate, and Providence. For my purposes all can be invoked to carry out the functions fate talk is mobilized to carry out.

8.   Wyrd oft nereð
    unfægne eorl,   þonne his ellen deah. (vv. 572–73)

This proverb has elicited considerable attention; see the bibliographical note to these lines in *Klaeber's Beowulf.*

9. Vv. 1056–1057a.

10. See Cook, "A Note on *Beowulf*"; and the discussion in Deskis, *Beowulf and the Medieval Proverb Tradition,* 73–75.

11. Chaucer, *The Legend of Good Women,* v. 1773, where it is a "hardy" rapist invoking the proverb.

12. See *Oxford English Dictionary,* s.v. "fey," a., and s.v. "fay," n.

13. On the intimate connections of drinking, boasting, and vows, see Robinson, *Beowulf and the Appositive Style,* 75–79.

14. Deskis, *Beowulf and the Medieval Proverb Tradition,* 76, humorously paraphrases Beowulf thus: "Fate often helps a brave man, but I deserve full credit for this victory."

CHAPTER 17. FRANKLY, I DO GIVE A DAMN

1. With not giving a damn, shit, fuck, or rat's ass compare one of the foundational principles of the cult of positivity: "putting it all behind you." That "behind" the "it" gets put is not the past as we think of it, one from which memory and obligation are recalled, but a behind of oblivion, in which even if a memory or an obligation should peek out, its moral force is to be denied. Your hands are forever self-cleansing, your soul self-forgiving, each day a new day, a fresh beginning. I concede that there are some practical virtues to this "put it all behind us" attitude. Great athletes have a way of divorcing themselves from every negative aspect of their very recent past; they have to have very short memories for failures.

2. *Hávamál* 76.

3. E.g., *Iliad,* 22.389, and frequent references to obliterating the enemy from memory, e.g., 6.60. See 2 Sam. 18.18, where Absalom raises a pillar in remembrance of his name since he has no son.

4. That fire also destroyed the only manuscript of the *Battle of Maldon,* noted in text at ch. 6, n. 1, but luckily it had been transcribed seven years before the fire.

5. MS C, Cotton Tiberius C.i version, asc.jebbo.co.uk/c/c-L.html#, entry for 1066.

6. Henry of Huntingdon, *Henry, Archdeacon of Huntington,* 7.1–4.

CHAPTER 18. GOING THROUGH ALL THESE THINGS TWICE

1. See ch. 2, n. 8.

2. 2 Æthelred, §6.1, Liebermann, *Gesetze,* 1.224.

3. Maimonides, "Laws of Repentance," 1.5.2.1, in *Mishneh Torah: The Book of Knowledge.*

4. Some would make the fall of the angels take place on day two, some day five, some before creation. For the Jewish traditions, see Ginzberg, *The Legends of the Jews,* 20–21n61. See the engaging essay by Carasik, "Three Biblical Beginnings."

5. Philo of Alexandria, *On the Creation,* 2.7.

6. Augustine, *Confessions,* 11.12.14.

7. See Jack Miles's prize-winning *God: A Biography* for his respectful account of God having to learn on the job of what it takes to be God to his creation. Miles assumes that God had no prior experience with other destroyed worlds.

8. Neusner, *Genesis Rabbah,* 3.vii, p. 33. Dating this midrashic text is uncertain, but fourth or fifth century is a reasonable assumption.

9. Compare the grim unwinding of creation that concludes Alexander Pope's *The Dunciad,* where the universe is undone not by disobedience but by bad poets and wits who think they are producing splendid stuff, their unjustifiable self-esteem bringing down the world:

> Lo! thy dread Empire, Chaos! is restor'd;
> Light dies before thy uncreating word:
> Thy hand, great Anarch! lets the curtain fall;
> And Universal Darkness buries all. (4.653–56)

10. These represent the J and P sources respectively, but the compilers of Genesis seem to have been intent on making redos and do-overs one of their themes. On carving up bodies and contract formation, see Faraone, "Molten Wax, Spilt Wine and Mutilated Animals"; also my *Eye for an Eye,* chs. 2–4.

11. See Exod. 3.6, where God identifies himself to Moses as "the God of your father, the God of Abraham, the God of Isaac, and the God of Jacob," as if it were not quite clear they were the same being. See *Jewish Study Bible,* Exod. 3.6n.

12. One of the matters that needed clarification in the first two generations was which of two sons was to succeed to the father's position; Ishmael and Esau, the elder in each case, it was determined, were to be excluded. By Jacob's death all sons by wives and handmaids inherit.

13. See *Jewish Study Bible,* Gen. 1.1, 12n1; see Orlinsky, "Enigmatic Bible Passages."

14. See Goffman on reruns and rerun signals in "Replies and Responses," 14, 25–27, 35–36, 40; and Clark and Wasow, "Repeating Words in Spontaneous Speech."

15. An accurate send-up of childhood games by argument, do-over, and rule change appeared in Bill Watterson's *Calvin and Hobbes* as "Calvinball."

16. T. S. Eliot, *East Coker,* §V, in *Complete Poems and Plays.* In old Slavic the same root gives rise to the word for both to begin and to end a legal claim. Ending the dispute invokes rules and understandings held to hold from the *beginning* of time; see Škrubej, "Historisch analysierte Lexik," 363–67. One could also see the idea of an end suggesting "old," as it does with death, and suggesting new or young, because more recent in time than the beginning. The same confusion occurs with beginnings; the world when young means the old world.

17. Herodotus, *The Histories,* I.33, p. 53. See too Aristotle, *Nicomachean Ethics,* I.x–xi; see discussion in *Eye for an Eye,* 99–101.

18. There is some small solace that you will not be held to much account for any generation past your grandchildren's.

19. I have chosen to use a legal example to touch briefly upon issues that have been treated quite well by literary critics and narratologists. On endings, on which there is an enormous literature, the classic is Kermode's *The Sense of an Ending.* On beginnings there is much less, but Nuttall's *Openings* is a tour de force; also see the engaging article by Kellman, "Grand Openings and Plain."

20. See Goffman, *Presentation of Self.*

21. The suffering of the figure skater, however, cannot be compared with the demand made on the high priest Aaron and his third and fourth sons to go on with the show after the Lord, in a fit of pique, consumed Aaron's sons, Nadab and Abihu, for deviating from the prescribed sacrificial script, with no bad intentions (Lev. 10).

22. *The Wire,* season 1, episode 9.

23. "Stuck inside a Mobile with the Memphis Blues Again," 1966.

CHAPTER 19. DO NOT GO GENTLE: A VALEDICTION

1. Psychological experiments confirm that young adults can pick up and recall a sentence if a competing speaker is talking at the same time, while older adults' recall is significantly more impaired by low levels of conversational noise. Thornton and Light, "Language Comprehension and Production in Normal Aging," 262, citing Tun and Wingfield, "Fast Noisy Speech." See also Kramer and Madden, "Attention."

2. W. B. Yeats, "The Tower," vv. 1–4.

3. "Do not go gentle into that good night," v. 2.

4. Some might be tempted to choose death when they felt they were best prepared to face it nobly; the early church discouraged "volunteer" martyrs. A true martyr, it was argued, is ready no matter when and how death comes to him; he was not to go looking for it, as jihadist suicide bombers do. See my *The Mystery of Courage,* 72 and accompanying notes; and also the chapter "Fixing to Die."

5. See Adam Smith, *Theory of Moral Sentiments,* 1.3.15: the Duke de Biron, Charles de Gontaut, much famed for his martial courage and strategic abilities in the French Wars of Religion, was beheaded in 1602.

6. On the legal significance of sending back the mangled corpse of an animal or bloody token as proof that the losses are due to a predator, and not to an employee's theft, see Daube, *Studies in Biblical Law,* 5–8, discussing Exod. 22.12–13 with reference to Joseph's bloody cloak.

7. 1 Kings 16 to 2 Kings 9: Jezebel's despicable securing of Naboth's vineyard

hovers over the narrative, but her forcefulness of character is consistently portrayed. Her grand end is consistent with her entire characterization.

8. And for fans of *The Wire,* Snoop.

9. E.g., Parker, "Jezebel's Reception of Jehu"; more sensible is Olyan, "2 Kings 9:31: Jehu as Zimri."

BIBLIOGRAPHY

Adam of Bremen. *History of the Archbishops of Hamburg-Bremen.* Translated by Francis J. Tschan, with new introduction and bibliography by Timothy Reuter. New York: Columbia University Press, 2002.

Aers, David. "The Christian Practice of Growing Old in the Middle Ages." In *Growing Old in Christ,* edited by Stanley Hauerwas et al., 38–62. Grand Rapids, MI: Eerdmans, 2003.

———. "The Self Mourning: Reflections on *Pearl.*" *Speculum* 68 (1993): 54–73.

Alcestis. Euripides. Vol. 1. Translated by D. Kovac. Loeb Classical Library 12. Cambridge, MA: Harvard University Press, 1994.

Amarna Letters. Translated and edited by William L. Moran. Baltimore, MD: Johns Hopkins University Press, 1992.

Ancient Laws of Ireland: Senchus Mor. Vol. 1. Dublin: Alexander Thom, 1865.

Appian. *The Civil Wars.* Translated by John Carter. London: Penguin, 1996.

Aquinas, St. Thomas. *Summa theologiæ.* Translated by the Fathers of the English Dominican Province. 2nd ed. 1920. http://www.newadvent.org/summa/.

Aristotle. *Nicomachean Ethics.* Translated by W. D. Ross. Revised by J. O. Urmson. In *The Complete Works of Aristotle,* edited by Jonathan Barnes, 2.1729–1867. Princeton, NJ: Princeton University Press, 1984.

————. *Rhetoric.* Translated by W. Rhys Roberts. In *The Complete Works of Aristotle.* 2.2152–2269.

Ármann Jakobsson. "The Specter of Old Age: Nasty Old Men in the Sagas of the Icelanders." *Journal of English and Germanic Philology* 104 (2005): 297–325.

Athanasius: The Life of St. Antony. Early English Church Texts. http://www.earlychurchtexts.com/main/athanasius/vita_antonii_01.shtml.

Augustine, St. *Confessions.* Translated by Henry Chadwick. Oxford: Oxford University Press, 1991.

Babel, Isaac. *Collected Stories.* Translated by David McDuff. London: Penguin, 1994.

Babylonian Talmud. Edited by I. Epstein. London: Soncino, 1935–48.

Baltes, M. M., and L. L. Carstensen. "The Process of Successful Ageing." *Ageing and Society* 16 (1996): 397–422.

Baltes, Paul B. "On the Incomplete Architecture of Human Ontogeny: Selection, Optimization, and Compensation as Foundation of Developmental Theory." *American Psychologist* 52 (1997): 366–80.

Baltes, Paul B., and M. M Baltes. "Psychological Perspectives on Successful Aging: The Model of Selective Optimization with Compensation." In *Successful Aging: Perspectives from the Behavioral Sciences,* edited by Paul B. Baltes and M. M. Baltes, 1–34. New York: Cambridge University Press, 1997.

Baltes, Paul B., Ursula M. Staudinger, Andreas Maercker, and Jacqui Smith. "People Nominated as Wise: A Comparative Study of Wisdom-Related Knowledge." *Psychology and Aging* 10 (1995): 155–66.

Battle of Maldon. Edited by E. V. Gordon. New York: Appleton-Century-Crofts, 1966. See also Peter S. Baker's hypertext: http://faculty.virginia.edu/OldEnglish/anthology/maldon.html. Reliable translation by Jonathan A. Glenn available at: http://faculty.uca.edu/jona/texts/maldon.htm.

Baumgartner, M. P. "Social Control from Below." In *Toward a General Theory of Social Control,* edited by Donald Black, 1.303–45. New York: Academic Press, 1984.

Bauschatz, Paul C. *The Well and the Tree: World and Time in Early Germanic Culture.* Amherst: University of Massachusetts Press, 1982.

Bengston, Vern L., Daphna Gans, Norella M. Pulney, and Merril Silverstein, eds. *Handbook of Theories of Aging.* 2nd ed. New York: Springer, 2009.

Beowulf. Klaeber's Beowulf. 4th ed. Edited by R. D. Fulk, Robert E. Bjork, and John D. Niles. Toronto: University of Toronto Press, 2008.

Bersani, Leo, and Ulysse Dutoit. *The Forms of Violence: Narrative in Assyrian Art and Modern Culture.* New York: Schocken, 1985.

Birren, James, and K. Warner Schaie, eds. *Handbook of the Psychology of Aging.* 6th ed. Burlington, MA: Elsevier Academic Press, 2006.

Blady, Ken. *Jewish Communities in Exotic Places.* Northvale, NJ: Jason Aronson, 2000.

Blanchard-Fields, Fredda, and Antje Kalinauskas. "Theoretical Perspectives on Social Context, Cognition, and Aging." In Bengston et al., *Handbook of Theories of Aging,* 261–76.

Boehm, Christopher. *Blood Revenge: The Anthropology of Feuding in Montenegro.* Lawrence: University Press of Kansas, 1984.

Bright, Timothy. *A Treatise of Melancholy.* London: John Windet, 1586. http://web2.bium.univ-paris5.fr/livanc/?cote=74473&do=pages.

Burke, Deborah M., and Meredith A. Shafto. "Language and Aging." In Craik and Salthouse, *The Handbook of Aging and Cognition,* 373–443.

Burkert, Walter. *Homo Necans: The Anthropology of Ancient Greek Sacrificial Ritual and Myth.* Translated by Peter Bing. Berkeley: University of California Press, 1983.

Burnett, Anne Pippin. *Revenge in Attic and Later Tragedy.* Berkeley: University of California Press, 1998.

Burrow, J. A. *The Ages of Man: A Study in Medieval Writing and Thought.* Oxford: Clarendon, 1986.

Bynum, Caroline Walker. *Jesus as Mother: Studies in the Spirituality of the High Middle Ages.* Berkeley: University of California Press, 1982.

———. *The Resurrection of the Body in Western Christianity, 200–1336.* New York: Columbia University Press, 1995.

Byrhtferth's Enchiridion. Edited by Peter S. Baker and Michael Lapidge. Oxford: Published for the Early English Text Society by Oxford University Press, 1995.

Cahan, Abraham. *The Rise of David Levinsky.* 1917. London: Penguin, 1993.

Carasik, Michael. "Three Biblical Beginnings." In *Beginning/Again: Toward a Hermeneutics of Jewish Texts,* edited by Aryeh Cohen and Shaul Magid, 1–22. New York: Steven Bridges, 2002.

Carstensen, Laura L., Derek M. Isaacowitz, and Susan T. Charles. "Taking Time Seriously: A Theory of Socioemotional Selectivity." *American Psychologist* 54 (1999): 165–81.

Carstensen, Laura L., and Joseph A. Mikels. "At the Intersection of Emotion and Cognition: Aging and the Positivity Effect." *Current Directions in Psychological Science* 14 (2005): 117–21.

Carstensen, Laura L., Joseph A. Mikels, and Mara Mather. "Aging and the Intersection of Cognition, Motivation, and Emotion." In Birren and Schaie, *Handbook of the Psychology of Aging,* 343–62.

Cato. *On Agriculture.* Translated by W. D. Hooper and H. B. Ash. Loeb Classical Library 283. Cambridge, MA: Harvard University Press, 1934.

Chaucer, Geoffrey. *The Works of Geoffrey Chaucer.* 2nd ed. Edited by F. N. Robinson. Boston: Houghton Mifflin, 1957.

Chazan, Robert. *European Jewry and the First Crusade.* Berkeley: University of California Press, 1987.

Christ Disputes with the Doctors in the Temple. N-Town Plays. http://www.umm.maine.edu/faculty/necastro/drama/ntown/21_christ_and_doctors.html.

Cicero. *Letters to Atticus.* Translated by D. R. Shackleton Bailey. Loeb Classical Library 7. Cambridge, MA: Harvard University Press, 1999.

———. *On Old Age.* Translated by W. A. Falconer. Loeb Classical Library 154. Cambridge, MA: Harvard University Press, 1923. 9–99.

Clark, Herbert H., and Thomas Wasow. "Repeating Words in Spontaneous Speech." *Cognitive Psychology* 37 (1998): 201–42.

Classen, Albrecht, ed. *Old Age in the Middle Ages and Renaissance: Interdisciplinary Approaches to a Neglected Topic.* Berlin: de Gruyter, 2007.

Coale, Ansley J, and Paul George Demeny. *Regional Model Life Tables and Stable Populations.* 2nd ed. New York: Academic Press, 1983.

Cook, A. S. "A Note on *Beowulf.*" *Modern Language Notes* 8 (1893): 117–18.

Craik, Fergus I. M., and Ellen Bialystok. "Lifespan Cognitive Development: The Roles of Representation and Control." In Craik and Salthouse, *The Handbook of Aging and Cognition,* 557–601.

Craik, Fergus I. M., and Timothy A. Salthouse. eds. *The Handbook of Aging and Cognition.* 3rd ed. New York: Psychology Press, 2008.

Curtius, Ernst Robert. *European Literature and the Latin Middle Ages.* Translated by Willard R. Trask. Princeton, NJ: Princeton University Press, 1953.

Cutler, Neal E., Nancy A. Whitelaw, and Bonita L. Beattie. *American Perceptions of Aging in the 21st Century.* Washington, DC: National Council on Aging, 2002. http://www.healthyagingprograms.org/content.asp?sectionid=75&ElementID=205.

Damasio, Antonio R. *Descartes' Error: Emotion, Reason, and the Human Brain.* New York: G. P. Putnam, 1994.

Dames, Nicholas. *Amnesiac Selves: Nostalgia, Forgetting, and British Fiction, 1810–1870.* Oxford: Oxford University Press, 2001.

Daube, David. *Studies in Biblical Law.* Cambridge: Cambridge University Press, 1947.

Dead Sea Scrolls. Translated by Geza Vermes. *The Complete Dead Sea Scrolls in English.* Rev. ed. London: Penguin, 2004.

Deskis, Susan E. *Beowulf and the Medieval Proverb Tradition.* Medieval and

Renaissance Texts and Studies 155. Tempe: Arizona State University Press, 1996.

Dostoyevsky, Fyodor. *Notes from the Underground.* 1864. Translated by Jessie Coulson. Harmondsworth, UK: Penguin, 1972.

Dove, Mary. *The Perfect Age of Man's Life.* Cambridge: Cambridge University Press, 1986.

Dronke, Ursula. "The Role of Sexual Themes in *Njáls saga.*" London: Viking Society for Northern Research, 1981.

Dukeminier, Jesse, James E. Krier, Gregory S. Alexander, and Michael H. Schill. *Property.* 6th ed. New York: Aspen, 2006.

Durham, Edith. *Some Tribal Origins, Laws and Customs of the Balkans.* London: George Allen and Unwin, 1928.

Egil's Saga. Egils saga Skalla-Grímssonar. Edited by Sigurður Nordal. Íslenzk fornrit 2. 1933. Translated by Richard Scudder. London: Penguin, 2002.

Ehrenreich, Barbara. *Bright-Sided: How the Relentless Promotion of Positive Thinking Has Undermined America.* New York: Holt, 2009.

Einstein, Gilles O., Mark A. McDaniel, Marisa Manzi, Bryan Cochran, and Meredith Baker. "Prospective Memory and Aging: Forgetting Intentions over Short Delays." *Psychology and Aging* 15 (2000): 671–83.

Eliot, T. S. *Complete Poems and Plays, 1909–1950.* New York: Harcourt, Brace, 1952.

Faraone, Christopher A. "The Agonistic Context of Early Greek Binding Spells." In *Magika Hiera: Ancient Greek Magic and Religion,* edited by Christopher A. Faraone and Dirk Obbink, 3–32. Oxford: Oxford University Press, 1991.

———. "Molten Wax, Spilt Wine, and Mutilated Animals: Sympathetic Magic in Near Eastern and Early Greek Oath Ceremonies." *Journal of Hellenic Studies* 113 (1993): 60–80.

Fazio, Sam, and David B. Mitchell. "Persistence of Self in Individuals with Alzheimer's Disease: Evidence from Language and Visual Recognition." *Dementia: The International Journal of Social Research and Practice* 8.1 (2009): 39–59.

Featherstone, Mike, and Mike Hepworth. "Images of Aging: Cultural Representations of Later Life." In Sokolovsky, *The Cultural Context of Aging,* 134–44.

Ferrante, Joan M., trans. *Guillaume d'Orange: Four Twelfth-Century Epics.* New York: Columbia University Press, 1974.

Frakes, Jerold C. *The Fate of Fortune in the Early Middle Ages: The Boethian Tradition.* Studien und Texte zur Geistesgeschichte des Mittelalters 23. Leiden: Brill, 1988.

Fredrickson, Barbara L. "Gratitude, Like Other Positive Emotions, Broadens and Builds." In *The Psychology of Gratitude,* edited by Robert A. Emmons and Michael E. McCullough, 145–66. New York: Oxford University Press, 2004.

———. *Positivity: Groundbreaking Research Reveals How to Embrace the Hidden Strength of Positive Emotions, Overcome Negativity, and Thrive.* New York: Random House, 2009.

Geary, Patrick. "Humiliation of Saints." In *Saints and Their Cults: Studies in Religious Sociology, Folklore and History,* edited by Stephen Wilson, 123–40. Cambridge: Cambridge University Press, 1983.

Georgianna, Linda. "King Hrethel's Sorrow and the Limits of Heroic Action in *Beowulf.*" *Speculum* 62 (1987): 829–50.

Gerald of Wales. Giraldus Cambrensis. *Speculum Duorum; or, A Mirror of Two Men.* Translated by Brian Dawson. Edited by Yves Lefèvre and R. B. C. Huygens. Cardiff: University of Wales Press, 1974.

Ginzberg, Louis. *The Legends of the Jews: From the Creation to Exodus; Notes for Volumes 1 and 2.* Vol. 5. Translated by Henrietta Szold and Paul Radin. 1925. Baltimore, MD: Johns Hopkins University Press, 1998.

Gluckman, Max. "Moral Crises: Magical and Secular Solution." In *The Allocation of Responsibility,* edited by Max Gluckman, 1–50. Manchester: Manchester University Press, 1972.

Goffman, Erving. *The Presentation of Self in Everyday Life.* New York: Anchor, 1959.

———. "Replies and Responses." In *Forms of Talk,* 5–77. Philadelphia: University of Pennsylvania Press, 1983.

Gopnik, Adam. *Angels and Ages: A Short Book about Darwin, Lincoln, and Modern Life.* New York: Vintage, 2009.

Grágás. Laws of Early Iceland: Grágás. The Codex Regius of Grágás. 2 vols. Translated and edited by Andrew Dennis, Peter Foote, and Richard Perkins. Winnipeg: University of Manitoba Press, 1980, 2000. *Grágás: Islændernes lovbog i fristatens tid.* Edited by Vilhjálmur Finsen. Copenhagen, 1852 (*Konungsbók, Ia, Ib*), 1879 (*Staðarhólsbók II*).

Gregory of Tours. *The History of the Franks.* Translated by Lewis Thorpe. Harmondsworth, UK: Penguin, 1974.

Grettir's Saga. Grettis saga Ásmundarsonar. Edited by Guðni Jónsson. Íslenzk fornrit 7. 1936. Translated by Denton Fox and Hermann Pálsson. Toronto: University of Toronto Press, 1974.

Hardy, Thomas. *The Complete Poems.* Edited by James Gibson. New York: Palgrave, 2001.

Harris, Joseph. "Beowulf's Last Words." *Speculum* 67 (1992): 1–32.

Harvey, Barbara. *Living and Dying in England, 1100–1540: The Monastic Experience.* Oxford: Clarendon, 1993.

Hávamál. In *Edda: Die Lieder des Codex Regius,* 3rd ed., edited by Hans Kuhn, 17–44. Heidelberg: Carl Winter, 1962. Translated by Patricia Terry as *Sayings of the High One,* in *Poems of the Vikings: The Elder Edda.* Indianapolis: Bobbs-Merrill, 1969.

Hávarðar saga Ísfirðings. Edited by Björn K. Þórólfsson and Guðni Jónsson. Íslenzk fornrit 6.289–358. 1943. Translated by Fredrik Heinemann as *The Saga of Havard of Isafjord,* in Hreinsson, *The Complete Sagas of Icelanders,* 5.313–47.

Hehman, Jessica A., Tim P. German, and Stanley B. Klein. "Impaired Self-Recognition from Recent Photographs in a Case of Late-Stage Alzheimer's Disease." *Social Cognition* 23.1 (2005): 118–23.

Henry of Huntingdon. *Henry, Archdeacon of Huntington: Historia Anglorum.* Translated and edited by Diana Greenway. Oxford: Oxford University Press, 1997. With some small modifications her translation is readily accessible in an Oxford World Classics edition: *Henry of Huntingdon: The History of the English People, 1000–1154.*

Herodotus. *The Histories.* Translated by Aubrey de Sélincourt. Harmondsworth, UK: Penguin, 1972.

Herzog, Don. *Cunning.* Princeton, NJ: Princeton University Press, 2006.

History of William Marshall. 3 vols. Edited by A. J. Holden. With English translation by S. Gregory and notes by D. Crouch. London: Anglo-Norman Text Society, 2002–6.

Hittite Prayers. Edited by Itamar Singer. Atlanta: Society of Biblical Literature, 2002.

Hobbes, Thomas. *Leviathan.* 1651. New York: E. P. Dutton, 1914.

Homer. *Iliad.* 2nd ed. Revised by William F. Wyatt. Loeb Classical Library 170–71. Cambridge, MA: Harvard University Press, 1999.

Hoyer, William J., and Paul Verhaeghen. "Memory Aging." In Birren and Schaie, *Handbook of the Psychology of Aging,* 209–32.

Hrafnkel's Saga. Hrafnkels saga Freysgoða. Edited by Jón Jóhannesson. Íslenzk fornrit 11.95–133. 1950. Translated by Hermann Pálsson in *Hrafnkel's Saga and Other Stories,* 35–71. Harmondsworth, UK: Penguin, 1971.

Hreinsson, Viðar, ed. *The Complete Sagas of Icelanders, Including 49 Tales.* 5 vols. Reykjavík: Leifur Eiríksson, 1997.

Hume, David. *A Treatise of Human Nature.* 1739–40. Edited by L. A. Selby-Bigge; 2nd ed. by P. H. Nidditch. Oxford: Clarendon, 1975.

Ingalls, Daniel H. H. "Cynics and Pasupatas: The Seeking of Dishonor." *Harvard Theological Review* 55 (1962): 281–98.

Íslendinga saga. In *Sturlunga saga,* 1.229–534. Translated by McGrew and Thomas, 1.115–447.

Íslenzk fornrit. Reykjavík: Hið Íslenzka Fornritafélag.

Jacobus de Varagine. "Life of St. Nicholas." In *Legenda Aurea, The Golden Legend.* Translated by William Caxton. London, 1483. http://www.aug.edu/augusta/iconography/goldenLegend/nicholas.htm.

James, Montague Rhodes, trans. *The Apocryphal New Testament.* Oxford: Clarendon, 1924.

James, William. *Psychology: Briefer Course.* 1892. In *Writings, 1878–1899.* New York: Library of America, 1992.

Jewish Study Bible. Edited by Adele Berlin and Marc Zvi Brettler. Oxford: Oxford University Press, 2004.

John of Trevisa, trans. *Bartholomaeus Anglicus: De proprietatib[us] re[rum].* London: Wynkyn de Worde, 1495. *Early English Books Online.*

Johnson, Paul, and Pat Thane, eds. *Old Age from Antiquity to Post-modernity.* London: Routledge, 1998.

Jolly, Julius. *Hindu Law and Custom.* Translated by Batakrishna Ghosh. Calcutta: Greater India Society, 1928.

Jones, George Fenwick. "The 'Signs of Old Age' in Oswald von Wolkenstein's *Ich Sich und Hör.*" *Modern Language Notes* 89 (1974): 767–86.

Jurasinski, Stefan. *Ancient Privileges: Beowulf, Law, and the Making of Germanic Antiquity.* Morgantown: West Virginia University Press, 2006.

Juvenal. *Juvenal and Persius.* Translated and edited by Susanna Morton Braund. Loeb Classical Library 91. Cambridge, MA: Harvard University Press, 2004.

Kellman, Steven G. "Grand Openings and Plain: The Poetics of First Lines." *SubStance* 6 (1977): 139–47.

Kempe, Margery. *The Book of Margery Kempe.* Edited by Lynn Staley. Kalamazoo, MI: Medieval Institute, 1996. http://www.lib.rochester.edu/camelot/teams/kemp1frm.htm.

Kermode, Frank. *The Sense of an Ending: Studies in the Theory of Fiction.* 1967. Oxford: Oxford University Press, 2000.

Kormáks saga. Edited by Einar Ól. Sveinsson. *Íslenzk fornrit* 8.201–302. 1939. Translated by Rory McTurk in *Sagas of the Warrior-Poets,* 3–67. London: Penguin, 2002.

Kramer, Arthur F., and David J. Madden. "Attention." In Craik and Salthouse, *The Handbook of Aging and Cognition,* 189–249.

Kryla-Lighthall, Nichole, and Mara Mather. "The Role of Cognitive Control in Older Adults' Emotional Well-Being." In Bengston et al., *Handbook of Theories of Aging,* 323–44.

Labouvie-Vief, Gisela. "Dynamic Integration Theory: Emotion, Cognition, and Equilibrium in Later Life." In Bengston et al., *Handbook of Theories of Aging*, 277–94.

Lambert, W. G. *Babylonian Wisdom Literature*. Oxford: Oxford University Press, 1960.

Landnámabók. Edited by Jakob Benedicktsson. Íslenzk fornrit 1. 1968. Translated by Hermann Pálsson and Paul Edwards as *The Book of Settlements: Landnámabók*. Winnipeg: University of Manitoba Press, 1972.

Langland, William. *The Vision of Piers Plowman*. B-text. Edited by A. V. C. Schmidt. New York: E. P. Dutton, 1978.

La Rochefoucauld. *Maxims*. Translated by Leonard Tancock. Harmondsworth, UK: Penguin, 1959.

The Law Code of Manu. Translated by Patrick Olivelle. Oxford: Oxford University Press, 2004.

Laxdæla saga. Edited by Einar Ól. Sveinsson. Íslenzk fornrit 5. 1934. Translated by Keneva Kunz as *The Saga of the People of Laxardal*. London: Penguin, 2008.

Leach, Barton. "Perpetuities in a Nutshell." *Harvard Law Review* 51 (1938): 638–71.

Lee, Richard B. *The Dobe Ju/'hoansi*. 3rd ed. Toronto: Wadsworth, 2002.

Leges Henrici Primi. Translated and edited by L. J. Downer. Oxford: Clarendon, 1972.

Levi, Primo. *Survival in Auschwitz*. Translated by Stuart Woolf. 1958. New York: Touchstone, 1996.

Lichtheim, Miriam. *Ancient Egyptian Literature: The Old and Middle Kingdoms*. 1973. Berkeley: University of California Press, 2006.

Liebermann, Felix. *Die Gesetze der Angelsachsen*. 3 vols. Halle: Niemeyer, 1903–16.

Linton, Ralph. "Age and Sex Categories." *American Sociological Review* 7 (1942): 589–603.

Little, Lester K. *Benedictine Maledictions: Liturgical Cursing in Romanesque France*. Ithaca, NY: Cornell University Press, 1993.

Ljósvetninga saga. Edited by Björn Sigfússon. Íslenzk fornrit 10.1–139. 1940. Translated by Theodore M. Anderson and William Ian Miller in *Law and Literature in Medieval Iceland*, 119–255. Stanford, CA: Stanford University Press, 1989.

Longinus. *On the Sublime*. Translated by W. H. Fyfe; revised by Donald Russell. Loeb Classical Library 199. Cambridge, MA: Harvard University Press, 1995.

MacDonald, Maryellen C., and Morten H. Christiansen. "Reassessing Working Memory: Comment on Just and Carpenter (1992) and Waters and Caplan (1996)." *Psychological Review* 109 (2002): 35–54.

Maimonides, Moses. *Mishneh Torah: The Book of Knowledge.* Vol. 1. Translated by Moses Hyamson. New York: Feldheim, 1981.

———. *Mishneh Torah: The Code of Maimonides, bk. 14; The Book of Judges.* Translated by Abraham M. Hershman. New Haven, CT: Yale University Press, 1949.

Maine, Henry Sumner. *Ancient Law.* 3rd ed. London: J. Murray, 1866.

———. *Lectures on the Early History of Institutions.* New York: Holt, 1875.

Mandeville, Bernard. *The Fable of the Bees; or, Private Vices, Publick Benefits.* 2 vols. Edited by F. B. Kaye. Oxford: Clarendon, 1924. Repr., Indianapolis: Liberty Fund, 1988.

Margalit, Avishai. *The Ethics of Memory.* Cambridge, MA: Harvard University Press, 2002.

McDaniel, Mark A., Gilles O. Einstein, and Larry L. Jacoby. "New Considerations in Aging and Memory: The Glass May Be Half Full." In Craik and Salthouse, *The Handbook of Aging and Cognition,* 251–310.

McDaniel, Mark A., Gilles O. Einstein, Amy C. Stout, and Zack Morgan. "Aging and Maintaining Intentions over Delays: Do It or Lose It." *Psychology and Aging* 18 (2003): 823–35.

McDonough, James. *Platoon Leader.* Novato, CA: Presidio, 1985.

McVay, Jennifer C., and Michael J. Kane. "Conducting the Train of Thought: Working Memory Capacity, Goal Neglect, and Mind Wandering in an Executive-Control Task." *Journal of Experimental Psychology: Learning, Memory, and Cognition* 35 (2009): 196–204.

Michalowski, Piotr. *Letters from Early Mesopotamia.* Atlanta: Scholars Press, 1993.

Middle English Dictionary. Edited by Hans Kurath. Ann Arbor: University of Michigan Press, 1952–2001. http://quod.lib.umich.edu/m/med/.

Mieszkowski, Gretchen. *Medieval Go-betweens and Chaucer's Pandarus.* New York: Palgrave, 2006.

———. "Old Age and Medieval Misogyny: The Old Woman." In Classen, *Old Age in the Middle Ages and Renaissance,* 299–319.

Miles, Jack. *God: A Biography.* New York: Knopf, 1995.

Miller, William Ian. *The Anatomy of Disgust.* Cambridge, MA: Harvard University Press, 1997.

———. *Audun and the Polar Bear: Luck, Law, and Largesse in a Medieval Tale of Risky Business.* Leiden: Brill, 2008.

———. *Bloodtaking and Peacemaking: Feud, Law, and Society in Saga Iceland.* Chicago: University of Chicago Press, 1990.

———. "Deceit in War and Trade." In *The Philosophy of Deception,* edited by Clancy Martin, 49–66. New York: Oxford University Press, 2009.

———. *Eye for an Eye.* Cambridge: Cambridge University Press, 2006.

———. *Faking It.* Cambridge: Cambridge University Press, 2003.

———. *Humiliation: and Other Essays on Honor, Social Discomfort, and Violence.* Ithaca, NY: Cornell University Press, 1993.

———. *The Mystery of Courage.* Cambridge, MA: Harvard University Press, 2000.

———. "Near Misses." *Michigan Quarterly Review* 38 (1999): 1–15.

Murray, Alexander. "Confession Before 1215." *Transactions of the Royal Historical Society,* 6th ser., 3 (1993): 51–81.

———. *Reason and Society in the Middle Ages.* Oxford: Clarendon, 1978.

Myerhoff, Barbara. *Number Our Days: A Triumph of Continuity and Culture among Jewish Old People in an Urban Ghetto.* New York: Touchstone, 1980.

Neusner, Jacob. *Genesis Rabbah: The Judaic Commentary to the Book of Genesis.* Atlanta: Scholars Press, 1985.

Nietzsche, Friedrich. *On the Genealogy of Morals.* 1887. Translated by Walter Kaufmann and R. J. Hollingdale. New York: Vintage, 1967.

Njal's Saga. Brennu-Njáls saga. Edited by Einar Ól. Sveinsson. Íslenzk fornrit 12. 1954. Translated by Magnus Magnusson and Hermann Pálsson. Baltimore, MD: Penguin, 1960.

Nuttall, A. D. *Openings: Narrative Beginnings from the Epic to the Novel.* Oxford: Clarendon, 1992.

Oliver, Lisi. "Sick-Maintenance in Anglo-Saxon Law." *Journal of English and Germanic Philology* 107 (2008): 304–26.

Olyan, Saul M. "2 Kings 9:31: Jehu as Zimri." *Harvard Theological Review* 78 (1985): 203–7.

Orderic Vitalis. *The Ecclesiastical History of Orderic Vitalis.* Translated and edited by Marjorie Chibnall. Vol. 2, bks. 3–4. Oxford: Clarendon, 1969.

Orlinsky, Harry M. "Enigmatic Bible Passages: The Plain Meaning of Genesis 1:1–3." *Biblical Archaeologist* 46 (1983): 207–9.

Orwell, George. *The Road to Wigan Pier.* 1937. New York: Harcourt, Brace, 1958.

Pardee, Dennis. *The Context of Scripture.* Edited by William W. Hallo. 3 vols. Leiden: Brill, 1997–2002.

Park, Denise C., and Doris Payer. "Working Memory across the Adult Lifespan." In *Lifespan Cognition: Mechanisms of Change,* edited by Ellen Bialystok and Fergus I. M. Craik, 128–42. New York: Oxford University Press, 2006.

Park, Denise C., and Patricia Reuter-Lorenz. "The Adaptive Brain: Aging and Neurocognitive Scaffolding." *Annual Review of Psychology* 60 (2009): 21.1–21.24.

Parker, Simon B. "Jezebel's Reception of Jehu." *Maarav* 1 (1978): 67–78.

Parkin, Tim G. *Old Age in the Roman World: A Cultural and Social History.* Baltimore, MD: Johns Hopkins University Press, 2004.

Philo of Alexandria. *On the Creation.* In *The Works of Philo,* translated by C. D. Yonge. Peabody, MA: Hendrickson, 1993.

Pitt, H. G. *Abraham Lincoln.* Phoenix Mill, UK: Sutton, 1998.

Plato. *Republic.* Translated by Paul Shorey. In the *Collected Dialogues of Plato,* edited by Edith Hamilton and Huntington Cairns, 575–844. Bollingen Series 71. New York: Pantheon, 1961.

Plummer, Charles, trans. and ed. *Bethada Náem Nérenn: Lives of the Irish Saints.* Oxford: Clarendon, 1922.

Pope, Alexander. *The Dunciad.* Edited by Valerie Rumbold. Harlow, UK: Longman, 1999.

Pratt, Karen. "De Vetula: The Figure of the Old Woman in Old French Literature." In Classen, *Old Age in the Middle Ages and Renaissance,* 321–42.

Rabbitt, Patrick, Ibrahim Said, Mary Lunn, Marietta Scott, Neil Thacker, Charles Hutchinson, Michael Horan, Neil Pendleton, and Alan Jackson. "Age-Associated Losses of Brain Volume Predict Longitudinal Cognitive Declines over 8 to 20 Years." *Neuropsychology* 22 (2008): 3–9.

Raphals, Lisa. "Fate, Fortune, Chance and Luck in Chinese and Greek: A Comparative Semantic History." *Philosophy East and West* 53 (2003): 537–74.

Raz, N., K. Rodrigue, and J. Acker. "Hypertension and the Brain: Vulnerability of the Prefrontal Regions and Executive Functions." *Behavioral Neuroscience* 17 (2003): 1169–80.

Reynolds, Andrew. *Anglo-Saxon Deviant Burial Customs.* Oxford: Oxford University Press, 2009.

Robinson, Fred C. *Beowulf and the Appositive Style.* Knoxville: University of Tennessee Press, 1985.

Rosaldo, Michelle. *Knowledge and Passion: Ilongot Notions of Self and Social Life.* Cambridge: Cambridge University Press, 1980.

Rosenberg, Harriet G. "Complaint Discourse, Aging and Caregiving among the Ju/'hoansi of Botswana." In Sokolovsky, *The Cultural Context of Aging,* 30–52.

Rosenthal, Joel T. *Old Age in Late Medieval England.* Philadelphia: University of Pennsylvania Press, 1996.

Rosenwein, Barbara. *To Be the Neighbor of Saint Peter: The Social Meaning of Cluny's Property, 909–1049.* Ithaca, NY: Cornell University Press, 1989.

Roth, Martha T. *Law Collections from Mesopotamia and Asia Minor.* 2nd ed. Atlanta: Scholars Press, 1997.

Rowe, John W., and Robert L. Kahn. *Successful Aging.* New York: Pantheon, 1998.

Rozin, Paul, and E. B. Royzman. "Negativity Bias, Negativity Dominance, and Contagion." *Personality and Social Psychology Review* 5 (2001): 296–320.

Sayers, William. "The Alien and Alienated as Unquiet Dead in the Sagas of the Icelanders." In *Monster Theory,* edited by Jeffrey Jerome Cohen, 242–63. Minneapolis: University of Minnesota Press, 1996.

Schapera, Isaac. "The Sin of Cain." *Journal of the Royal Anthropological Institute* 85 (1955): 33–43.

Schniedewind, William M., and Joel H. Hunt. *A Primer on Ugaritic: Language, Culture, and Literature.* Cambridge: Cambridge University Press, 2007.

Scott, James C. *Domination and the Arts of Resistance: Hidden Transcripts.* New Haven, CT: Yale University Press, 1990.

Sears, Elizabeth. *The Ages of Man: Medieval Interpretations of the Life Cycle.* Princeton, NJ: Princeton University Press, 1986.

Seneca. *Lucius Annaeus Seneca, Moral Epistles.* Vol. 1. Translated by Richard M. Gummere. Loeb Classical Library 214. Cambridge, MA: Harvard University Press, 1917.

Shahar, Shulamith. *Growing Old in the Middle Ages: "Winter Clothes Us in Shadow and Pain."* London: Routledge, 1997.

———. "Old Age in the High and Late Middle Ages: Image, Expectation, and Status." In Johnson and Thane, *Old Age from Antiquity to Post-modernity,* 43–63.

Shakespeare, William. *Hamlet.* Edited by Harold Jenkins. Arden Shakespeare. New York: Methuen, 1982.

Shklar, Judith. *Ordinary Vices.* Cambridge, MA: Harvard University Press, 1984.

Singer, Itamar, ed. *Hittite Prayers.* Atlanta: Society of Biblical Literature, 2002.

Škrubej, Katja. "Historisch analysierte Lexik: Relevante Quelle für die rechtsgeschichtliche Forschung? (Am Beispiel der altslawichen Bezeichnung zakonik." In *Ad Fontes. Europäisches Forum junger Rechtshistorikerinnen und Rechtshistoriker,* edited by B. Feldner et al., 357-70. Frankfurt: Peter Lang: 2002.

Smith, Adam. *The Theory of Moral Sentiments.* 1759. Edited by D. D. Raphael and A. L. Macfie. Oxford: Clarendon, 1976.

Smith, Jacqui, Ursula M. Staudinger, and Paul B. Baltes. "Occupational Settings Facilitating Wisdom-Related Knowledge: The Sample Case of

Clinical Psychologists." *Journal of Consulting and Clinical Psychology* 62 (1994): 989–99.

Smith, R. M. "Ageing and Well-being in Early Modern England: Pension Trends and Gender Preferences under the English Old Poor Law, c. 1650–1800." In Johnson and Thane, *Old Age from Antiquity to Post-modernity,* 64–95.

Sokolovsky, Jay, ed. *The Cultural Context of Aging.* 3rd ed. Westport, CT: Praeger, 2009.

Spiegel, Shalom. *The Last Trial: On the Legends and Lore of the Command to Abraham to Offer Isaac as a Sacrifice: The Akedah.* Translated and introduction by Judah Goldin. 1950. Woodstock, VT: Jewish Lights, 1993.

Stalsberg, Anne. "Women as Actors in North European Viking Age Trade." In *Social Approaches to Viking Studies,* edited by Ross Samson, 75–86. Glasgow: Cruithne, 1991.

Steinsaltz, Adin. *The Talmud: The Steinsaltz Edition.* Vol. 14, *Tractate Ta'anit, Part II.* Translated by Israel V. Berman. New York: Random House, 1995.

Stone, Suzanne Last. "Rabbinic Legal Magic: A New Look at Honi's Circle as a Construction of Law's Space." *Yale Journal of Law and Humanities* 17 (2005): 97–123.

Strouse, Anne, Daniel H. Ashmead, Ralph N. Ohde, and D. Wesley Grantham. "Temporal Processing in the Aging Auditory System." *Journal of the Acoustical Society of America* 104 (1998): 2385–99.

Sturlunga saga. 2 vols. Edited by Jón Jóhannesson, Magnús Finnbogason, and Kristján Eldjárn. Reykjavík, 1946. Translated by Julia H. McGrew and R. George Thomas as *Sturlunga saga.* 2 vols. New York: Twayne, 1970–74.

Sturlu saga. In *Sturlunga saga,* 1.63–114. Translated by McGrew and Thomas as *The Saga of Hvamm-Sturla,* 1.59–113.

Taylor, Shelley E., and Jonathan Brown. "Illusion and Well-being: A Social Psychological Perspective on Mental Health." *Psychological Bulletin* 103 (1988): 193–210.

Thane, Pat. "Social Histories of Old Age and Aging." *Journal of Social History* 37 (2003): 93–111.

Thomas, Dylan. *Selected Poems, 1934–1952.* New York: New Directions, 2003.

Thornton, Robert, and Leah L. Light. "Language Comprehension and Production in Normal Aging." In Birren and Schaie, *Handbook of the Psychology of Aging,* 261–87.

Thorstein the Staff-Struck. Þorsteins þáttr stangarhöggs. Edited by Jón Jóhannesson. Íslenzk fornrit 11.67–79. 1950. Translated by Hermann Pálsson in *Hrafnkel's Saga and Other Stories,* 72–81. Harmondsworth, UK: Penguin, 1971.

Tremblay, Kelly L., Michael Piskosz, and Pamela Souza. "Aging Alters the Neural Representation of Speech Cues." *NeuroReport: For Rapid Communication of Neuroscience Research* 13 (2002): 1865–70.

Trilling, Renée R. *The Aesthetics of Nostalgia: Historical Representation in Old English Verse.* Toronto: University of Toronto Press, 2009.

Trollope, Anthony. *Barchester Towers.* 1857. Harmondsworth, UK: Penguin, 1983.

Tun, P. A., and A. Wingfield. "Fast Noisy Speech: Age Differences in Processing Rapid Speech with Background Noise." *Psychology and Aging* 13 (1998): 424–34.

Van Caenegem, R. C., ed. *English Lawsuits from William I to Richard I.* 2 vols. London: Selden Society, 1990.

Vatnsdœla saga. Edited by Einar Ól. Sveinsson. Íslenzk fornrit 8.1–131. 1939. Translated by Andrew Wawn as *The Saga of the People of Vatnsdale,* in Hreinsson, *The Complete Sagas of Icelanders,* 4.1–66.

Viga-Glúms saga. Edited by Jónas Kristjánsson. Íslenzk fornrit 9.1–98. Translated by John McKinnell as *Killer-Glum's Saga,* in Hreinsson, *The Complete Sagas of Icelanders,* 2.267–314.

Villehardouin, Geoffrey de. *The Conquest of Constantinople.* Translated by M. R. B. Shaw. Harmondsworth, UK: Penguin, 1963.

Vita Anskarii. Monumenta Germaniae Historica. SS Rer. Germ. 55. Edited by G. Waitz. Hanover, 1884. Translated by Charles H. Robinson. http://www.fordham.edu/halsall/basis/anskar.html.

Wack, Mary F. *Lovesickness in the Middle Ages: The Viaticum and Its Commentaries.* Philadelphia: University of Pennsylvania Press, 1990.

Wehlau, Ruth. "'Seeds of Sorrow': Landscapes of Despair in *The Wanderer, Beowulf's* Story of Hrethel, and *Sonatorrek.*" *Parergon* 15 (1998): 1–17.

Weinfeld, Moshe. "Covenant Terminology in the Ancient Near East and Its Influence on the West." *Journal of the American Oriental Society* 93 (1973): 190–99.

Wente, Edward. *Letters from Ancient Egypt.* Atlanta: Scholars Press, 1990.

Whitelock, Dorothy. *English Historical Documents, 540–1041.* 2nd ed. New York: Oxford University Press, 1979.

Whitman, James Q. "The Seigneurs Descend to the Rank of Creditors: The Abolition of Respect, 1790." *Yale Journal of Law and Humanities* 6 (1994): 249–83.

William of Malmesbury. *Gesta Regum Anglorum.* Vol. 1. Translated and edited by R. A. B. Mynors, R. M. Thomson, and M. Winterbottom. Oxford: Clarendon, 1998.

Willis, Sherry L., K. Warner Schaie, and Mike Martin. "Cognitive Plasticity."
    In Bengston et al., *Handbook of Theories of Aging,* 295–322.

Wills, Gary. *Lincoln at Gettysburg: The Words That Remade America.* New
    York: Simon and Schuster, 1992.

Wilmot, John. *The Complete Poems of John Wilmot, Earl of Rochester.* Edited
    by David M. Vieth. New Haven, CT: Yale University Press, 1968.

Wyatt, N., trans. and ed. "The Story of King Keret." In *Religious Texts from
    Ugarit: The Words of Ilimilku and His Colleagues.* Sheffield, UK: Sheffield
    Academic Press, 1998.

Yeats, William Butler. *Collected Poems.* New York: Macmillan, 1956.

Zarit, Steven. "A Good Old Age: Theories of Mental Health and Aging." In
    Bengston et al., *Handbook of Theories of Aging,* 675–92.

Zelizer, Viviana A. *Morals and Markets: The Development of Life Insurance
    in the United States.* New York: Columbia University Press, 1979.

INDEX

Tantalus, 202

tantrums, 115, 122, 241

teachers, teaching, 55–56, 64, 66, 189,
    195, 197; complaining and, 83–84;
    praising and, 110

thankfulness, 192–99, 294n5

thank-you notes, 197–98

Thatcher, Margaret, 44

Thomas, Dylan, 251, 261

Thor, bludgeoned by Wolfred, 100

tip of the tongue, 29–30, 273n10

Tollund Man, 157–58

tragedy, 14, 88, 202, 212, 218, 223;
    revenge and, 127–28

Trollope, Anthony, 153

Ugarit, 81, 166. *See also* curses

Underground Man, 83, 86, 102

universals. *See* complaining; singing
    in the shower

unwinding. *See* do-overs

vanity, 15–18, 91, 173; of clueless
    forty-year olds, 208; as emptiness
    and worthlessness, 60, 65, 70–
    71; of human wishes, 89, 225.
    See also biblical citations: Eccles.

Viagra, 34, 51, 247

Vikings, 64, 97, 130, 148, 223; as
    booksellers, 97, 282n2

Villa, Pancho, 253

vocabulary, 23, 27, 29, 203, 273n10

voicing, onset, 271n7

waiting, 33–34

whatifness, 200–202, 212–13

whining. *See* complaining

William I the Conqueror, 180; flop-
    ping, 286n39

William II Rufus, 143

Williams, Hank, 261

Wilmot, John, 52–53

Wire, The, 246–47, 299n8

wisdom, 2, 38, 64, 49–76; clinical
    psychologists claimed as exemplars
    of, 276–77n3; cunning, deception,
    and skill as, 64–70; David and
    Solomon's lethal version of, 71–76;
    despair and, 70–71; etymology of,
    64; insipidness of contemporary
    research in, 50–51, 69, 76; as
    look-before-you-leap prudence,
    50. *See also* Humpty Dumpty;
    positivity

wisdom literature, 55; Norse, Egyp-
    tian, Babylonian, biblical, 64–65.
    See also biblical citations: Eccles.,
    Job, Prov.; Egypt; Odin; proverbs

wishful thinking, 23, 76, 161, 189,
    250, 274n7

wistfulness, 57, 91, 198, 206

women, 43, 50–51, 59, 133–34, 139,
    156; as Fates, 217; marriage as
    hostage taking and, 239; taking to
    bed, 153–54; Thorgerd Egilsdottir,
    149, 151–52; witches and cunning,
    42, 128, 158, 276n14

Wordsworth, W., 59

Wyrd, 217–20. *See also* fate

Yahweh, 43–44, 71, 88, 110–11, 117,
    259

Yeats, W. B., 250–51

Yiddish. *See* Jews

Zoloft, 35–36